THE SUFI MESSAGE

VOLUME VIII

5th Reprint : Delhi, 2018
First Indian Edition: Delhi, 1990

Vol. VIII	ISBN : 978-81-208-0683-2	(Cloth)
	ISBN : 978-81-208-0684-9	(Paper)
Set	ISBN : 978-81-208-0494-4	(Cloth)
	ISBN : 978-81-208-0495-1	(Paper)

Also available at :

MOTILAL BANARSIDASS

41 U.A. Bungalow Road, Jawahar Nagar, Delhi 110 007
1B, Jyoti Studio Compound, Kennedy Bridge, Nana Chowk, Mumbai 400 007
203 Royapettah High Road, Mylapore, Chennai 600 004
236, 9th Main III Block, Jayanagar, Bengaluru 560 011
8 Camac Street, Kolkata 700 017
Ashok Rajpath, Patna 800 004
Chowk, Varanasi 221 001

Printed in India
by RP Jain at NAB Printing Unit,
A-44, Naraina Industrial Area, Phase I, New Delhi–110028
and published by JP Jain for Motilal Banarsidass Publishers (P) Ltd,
41 U.A. Bungalow Road, Jawahar Nagar, Delhi-110007

CONTENTS

PART III

PREFACE TO THE SERIES

THE present volume is the first of a series including all the works intended for publication of Hazrat Inayat Khan (Baroda 1882-New Delhi 1927), the great Sufi mystic who came to the Western world in 1910 and lectured and taught there until his passing away in 1927.

A new edition of this series, which was published for the International Headquarters of the Sufi Movement in the West in the '60s, is now made available in the Indian subcontinent and the Middle East. In this way Hazrat Inayat Khan's inspired and universal vision of the Sufi Message returns to his own beloved country, where it originated and where interest in it is growing.

This book and other volumes of this series have not been written down by the author. They contain his lectures, discourses and other teachings as taken down in shorthand and other handwriting. When preparing for publication great care was taken, not only to avoid distortion of their intent and meaning, but also to leave intact, as far as possible, the flow of mystical inspiration and poetical expression which add so much to their spell, and without which a significant part of his message would be lost. Although speaking in a tongue foreign to him, he moulded it into a perfect vehicle for his thought, at times somewhat ungrammatical and unusual, but always as clear and precise as his often difficult and abstruse subjects would allow.

It goes without saying that neither in the present nor in the previous edition anything has been altered which would involve even the slightest deviation from the author's intention and no attempt has been made to transform his highly personal and colourful language into idiomatically unimpeachable English. Already so much is necessarily lost by the transfer of the spoken word to the printed page, that every effort has been made, as it should, to preserve the Master's melodious phrasing, the radiance of his personality, and the subtle sense of humour which never left him.

Hazrat Inayat Khan's teaching was nearly all given during the years 1918-1926. It covers a great many subjects, several of which were grouped in series of lectures and taken up again some years later. Certain subjects may cover nearly the same ground as others; stories and examples which abound in most of his works are met again elsewhere; and much of what he taught one finds repeated in several places. This was intentional, as repetition belonged to Hazrat Inayat Khan's method of teaching; it is for the student to become aware of the subtle differences in each context. For these and other reasons it would be difficult to follow a rigid system in publishing Hazrat Inayat Khan's works; a chronological grouping of his lectures would be very unsatisfactory, and a stringent classification according to subject-matter hardly feasible.

The complete series contains fourteen volumes. The last volume is the Index. This edition is the first one to present an index to the Sufi Message of Hazrat Inayat Khan.

Each volume is complete in itself, and therefore may be read without any necessity to study following or previous ones. However, one may get a spiritual and mental appetite to continue reading. One will find that a meditative way of reading will convey not only the words but also the spiritual power emanating from them, tuning mind, heart and soul to the pitch which is one's own.

PREFACE TO VOLUME VIII

HERE IS AN exceptional collection of 68 papers covering a wide range of topics under the heading Sufi Teachings. And indeed when read by an open mind and a responsive heart one feels enriched. Usually teachings consist of external information which has to be learnt. Reading these papers, however, gives the feeling of one's consciousness being reawakened, of recollecting forgotten knowledge, of experiencing life itself. .

The papers represent lectures and meditations given by Hazrat Inayat Khan mainly in the early yeas of his mission in the West, particularly during the first world war, when he lived in London.

They form a further exposition of Sufi thought, at the same time forming a real introduction into some major aspects of the Sufi Message of Hazrat Inayat Khan. This book presents its essence running as a firm thread through all the chapters whilst at the same time highlighting its immense variety of themes and subjects.

As very often general perspective adopted is an analysis of man's situation in and his conduct of life. Invariably this analysis leads to proposals and solutions for the problems of both the individual and mankind at large.

The book may be read in the sequence of chapters as given. But you may as well select some items which strike your mind, heart or soul. Or you might be looking for some order in the embarrassing variety of themes. To provide some assistance we will now propose some general themes, and suggest which chapters may come under each heading. This may help you in structuring the book, and find your way in it. However, the best way remains your inner guidance and intuition.

The book opens with some introductory chapters on SUFISM (*History of the Sufis, Sufism, The Sufi's Aim*). The general theme covered most frequently is HUMAN LIFE. This is generally treated from a practical and spiritual point of view: in Part II we mention *Resist not evil, Judging, The privilege of being human.* Our God part and our man part, Man the seed of God, in Part III Holiness, The ego, The birth of the new era, Character building, Respect and consideration, Graciousness, Overlooking. Conciliation, Optimism and pessimism, Happiness; two chapters from Part I may also be brought under this theme: The prophetic tendency and Seeing. As is easily seen many items have a touch of morals; interestingly, morals are not seen as do's and dont's but rather in the form of an inspiring ideal which may change your attitude in life:

Related to this is the theme of the WILL: Self-discipline, Physical control, Struggle and resignation, Renunciation, The difference between will, wish and desire (all coming under the heading of Part I) and in Part II Resist not evil and Destiny and free will. Also the next papers go under the same heading: Selflessness, Consciousness, Conscience; after reading Vaccination and Inoculation one may feel that it should be classified here too (all in Part III).

Under the heading of PHILOSOPHY are coming the lectures on the law of attraction, Pairs of opposites, Evolution, Spiritual circulation through the veins of nature, Manifestation, gravitation, assimilation and perfection, Karma and reincarnation (all to be found in Part II); moreover in III Life in the hereafter and the conservative spirit.

Some RELIGIOUS papers are to be found in part III; on Resurrection, on the Cross and on Orpheus.

The general theme of BALANCE contains the papers on Health, Harmony and Balance in Part I, on the law of life in II, and on the gift of eloquence, the power of silence and the mystery of sleep (Part III). INNER LIFE AND SPIRITUALITY could be the caption over the complete Part IV containing the most inspiring lectures of this volume (see the table of contents) other papers under this heading are the different stages of spiritual development (I), Divine Impulse (II), Marriage (III). Besides, we would think that this caption may very well go over the following as well: The deeper side of life, Life's mechanism, the smiling forehead, the spell of life (all in III).

W.v.L.

SUFISM has never had a first exponent or a historical origin. It existed from the beginning, because man has always possessed the light which is his second nature; and light in its higher aspect may be called the knowledge of God, the divine wisdom—in fact, Sufism. Sufism has always been practised and its messengers have been people of the heart; thus it belonged to the masters as well as to others.

Tradition states that Adam was the first prophet, which shows that wisdom was already the property of the first man. There have always been some among the human race who have desired wisdom. These sought out spiritual beings in their solitude, serving them with reverence and devotion, and learning wisdom from them. Only a few could understand those spiritual beings, but many were attracted by their great personalities. They said, 'We will follow you, we will serve you, we will believe in you, we will never follow any other', and the holy ones said to them, 'My children, we bless you. Do this; do that. This is the best way to live.' And they gave their followers precepts and principles, such as might produce in them meekness and humility. In this way the religions were formed.

But in the course of time the truth was lost. The tendency to dominate arose, and with it the patriotism of the community and prejudice against others; and thus wisdom was gradually lost. Religion was accepted, though with difficulty, but the evolution of the world at that time was not such as could understand the Sufis. They were mocked at, ill-treated, ridiculed; they were obliged to hide themselves from the world in the caves of the mountains and in the solitude.

At the time of Christ there were Sufis among the first of those who gave heed to him, and in the time of Mohammad the Sufis on Mount Zafah were the first to respond to his cry. One of the explanations of the term Sufi is this association with Mount Zafah. Mohammad was the first to open the way for them in

Arabia, and they had many followers, among them Sadik and Ali.

Sufism then spread to Persia. But whenever the Sufis expressed their free thought, they were attacked by the established religions, and so Sufism found its outlet in poetry and music. Thus it happened that the great Sufi poets, such as Hafiz, Rumi, Shams-e Tabrèz, Sa'di, Omar Khayyám, Nizami, Farid, Jami, and others, gave the wisdom of Sufism to the world. Rumi's work is so great that if one has read and understood it one has learnt every philosophy there is. His poems are sung in the sacred assemblies of the Sufis as part of their worship. The lives of the Sufis were marvellous in their piety, in their humanity.

It was in India that the art of Sufism was brought to perfection: India has been a spiritual land for a very long time. Mysticism was a science to the Indians and their first object in life. This was so in the time of Mahadeva, and later in the time of Krishna. When Sufism had found this soil in which to sow the seed it reached perfection, and many highly talented people became followers, amongst them Khwaja Moin-ud-Din Chishti. Music played an important part in their lives and training. In these Sufis the art of devotion, of idealization, reached its highest development, and their consciousness attained freedom from the external plane.

The translators and readers of the Persian poets, while admiring and praising them highly, have often made the mistake of not giving credit where it was due. They have spoken of the poets as if they had produced everything out of themselves, and inherited nothing from the lore of the past. But Persia, lying between Greece, Egypt, Arabia, and India, came under the influence of Plato and Socrates, of Hinduism and Buddhism, and especially of their poetry and philosophy. Everything in the world is influenced in some way by other things, so it cannot be said that Sufism was born in Persia and that it did not exist before; it is an undeniable fact that Sufis existed in the time of Mohammad and even previously, and that Mohammad liked to converse with them and advise them. Thus Sufism in the course of time absorbed the influence of many religions, and in its turn also influenced many other religions. Though very little of the ancient writings survives, and though that little has lost much through wrong interpretation, yet traces of this ancient Sufism can still be found.

In very ancient times the *Sáfa* was founded, the Brotherhood of Purity. Its doctrine was: Know thyself and thou wilt know God. These students of the self were Sufis, for Sufism is the study of the self.

Sufis and Yogis can respect each other, as the only difference between the Yogi and the Sufi is that the Yogi cares more for spirituality and the Sufi more for humanity. The Yogi thinks that it is better to be God; the Sufi thinks that it is better to be man, because if one is only spiritual, there is always the danger of a fall; our body has the tendency to fall down. The Sufi says that as all the needs and desires of this body and its senses exist, one should satisfy them; he says that we should have whatever we can have, but if we cannot have it, we should not care. Yet there is no inner difference between the Sufi and the Yogi. In wisdom there is no difference; if there seems to be any it is only a difference of form.

Joy is in union; neither in the spiritual nor in the material realm alone, but in both. Why does one join one's hands? Because where there are two the joy is in meeting. The eyes are two; when they are closed there is a joy. When the breath goes through both nostrils the mystic feels an ecstacy. Why do people shake hands? Why do people enjoy it when they embrace? Why do people seek the society of a scientist or a sage? Because a soul is attracted to and united with another soul. The joy is not in spirituality alone, but in the union of the spiritual and the material.

To be all animal is not good; and to be all angel is not good either, because we are made with an animal body which needs to eat, drink, and sleep, and whose senses have a thousand needs. We should keep those animal attributes that are harmless, and give up those that are harmful. To eat is not bad and to drink is not bad, but to snatch the food from another's plate when we already have food on our own, that is a bad thing.

The central theme of the Sufi's life is the freedom of the soul. As the great Persian Sufi poet Rumi says, 'The soul on earth is in a prison, and it remains there as long as it lives on earth'. Man may or may not realize it, but there is a deep yearning in every soul to rise above this imprisonment, to escape from this captivity; and the answer to this yearning is spiritual attainment.

There are two aspects of Sufis: one is called *Rind* and the other *Salik*. The aspect which is called Rind is very well expressed in Fitzgerald's translation of Omar Khayyám: 'O my Beloved, fill the cup that clears today of past regrets and future fears. Why, tomorrow I may be myself, with yesterday's sev'n thousand years!' By this he means: Make the best of this moment; it is now that you can clearly see eternity, if you live in this moment. But if you keep the world of the past or the world of the future before you, you do not live in eternity but in a limited world. In other words, live neither in the past nor in the future, but in eternity. It is now that we should try to discover that happiness which is to be found in the freedom of the soul.

This is the central theme of all great poets who may be called Rind. Their lives are not bound by so-called principles, such as those known to the orthodox. They are free from every kind of bigotry, dogma, and principle urged upon mankind. At the same time they are men of high ideals and great morals, deep thoughts, and very advanced realization. They live a life of freedom in this world of imprisonment where every being is a captive.

Then there are the Salik among the Sufis, who study and meditate and ponder upon ethics, living according to certain principles. Life teaches them and guides them on the right path, and they live a life of piety and renunciation. The way of the Salik is to understand whatever religion a person may have, and to follow it from his own point of view. The Salik makes use of religious terminology as the orthodox do, and he attends the same ceremonies; but to him their meaning is different. Thus every line of the sacred scriptures has a particular meaning for a Salik, for he sees it in a special light.

Higher and more subtle thoughts about God and man and life can be understood only according to the evolution of man; and therefore it is natural that those Sufis who are called Salik accept the religious form first in order to be in harmony with other people; and then they interpret the true wisdom found in that religion.

Most of the Sufi literature is written in such a way that to someone who does not know the inner, underlying meaning, it will be very surprising. If we take the poems of Hafiz, we notice that the name of God is scarcely mentioned in any of them. If we take the poems of Omar Khayyám, which are so much appreciated in the Western world, we shall see that he is always speaking of wine, of the beloved, of the goblet, of the solitude. A person might say, 'What kind of spirituality is this? He speaks of nothing but wine and the goblet! If this were spirituality it would be a great pity for humanity!' Indeed, in these poems there is little devotional expression. In the poems of Jami there is no expression of devotion at all; nor in those of a hundred other Sufi poets who are considered great sages and mystics. They feared that if once they got the name of being spiritual, they would always have to appear as a spiritual person, look like a spiritual person, speak like a spiritual person; and they feared that in this way their freedom would be lost and they would be considered hypocritical.

SUFISM

THERE ARE three principal schools of philosophical thought in the East: Sufism, Vedantism and Buddhism. The Sufi school of thought was that of the prophets of Beni Israel: Abraham, Moses, David, Jonah and others, Zarathushtra, Christ, Mohammad; these and other prophets came from that part of the world which includes Syria, Arabia, Persia, Egypt, and what is now Turkey and south-east Russia.

Sufism is the ancient school of wisdom, of quietism, and it has been the origin of many cults of a mystical and philosophical nature. Its roots can be traced to the school which existed in Egypt and from which source all the different esoteric schools have come. Sufism has always represented that school and has worked out its destiny in the realm of quietude.

From this school of Sufism came four schools: the first was the *Naqshibandi* which works mostly with symbolism, ritual, and ceremony. The second was the *Qadiri*, which taught wisdom within the realm of the existing Islamic religion in the East. The third was the *Sohrwardi* which taught the mystery of life by the knowledge of metaphysics and the practice of self-control. The fourth was the *Chishtia* which represented the spiritual ideal in the realm of poetry and music. From these schools many branches sprang forth in Arabia, Turkey, Palestine, Tartary, Russian Turkestan, Bokhara, Afghanistan, India, Siberia, and other parts of Asia.

In the different schools the ideal remained the same, although the methods varied. The main ideal of every Sufi school has been to attain that perfection which Jesus Christ has taught in the Bible, 'Be ye perfect, even as your Father in heaven is perfect.' The method of the Sufis has always been that of self-effacement. But which self? Not the real, but the false self upon which man depends, and upon which he prides himself as being something special; and by effacing this false self he allows that real Self to manifest in the world of appearance. Thus the Sufi method works towards the unfoldment of the soul, that self which is eternal and to which all power and beauty belong.

Sufism has understood what is behind the ideal of Ahura Mazda and Ahriman, the good principle and the evil principle. One finds this in the words of Christ and in the Qur'an as well as in the Zend Avesta. It has understood what is behind the idea of angels. And it has idealized God and the Master, the deliverer of the divine message. It may be called Jewish mysticism, without omitting the influence of Christianity. It may be called the wisdom of the Christians, without omitting the wisdom of Islam which is to be found in it. It may be called the esoteric side of Islam, without neglecting the influence of philosophies as foreign as those of the Vedanta and Buddhism. This is the reason why it is so wide, perfect, and universal.

The Sufi's worship of nature is due to the influence of Zarathushtra. His tendency towards sacrifice is the lesson taught by Abraham. His miraculous power is due to the influence of Moses. As one who warns of coming dangers he represents the great warner of the past, Noah. His independence of asceticism shows the influence of Solomon. His sacred music tells us of the song of David. His tendency towards renunciation is learnt from the example Christ gave. The humanity the Sufi shows is influenced by the personality of Mohammad. This makes the Sufi the disciple of every master, the follower of every religion, the knower of every aspect of wisdom. Thus it is that in spite of his spiritual attainment he remains sociable in the world.

Many people have said, 'We believe only in Moses, or in Christ.' Some say that they believe only in the Vedas, or in other ancient scriptures. But the Sufi does not care who has said something; he cares only about what has been said. If he finds truth in the words of Zarathushtra he accepts it; if he finds truth in the Kabala he accepts that. He accepts the words of Christ and the Bible; he sees truth in the Qur'an. He accepts the Vedanta; some of the Sufis have been greater students of the Vedanta than many Hindus. In all he sees one scripture.

Dara, the brother of Aurangzeb, was one of the first foreigners to study the Vedanta and spread the knowledge found therein. And in Akbar's reign there were Christian churches in his dominions, Jewish synagogues, and mosques; and he went to all. This was evident proof of his Sufi outlook. And when the great poet Kabir died, Hindus and Muslims both claimed him. The Hindus wanted to cremate him; the Muslims wanted to bury him. They both claimed that he belonged to their religion. The Sufi sees the truth in every religion. He never says that a religion is not his. Hindus and Muslims alike visit the tombs of the great Sufi saints; for instance they all go to the tomb of Khwaja Moin-ud-Din Chishti in Ajmer.

The Sufi sees the one truth in all forms. If anyone asks a Sufi to come and offer prayer in the Christian church, he is ready to do so. If some one would like to take him to the synagogue and ask him to pray as the Jews do, he would be quite willing; and among Muslims he will offer Nimaz as they do. In the Hindu temple he sees the same God, the living God, in the place of the idol; and the temple of Buddha inspires him instead of blinding him with idolatry. Yet his true mosque will be his heart in which the Beloved lives, who is worshipped by both Muslim and Kufr alike.

At the present time the object of the Sufi Movement is to bring about a better understanding among individuals, nations, and races; and to give help to those who are seeking after truth. Its central theme is to produce the consciousness of the divinity of the human soul; and towards this end the Sufi teaching is given.

It is not only the misunderstanding between East and West or between Christians and Muslims which has brought Sufism to the West, but the misunderstandings among Christians themselves and between individuals in general. Sufism, as a school, has come from the East to the West, but Sufism as a message has come from above to the earth; and in that sense Sufism belongs neither to the East nor to the West. The Sufi esoteric school has behind it the tradition of the ancient Sufi schools which existed in all the various periods, but the Sufi message has its own tradition. It is more than a school: it is life itself; it is the answer to the cry of the whole of humanity.

Sufism is a religion if one wants to learn religion from it; it is a philosophy if one wants to learn wisdom from it; it is mysticism if one wishes to be guided by it in the unfoldment of the soul. And yet it is beyond all these things. It is the light, it is the life which is the sustenance of every soul, and which raises a mortal being to immortality. It is the message of love, harmony, and beauty. It is a divine message. It is the message of the time; and the message of the time is an answer to the call of every soul. The message, however, is not in its words, but in the divine light and life which heals the souls, bringing to them the calm and peace of God.

Sufism is neither deism nor atheism, for deism means a belief in a God far away in the heavens and atheism means being without belief in God. The Sufi believes in God. In which God? In the God from whom he has become separated, the God within him and outside him; as it is said in the Bible, we live and move and have our being in God. That teaching is the teaching of the Sufis.

The Sufi believes in God as the idealized Self within the true life, as the collective Consciousness, and also as the Lord of both worlds, the Master of the day of judgment, the Inspirer of the right path, and the One from whom all has come and to whom all will return.

In reality there cannot be many religions; there is only one. There cannot be two truths; there cannot be two masters. As there is only one God and one religion, so there is only one master and only one truth. The weakness of man has always been that he only considers as truth that to which he is accustomed, and anything he has not been accustomed to hear or to think frightens him. Like a person in a strange land, away from home, the soul is a stranger to the nature of things it is not accustomed to. But the journey towards perfection means rising above limitations; rising so high that not the horizon of one country or of one continent only is seen, but that of the whole world. The higher we rise the wider becomes the horizon of our view.

The Sufi does not prescribe principles for anybody, but this is not as in ordinary life, where to have no principles means to be a very wicked person. Some wonder how Sufism can be followed if it has no principles. But the answer is that what is good for one may be very bad for another. For one it may be very good to be a nun or to sit all day in a church or in a mosque, but for another it may be very bad; and yet another may need to go to the cafés and restaurants and learn the meaning of the experiences gained there.

In the East, in a place where respect must be shown people wear a hat or a turban, whereas in the West in the same kind of place the hat is taken off. It is simply the opposite principle. In the East, in Hindu temples, mosques, and other holy places, one must take off one's shoes before entering; in the West one could not be in a church without shoes. If Brahmins had to wear heavy shoes, such as Europeans wear, they would become ill; they would always be tired; they must have thin shoes which they can take off easily. The principles of the religions have been given to suit the time and place.

People have always fought over principles, saying that they adhere to a certain principle, and that this is what makes them superior, while those who adhere to another principle are inferior. But to the Sufi there is no good and bad; his only moral is to be kind to others. That is what the world cannot understand, because the world always wishes for principles and wants to be told that this is good and that is bad. But we make a thing good or bad by the way we look at it, so it is our viewpoint that should be trained first. The Sufi makes everything that he does spiritual. He sees only unity and harmony. The Sufi's religion is love alone; therefore the principles of the different religions are nothing to him. He leaves the fight about principles to those who cannot see beyond the narrow limit of their own ideas.

When the word philosophy is mentioned a person thinks at once of the philosophy of the Vedanta, say, or of Plato and Aristotle. These and other philosophers have studied the physical universe, matter; they have studied how the spirit became matter, and they have studied metaphysics; but in these philosophies we find no idealization, no devotion, whereas in Sufism one finds the idealization of God.

The Sufis believe also in encouraging every kind of worship; but even the worshipping of an idol cannot make the Sufi a Kufr, an unbeliever, because besides the idol he worships everything else at the same time. To the world it might seem that he worships the idol, but in reality he is worshipping God in all. The idolater is he who says, 'This is God and that is not God; God is in this idol; God is not in you.'

The Sufi also has an idol, but it is a living idol. I once met a faqir in the street of Hyderabad. He said to me: 'Hey, Murshid, what is the way to such a street?' I was at that time studying philosophy. I thought, 'He calls me murshid; perhaps he sees something great in me!' But then I heard him ask a policeman, 'Hey, Murshid, is this the way to such a house?' and I understood that he said 'murshid' to everyone. When I asked my murshid about it, he said that this was the grade of Fanà-fi-Shaikh, in which the disciple sees his murshid in everyone and everything. The one who has reached it learns from everything, from every being, old or young, foolish or wise, even from a cat, from a dog, from a tree, from a stone. But the man who sees God in one object only and not in all things and beings, it is he who is the idolater; it is only when one sees God in all that one really sees God.

Sufism is a philosophy among the religions and it is a religion among the philosophies. Among the religions it is a philosophy by reason of the Sufi's freedom of thought; among the philosophies it is a religion because of the Sufi's idealization of God, his devotion and worship. The Sufis were called Sufis by others, they did not give themselves any name. They were free from name, from label, from distinction of personality, and for this the world called them Sufi, from *Sáf* which in Arabic means 'pure'.

THE SUFI'S AIM

THE SUFI'S aim in life is not to differ from any religion, nor to abuse any society. Whatever it be, Christianity, Buddhism, Judaism, Hinduism, or any other religion, whether it be the Theosophical Society, New Thought, or Christian Science, he does not see what weaknesses, what faults may be in them, but he sees the good in all; for every being in the world does what is best for him, if not, at least he thinks he is doing so. The Sufi's aim is the aim of the whole world: knowledge; but at the same time he wants to harmonize and to unite with others, not to seek differences. Thus his aim is to see not duality but unity, and this is in fact the aim of all religions; the only difference being that this aim has been declared either more or less plainly at different stages of the world's evolution.

God exists as the inactive, perfect Consciousness, whose perfection lies in His self-sufficiency; He appears active in manifestation. There also the Sufi sees the unity of God. He keeps God always before his eyes. Any kindness he receives, from friends, from father or mother, he recognizes as having been received from God: God is working through the father and the mother or the friend. Any obligation, any gratitude he feels, he feels towards God. The friendship, the love that he feels for his parents, relations, friends, or beloved, he attributes to God.

In the poems of the Sufi poets the curls of the beloved are often referred to. The poet sees God appearing as the beloved. He recognizes God appearing as the parent or the friend. With every breath he repeats the name of God, and therefore he thinks every breath so valuable that nothing in the world can equal it. One may say, 'Why repeat the same thought a million times? If there were some variation in thought it might be better!' But it is only by one thought, by the same thought, that a person can unite with his origin.

The question may arise as to whether the Sufi aims at becoming a healer or clairvoyant, at communicating with spirits, at analysing the world of phenomena, or whether he wishes to attach himself to any prophet or master; whether he seeks the presence of God or wishes to reach heaven, or whether he follows a certain religion. The answer is, he does not aim at any of these things.

There are many who desire mystical knowledge so that they may become healers, so that they may heal themselves and their friends without presenting a doctor's bill, and may be cured without the help of a physician. These things may come to a Sufi on his path towards a higher aim. He may encounter them all upon his journey, but to remain among them would be just as if one intended to go to the station to meet a friend, but stopped on the way to talk to other acquaintances and so arrived at the station too late.

Does the Sufi seek the presence of God? Does he depend upon the mediation of any prophet or master? To this also the answer is no. He does not seek the presence of God, because where there is a presence there is duality, and his aim is unity. In unity there can be no presence. He does not seek to attach himself to any master for ever. He has no wish to go to heaven, because he sees that heaven is everywhere.

Once imagination has helped a man to bring the presence of God before him, God is awakened in his own heart. Then before he utters a word it is heard by God; when he is praying in a room, he is not alone: he is there with God. To him God is not in the highest heaven, but beside him, before him, in him; then heaven is on earth and earth is heaven; then no one is as living to him as God, as intelligible to him as God, and the names and forms before his consciousness are all covered by Him. Then every word of prayer he utters is a living word. It not only brings a blessing to him, but it brings blessings to all those around him. This kind of prayer is the only true way of praying, and by it the object that is to be fulfilled by prayer is accomplished.

What then is his aim? He seeks to reach that experience in which there is no experience in the usual sense of the word. There are two tendencies: the tendency towards manifestation which has brought us to this world of variety, and the tendency towards inactivity which takes us back to the state from which we have come. Perfection is not in the unmanifested alone, nor in manifestation alone, but in the union of both.

The soul upon its way towards manifestation has gathered around it on all the different planes the vibrations with which it has come in contact, from the finest vibrations to the grossest physical vibrations. But this also is the perfection of the Creator. We could not enjoy the higher if it were not for the lower; we could not enjoy the sweet if it were not for the bitter. If all were best, we would not enjoy the best. If there were only one colour, we would not enjoy any colour. I remember the words of a poet who says, 'Lord, let me not live in this world where camphor, cotton, and bone are all considered white!' The more colours there are, the more shades, the greater is our enjoyment. A thousand, a hundred thousand imperfections are created in order that one whole perfection may be made. It is just like an artist painting a picture. He has his colours and his brushes; he draws the figure; and either at the first stroke or at the tenth, the hundredth, or the thousandth he makes it right.

The task of the Sufi is to remove covers. One's soul is so covered with different vibrations that it cannot see itself. The Sufi by his meditations, by his practices, first takes off the physical body, and observes what he can see without it. Then he rids himself of the astral plane, where man lives in his thoughts and feelings, and he sees what he is conscious of without that plane. The consciousness is like a curtain before which one stands with a small lantern. The reflection of the lantern is cast upon the curtain and it detaches or it limits a certain part of the curtain which receives the impressions.

The Sufi strives for self-realization, and he arrives at this self-realization by means of his divine ideal, his God. By this he touches that truth which is the ultimate goal, and which is the yearning of every soul. It is not only realization; it is a happiness which words cannot explain. It is a peace, the peace which is yearned for by every soul.

And how does he attain to it? By practising the presence of God; by realizing the oneness of the whole being; by working every moment of the day, consciously or sub-consciously, holding the truth before his vision in spite of the waves of illusion which arise continually, diverting his glance from the absolute truth. And no matter what any sect, cult, or creed may be called, as long as souls are striving towards that object, to a Sufi they are all Sufis. The attitude of the Sufi towards all the different religions is one of respect. His religion is the service of humanity, and his only object of attainment is the realization of truth.

THE DIFFERENT STAGES OF SPIRITUAL DEVELOPMENT

IN SANSKRIT there are three distinct words: *Atma,* which means the soul, or a soul, an individual, a person; *Mahatma,* a high soul, an illuminated being, a spiritual personality; and *Paramatma,* the divine man, the self-realized person, the God-conscious soul. As it is said in the Gayan, 'If you only explore him, there is a lot in man', therefore man—and I mean every man—has a very wide scope of development in the spiritual spheres, a scope that an ordinary mind cannot imagine.

The term 'divine man' has always been chiefly connected with man, and very few realize that in fact it means God-man. The reason for this is that certain religiously inclined people have separated man so much from God that they have filled the gap between man and God with what they call religion, a faith that stands for ever as a dividing wall between God and man, and in which all sins are attributed to man and all purity to God. It is a good idea, but far from the truth.

Regarding the first word, Atma, mankind can be divided into three principal categories. In one category he is the animal man, in another he can be the devil man, and yet another he can be the human man. A Hindustani poet says, 'There are many difficulties in life, because even for a man it is difficult to be a person.'

The animal man is the one who concerns himself only with food and drink and whose actions are in no way different from those of an animal, who is content with the satisfaction of his natural appetites. The man who represents devilish qualities is the one in whom the ego, the self, has become so strong and powerful, and therefore so blind, that it has almost wiped out any sense of gentleness, of kindness, of justice. He is the one who takes pleasure in causing harm or hurt to another person, the one who returns evil for the good done to him, the one whose pleasure is to do wrong. The number of those belonging to this category is large.

Then there is the human man, in whom sentiment is developed. Perhaps he is not the physician's idea of a normal person. But from the point of view of the mystic, a person in whom there is a balance between thought and sentiment, who is awakened to the feeling of another, and who is conscientious in everything he does and aware of the effect that it produces on others, is beginning to become human. In other words, it is not an easy thing even for a man to be a man. Sometimes it takes a lifetime.

The Mahatma is an illuminated soul. He looks at life from another point of view. He thinks about others more than about himself; his life is devoted to actions of beneficence; he expects no appreciation or reward for all that he can do for others; he does not look for praise and he is not afraid of blame. On one side connected with God and on the other side connected with the world, he lives his life as harmoniously as possible. Why does he tread the path of righteousness and piety? Why does he spend his life teaching and preaching to humanity? He does it because it is natural; every loving and illuminated heart has a desire to see others partake of its vision of glory.

There are three categories of Mahatmas. One is busy struggling with himself and with conditions before him and around him. Why should he struggle? The answer is that there is always a conflict between the person who wishes to go upward and the wind that blows him downward. The wind that blows a person downward is continually felt by anyone who takes a step on the path of progress. This wind is conflict with the self, it is conflict with others, it is conflict with conditions; conflicts that come from all around, till every part of that Mahatma is tested and tried, till his patience is almost exhausted and his ego is crushed. It is a hard rock that is turned into a soft paste. Just as a soldier in war may receive many wounds, and still more impressions which remain in his heart as wounds, so is the condition of this warrior who walks on the spiritual path; for everything is against him; his friends though they may not know it, his foes, conditions, the atmosphere, the self. And the wounds that he has to experience and the impressions that he receives in the struggle, make him into a spiritual personality, a personality which is difficult to resist, which is overwhelming.

The next category of Mahatma is the one who learns his lesson by passiveness, resignation, sacrifice, love, devotion, and sympathy. There is a kind of love that is like the flame of a candle: blow, and it is gone. It can only remain as long as it is not blown out; it cannot withstand blowing. And there is a love that is like the sun that rises and reaches the zenith, and then sets and disappears; this love endures longer. But then there is a love that is like the divine Intelligence, that was and is and will be. The closing and the opening of the eyes will not take away intelligence; the rising and the setting of the sun will not affect intelligence. When that love is created which endures wind and storm, and stands firm through rise and fall, then a person's language becomes different; the world cannot understand it. When love has once reached the Sovereign of love, it is like the water of the sea that has arisen as vapour and has formed the clouds over the earth and then pours down as rainfall. The continual outpouring of such a heart is unimaginable; not only human beings but even birds and beasts must feel its influence, its effect. It is a love that cannot be put into words, a love that radiates, proving its warmth by the atmosphere it creates. The resigned soul of the Mahatma may appear weak to someone who does not understand him, for he takes praise and blame in the same way, and he accepts all that is given to him, favour or disfavour, pleasure or pain. All that comes he accepts with resignation.

For the third category of these highly evolved souls there is struggle on the one hand and resignation on the other. And this is a most difficult way to progress: to go one step forward, and another step backward, and so on. There is no mobility in the progress because the one thing is contrary to the other. On one side power is working, on the other side love; on one side kingliness, on the other side slavery. As the Emperor Ghasnavi said in a Persian poem, 'I as an emperor have thousands of slaves ready at my call. But since love has kindled my heart, I have become the slave of my slaves.' On the one hand there is activity, on the other hand passivity.

The first example of the Mahatma may be called the Master, the next the Saint, and the third the Prophet.

With the Paramatma we come to the highest stage of the awakening of the consciousness. An ordinary person gives greater importance to the world and less to God; the illuminated one gives greater importance to God and less to the world; but the Paramatma gives, and yet at the same time does not give, importance to God or to the world. He is what he is. If one says to him, 'It is all true', he says, 'Yes, it is all true.' If one says, 'It is not true', he says, 'Yes, it is not true.' If one says, 'All is both false and true', he says, 'Yes, all is false and true.' His language becomes gibberish and very puzzling to an ordinary person. For it is easier to communicate with someone who speaks our language, but as soon as the sense of someone's words is different, his language becomes different; it becomes a foreign language compared with one's everyday speech. Words mean nothing to the Paramatma, but only their inner sense. And one cannot even say that he understands the sense: he is the sense; he becomes that which others pursue.

THE PROPHETIC TENDENCY

THE PROPHETIC tendency exists throughout the whole of manifestation. It exists among the jinns and the heavenly beings, and also in every part of nature, in the mineral and vegetable kingdoms and among the animals as well as among men.

There would be no diamond mines if there were not a spark in the diamond. One spark of a diamond may cause any other atom of the earth with which it comes in contact to become a diamond; it is the same with the ruby. The diamond wants to make everything else become a diamond, and the ruby wants to make every other atom into a ruby.

As for the plants, if one goes into the jungle—not where man has planted and sowed, but in the real jungle which has not been touched—one will see that where there is one mango tree, many mango trees will grow. If there is one fragrant flower, a thousand fragrant flowers will be near it; if there is a sweet fruit, there will be hundreds of sweet fruits.

Among the animals too there are many examples of this phenomenon. For instance, in India the monkeys sometimes come to a village from the forest and destroy all the roofs of the houses. There is always one among them which is the leader. When he jumps, all the other monkeys jump after him. When he wants to go back to the forest, they all go back to the forest.

In the northern provinces near Nainital and Nepal, at the foot of the Himalayas, there is jungle in which there are elephants. The natives have many different ways of catching these elephants, and one way is to dig a pit and cover it over with a net and branches; then they hang their hammocks up in the trees, and there they stay for some days watching for the elephants. They are quite happy in the trees, because the climate is pleasant. If a herd of elephants happens to go that way, one elephant puts his foot in the net and falls into the pit; he cannot help himself. When he cries out, the other elephants look on from a distance, but are afraid to go near, and the men have a kind of firework with which they frighten them away if they do.

Now in a troop of elephants there is always one which walks in front. He holds a stout branch in his trunk, and he knocks on the ground with it before every step to see whether there is a pit. Then, if the ground is safe, he goes forward and all the others follow him. He knows about a thousand other dangers. The herd have such confidence in him that wherever he goes, they go too. This shows that the quality of leadership exists among elephants, and also the tendency to self-sacrifice. The elephant that is the leader goes first, realizing that if there is a pit he may fall in and the other elephants will be safe. He is careful, however, not to go anywhere where it is not safe, and if an elephant is caught it is generally some small elephant which has no sense and does not follow the leader.

In Nepal, the Maharaja had an elephant which was just such a leader. He lived in the Maharaja's palace, and the Maharaja gave orders that no one should ride him but himself, because he honoured the elephant, recognizing his qualities. I have seen this myself. Whenever Maharaja Bir Shamsher went into the forest elephant hunting, this elephant was taken too. The Maharaja had named him Bijili, which means 'lightning'. He was very small, but if they failed to make a catch, Bijili was sent out, and he always came back with another elephant, such was his magnetism. He did not like to catch elephants, because he possessed the quality of mercy, he would never go unless he was forced by the mahouts, and when he saw the other elephants, at first he turned his head away. This shows that even among animals the prophetic tendency exists.

Sometimes we see this prophetic tendency in parents. Whatever way they themselves have had to follow, they wish to train their child for the best way, for a higher way. Sometimes we see it in a friend. Whatever undesirable experiences he may have had himself, he wishes to save his friend from them. It is only the chosen ones, the blessed souls who have this tendency; it is not found in all parents, nor in every friend. To have such parents, such a friend, is the greatest blessing.

What was the object of the prophetic mission? The evolution

of man has been such that he was very much nearer to the
animals in ancient times than now. Then he thought only of eating and drinking and his chief aim was to take whatever he wanted
from other people, caring nothing about the result of his actions,
until he was awakened from this animal existence.

The prophets were sent to awaken man; just as someone who
cannot wake up of his own accord in the morning is wakened by
the alarm-clock. The prophets were this alarm. Sometimes
power was needed to arouse people, and in such a case the
prophet was a king, like Solomon. Sometimes beauty appealed,
and thus Joseph came, whose appearance, whose face was so
beautiful that all hearts were melted by his magnetism.

It has always been the way of the divine Power to send that
prophet who was needed at the time. When a venerable life was
needed there was Jacob, in whom everything was so worthy of
veneration that all bowed before him. At a time when music
was deeply felt and admired David came; gifted with a beautiful
voice and playing the harp, he gave his message in songs. In this
way every prophet came in the guise that the people of the age
could understand. At first, however, the people's intelligence
would not be sufficiently developed for this, and their self was too
much before their eyes. The prophets had renewed their own
self, and that is why they were prophets. When the self is before
the eyes of the soul, then the soul is blinded.

There is a saying that the words of the prophet are as seals on
the secret of God. This means that just as the seal protects the
contents of a letter, and when that seal is broken the matter
which one wants to read is disclosed, so it is with the words of the
prophet. The seal is not a letter; it is only a seal; and so are the
prophet's words. And again there comes a moment in one's life
when one is able to open that seal. It may be opened after one
month, after five months, five years, or more, but the time will
come; and when the seal is opened, then everything is disclosed,
just as in an opened letter.

Once I put to music a verse of an inspired poet of Persia, and I
sang it with great joy for the words had a beautiful meaning;
yet at the same time I always felt that the verse had a meaning
beyond the apparent one, which I did not understand. I had a

distinct feeling that something was sealed and hidden there. And after fifteen years it happened, when my mind was searching for a simile for a certain revelation, that a voice came, bringing it to my mind. There was no end to my joy in opening that seal which had been closed for fifteen years! For everything there is an appointed time; and when that time comes it is revealed. That is why, although on one hand we may be eager to attain to a certain revelation, yet on the other hand we must have patience to wait for the moment of its coming.

Although the tongue of God is continually speaking through all things, yet in order to speak to the deaf ears of many among us, it is necessary for Him to speak through the lips of man. He has done this all through the history of man, every great teacher of the past having been this guiding spirit living the life of God in human guise. In other words, their human guise has been various coats worn by the same being, who only appeared to be different in each. Shiva, Buddha, Rama, Krishna on the one side; Abraham, Moses, Jesus, Mohammad on the other; and many more, known or unknown to history, have always been in reality one and the same person.

Those who knew the messenger when they saw him, recognized him in whatever form or guise; those who could only see the coat went astray. To the Sufi, therefore, there is only one teacher, whatever name he may be given at different periods in history; and he comes constantly to awaken humanity from the slumber of this life of illusion and to guide man onward towards divine protection. As the Sufi progresses in this view he recognizes his Master not only in the holy ones, but in the wise and in the foolish, in the saint and in the sinner, and he has never allowed the Master, who is the one and only Master and who alone can be and who ever will be, to disappear from his sight.

Is not the source of all truth hidden in every man's heart, whether he be Christian, Muslim, Buddhist, or Jew? Are we not all part of that life which we call spiritual or divine? To be only this or that, is the same as not going further than this or that. The bliss found in the solitude is hidden within every human being; he has inherited it from his heavenly Father. In mystical terms it is called the All-pervading Light. Light is the source and origin of every human soul and of every mind.

The Sufi looks upon all life as one life, upon all religions as his religion: call him a Christian and he seeks to be that, call him a Muslim and he is that, a Hindu and he feels he is that; call him whatever you like, he does not mind. A Sufi does not desire to be called anything. Who calls him a Sufi? It is not he. But if he does not call himself something, someone else is sure to find a name for him.

Man is the aim of creation, and he is the highest being because he is man. He alone knows the purpose for which he was manifested, the reason why he is here. Cats and dogs do not know this. Every other being in manifestation wants to become man. The jinns want to become man, and also the rocks, the plants, and the animals.

But it is not man as he usually is that the divine Power wishes to produce; the man that God wants is not the man who only eats, drinks, and sleeps like the animals. If a man wishes to know what he should be he should compare himself with the animals. If he eats, they also eat; if he drinks, they also drink; if he sleeps, they also sleep. They have their passions and hatred and anger just as he has. If he is only that, then he is not man. Only in man do we find kindness, sympathy, discipline, self-sacrifice, meekness and such qualities; and if we see any of them in the animals, in dogs and cats or horses and cattle, such as faithfulness in the dog, and obedience and courage in the horse, it is only through the reflection of man, through association with man. If we go to a river-bed and pick up pebbles, how many pebbles do we not find that show the likeness of a human face! Sometimes the nose is absent, sometimes the lips, but we very often find marks and lines resembling a face. What a wonderful thing this is, for it shows us that everything is striving to become like the human face, in fact to become man.

It is also true that man alone has the sense of responsibility. The animals do not have it. Regarding this the Qur'an says, 'We offered our burden to the heavens, to the earth, and to the mountains, but they refused to bear it and were afraid of it; then we offered our burden to man, and he accepted it.' This means that only man has accepted the responsibility for his actions. Then the sura goes on to say, 'Verily, man is cruel and foolish.' Foolish, because he has taken upon himself that which is God's. There are, for instance, many who run away from marriage, because they think a wife and children are a responsibility. They do not realize that a wife and children are God's, and that He takes care of what is His. And man is cruel because he uses his will and power, which in reality are God's, to harm others. Our will, our strength, are God's and yet we say 'my' and 'mine'; we claim them for ourselves.

The watchman calls from evening till morning. In the day the alarm-clock is not needed, because it is day. The prophets were sent during the night. They came with the same message under different names; the same divine wisdom spoke in each of them. But if a Hebrew had been asked, 'Do you recognize Krishna and Rama?' he would have said, 'I never heard of Krishna and Rama; I recognize Moses, because that is written in my book.' If a Hindu were asked, 'Do you recognize Moses or Christ?' he would say, 'No, I recognize Rama and Krishna and Vishnu and the Vedanta. You may keep Christ and Moses, I will keep Rama and Krishna and Vishnu.' There are some who prefer the Kabala to the Bible and recognize only the Kabala. If you ask a Roman Catholic, he will say, 'There is only one Church, and that is mine.' They have all recognized the name, the personality, but they have not recognized the truth. They want to keep Krishna in the temple, Christ in the church, and Moses shut up in the synagogue. That is why there are so many now seeking for truth.

In each age the message was revealed more and more clearly according to the capacity of the world to bear it; and this went on until the last and clearest revelation, the message of Mohammad, the seal of the prophets. After this no more prophets were needed; the world was awakened to the understanding of true reality. This is not the time to wait for the coming of another prophet; now is the time to awaken to the truth within ourselves. And if there is a friend who has gone this way already, now is the time to ask his advice.

It is not the Sufi's work to interfere with anyone's religion, nor to force a belief upon anyone. He does not tell one to believe this or that. The murshid is a friend and guide. He advises, he does not force anything upon one. I was not born in a Christian family, but no Christian could be more touched than I am by the words of Christ that I read. If they are rightly understood, they alone are enough to make one a saint. It is written that finally he was crucified; but from his birth onward every moment of his life was a crucifixion. The world is too rough for the souls of the prophets; their hearts are too tender for it.

No Brahmin has studied the Vedanta with more interest than I have. If one knows Brahma one knows God, and one is in fact Brahmin, although whether the Brahmin recognizes this or not is another matter. The Sufi says, 'You wish to know about revelation? You wish to know about inspiration? This is the way for you to follow: believe as much as your intelligence allows you to believe, as much as you can reach; do not believe what your intelligence does not allow you to believe.'

He recognizes one divine wisdom in all the prophetic messages. He sees the same infinite Being through all, in different forms through all ages. It is just as if one had the photographs of one's sweetheart at different ages: at twelve years, at twenty, at thirty, at forty. The photographs are different, but it is the same sweetheart.

SEEING

ONE CAN see, one can look, and one can observe. These three words denote the same action, yet each word suggests something different. By observing we understand something about what we see; by seeing we take full notice of it; but by looking we glance at it without necessarily understanding it or taking notice of it. And so there are three conditions: looking at the surface of a thing, looking at a thing properly, and looking at a thing with real observation and understanding it at the same time.

Everyone notices things in one of these three ways. That which interests a man most, he observes most keenly; that which attracts his mind, he sees and takes notice of; and that upon which his glance happens to fall, he only looks at. And there are, therefore, three different effects made upon man by all he sees: a deeper effect of that which he has observed fully, a clear effect of that which he has seen, and a passing effect of that which had just caught his glance. This is the reason why there are seers, thinkers, and those who have only their two eyes.

There is another side to this question: a person who is walking gains a certain kind of impression of the route he takes; one who drives the same way in a motor-car has a different kind of experience, and the experience of the one who flies in an aeroplane is different again. Perhaps the one who was walking was not able to reach his goal as quickly as the one in the motor-car or the one in the aeroplane, but the observations that he was able to make, the sights that he saw, and all the experiences that he had there, were far beyond those of the other two. And in just the same way our mind works. There is one man whose mind works at the rate of an aeroplane; there is another man whose mind works like an automobile; and there is a third whose mind works at the speed of a man walking. The one whose mind is working at that speed will not perhaps react as quickly as the others, but what he thinks he will think thoroughly; what he sees he will see thoroughly. It is he who will have insight into things, it is he who will understand the hidden law behind things, because the activity of his mind is normal. Thinking does not always depend upon quickness of the mind; sometimes it is the quality of the mind which is more important.

An intelligent person thinks swiftly too, but that is another thing. There can be a great difference between two stones, for instance between a diamond and a pebble. They are both stones, but one is precious and the other dull. In the same way there are two different qualities of mind: one man thinks quickly and intelligently, the other thinks quickly but is very often mistaken. He is mistaken because he thinks quickly, while in the other case it is the quality of mind which even in quick thinking makes that person think rightly. Nevertheless the rhythm of thinking has a great deal to do with one's life. When the three who have travelled the same way on foot, in the car and by aeroplane, meet together and speak of their experiences, we shall find a great difference in what they tell; and this explains why people who have gone through the same life, who have lived under the same sun, who have been born on the same earth, are yet so different in their mentality. The reason is that their minds have travelled at different speeds. Their experiences are quite different though they have travelled the same way.

A seer is the one who has not only looked, but who has seen. And how has he seen? By controlling the impulse of walking too quickly, by resisting the temptation of going to the right or to the left, by going steadily towards the object that he wants to reach. All these things help to make one a seer.

The seer sees more than for instance the astrologer; much more. There is no comparison. But the seer does not speak about what he sees; if he did he would become just like the astrologer. To the seer every person's soul is just like an open letter; but if he were to divulge its secrets his sight would become dimmer every day because it is a trust given to him by God. Spiritual trust is given to those who can keep that trust and who are able to keep a secret.

There are many wrong interpretations of the word seer. Sometimes people think that a seer is a clairvoyant or a spiritist, but that is a different kind of person and not a seer. The seer need not see the unseen world; there is so much to be seen here in the visible world! There is so much that man could see in this objective world, but which is hidden from his eyes, that if he were to concentrate all his life upon seeing all that is to be seen he would find more than enough to think about. It is childish curiosity on the part of some people when they want to see something that they think no one has seen before. It is also vanity, for the sake of telling that they see something which others do not see. But the world seen and the world unseen are one and the same; and they are both here. And when we cannot see the world unseen, it is not because it hides itself from our eyes, it is because we close our eyes to it.

Then there is long sight and short sight and medium sight. There are some who can see far beyond, or long before events, and there is the person who only sees what is immediately before him and what is next to him; he sees nothing of what is behind him. His influence reaches only as far as the thing that is just beside him, and it is that which influences him. But there is another person who reasons about what he sees; his can be called medium sight. He reasons about it as far as his reason allows. He cannot see beyond his reasoning; he goes so far and no further. Naturally if these three persons meet and speak together, each has his own language. It is not surprising if one does not understand the point of view of the other, because each one has his own vision according to which he looks at things. No one can give his own sight to another person in order to make him see differently.

If the spiritual people of all ages taught faith, it was not because they wished that no one should think for himself but should accept everything in faith which was taught him. If they had had that intention they would not have been spiritual people. Nevertheless, however clever a person may be, however devoted and enthusiastic, if he is without faith the spiritual souls cannot impart their knowledge to him, for there is no such thing as spiritual knowledge in the sense of learning. If there is anything spiritual that can be imparted to the pupil, it is the point of view, the outlook on life. If a person already has that outlook on life, he does not need spiritual guidance; but if he has not, then words of explanation will not explain anything to him, for it is a point of view and it cannot be explained in words.

However much a person may try to describe the light that he saw when he was on top of a mountain to the man who has never climbed that mountain, that man may refuse to believe all that the other says; but perhaps, if he trusts him, he will begin to listen to his guidance. He may not see it, but he will listen, and he will benefit by the experience of the one who has seen the light from the top of the mountain. But the one who goes to the top of the mountain will have the same experience himself.

There is still another side to this question, and that is from which height one looks at life. There is one view when a person looks at life standing on the ground; it is different when he is climbing the mountain, and it is a different outlook again when he has reached the top. And what are these degrees? They are degrees of consciousness. When a person is looking at life and says, 'I, and all else', that is one point of view; when a person sees all else and forgets 'I', that is another point of view; and when a person sees all and identifies it with 'I', that is another point of view again. And the difference these points of view make in a person's outlook is so vast that words can never explain it.

Reaching the top of the mountain means entering what is called *Nirvana*, cosmic consciousness; the idea of communicating with God is symbolized by a person who has climbed a part of the mountain, and who therefore already has a less clearly defined idea of *I* and *you*, and of *he, she*, and *it* than the one who is standing on the ground.

Spiritual progress is expansion of the soul. It is not always desirable to live on the top of the mountain, because the ground also is made for man. What is desirable is to have one's feet on the ground and one's head as high as the top of the mountain. A person who can observe life from all sides, from all angles, will have a different experience from each angle; and every side he looks at will give him new knowledge, a different knowledge from that which he had before.

Finally there is the question of seeing and not seeing. This is understood by the mystics as being able to see at will, and also being able to overlook. It is not easy for a person to overlook, it is

something one must learn. There is much that man is able to see
and that he must see; and there is much that he should not see,
that it is better he does not see. If we cannot see, that is a disadvantage; but there is no disadvantage in not seeing something
that we should not see. There are so many things that can be seen
that we may just as well avoid seeing those we should not.

The one who is held by what he sees lacks mastery. Although
he does not want to see it, he cannot help seeing it; but the one
who has his sight under control, sees what he wants to see, and
what he does not want to see he does not see. That is mastery.
And as it is true of the eyes, that we see what is before us and
we do not see what is behind us, so it is true of the mind: what is
before it, it sees and what is behind it, it does not see. Naturally,
therefore, if this objective world is before a person's eyes, the
other world is hidden from his sight, because he sees what is
before him and not what is behind him. And as it is true that
what is behind us we can only see by turning our head, so also it is
true that what the mind does not see can only be seen when the
mind is turned the other way. What is learned in esotericism and
in mysticism is the turning of the mind from the outer vision to
the inner vision.

One might ask, what profit do we derive from this? If it is
profitable to rest at night after a whole day's work, so it is
profitable to turn one's mind from this world of variety in order
to rest it and to give it another experience which belongs to it,
which is its own and which it needs. It is this experience which is
attained by the meditative process. A person who is able to think
but not able to forget, a person who is able to speak but not able
to keep silent, a person who is able to move but not able to keep
still, a person who is able to cry but not able to laugh—that person
does not know mastery. It is like having one hand, it is like standing on one foot. To have complete experience of life one must be
able to act and to be still, one must be able to talk and to keep
silent.

There are many precious things in nature and art, things that
are beyond value, yet there is nothing in this world that is more
precious than sight; and the most precious of all is insight, to be
able to see, to be able to understand, to be able to learn, to be

able to know. That is the greatest gift that God can give, and all other things in life are small compared with it. If there is anything that one can do to enrich one's knowledge, to raise one's soul to higher spheres, to allow one's consciousness to expand to perfection, it is to do everything one possibly can to open one's sight, which is the sign of God in man. It is the opening of the sight which is called the soul's unfoldment.

SELF-DISCIPLINE

WHAT COUNTS most in the path of truth is self-discipline, for without this our studies and practices cannot produce great results. This self-discipline has many different aspects. By studying the lives of the ascetics who lived in the mountains and forests and in the wilderness, we learn that those who have really sought after truth have done their utmost to practise self-discipline; without it no soul in the world has ever arrived at a higher realization. No doubt it frightens people living in the world, accustomed to a life of comfort, even to think of self-discipline; and when they do think of it they imagine it only in its extreme forms. But it is not necessary for us to go to the mountain caves or to the forest or to the wilderness in order to practise self-discipline; we can do so in our everyday life.

There are four principal ways in which self-discipline can be practised. One way is the physical way, the practice of remaining in the same position, of sitting in the same posture for a certain time. And when one begins to do it one will find that it is not as easy as it seems. One may sit without realizing it in the same posture or stand in one position for a certain time, but as soon as one begins consciously to practise it one finds it very difficult. There are various positions in which to hold one's hands or legs or eyes or head; and these practices help one to develop the power of self-discipline.

The fantasy of the whole of creation is apparent in the direction of every movement; it is in accordance with that direction that a thing takes form. Where do all the opposites such as sun and moon, man and woman, pain and joy, negative and positive, come from? Since the source and the goal are one, why such differences? They belong to their direction, the secret of every difference is direction. It is an activity, an energy working in a certain direction which makes a certain form. That is why the way one sits makes a difference; it makes a difference whether one sleeps on the right side or on the left, whether one stands on one's feet or on one's head. Mystics have practised various postures for many, many years; and they have discovered different ways of sitting while doing certain breathing exercises. They have made a science out of this; there is a warrior's posture, a thinker's posture, an aristocratic posture, a lover's posture, a healer's posture; different postures for the attainment of different objects. These postures make it easier for man to learn the science of direction; posture does not denote anything but direction.

Then there is another aspect of self-discipline which is connected with eating or drinking: one avoids certain things in one's everyday food or drink, and makes a practice of being able to live without them, especially things that one feels one cannot live without. This is one of the reasons, apart from the psychological and physical ones, that some adepts live on a diet of fruit and vegetables; that for days or weeks or months they go without certain things that they are accustomed to eat or drink.

Fasting is also one of the ways by which the denseness of the body can be diminished. And when one knows the right way of fasting, when one is under the direction of someone who really knows when and why and how a person should fast so that he is benefited by it, a great deal can be achieved by fasting. Surgeons keep their patients without food for several hours or days knowing that it will help them to heal more quickly. In the same way spiritual teachers may prescribe a fast for their pupils; sometimes going without meat and sometimes without bread; sometimes living on milk or fruits and sometimes for a limited time without anything at all, according to the capacity and endurance of the pupil. But in point of fact, I am myself the last person to prescribe fasting. I hardly ever do so; I only give some advice to my pupils if they themselves wish to fast. I once knew a disciple who went to a murshid, and the murshid told him that in order to begin his practices he should start with a three days' fast; but after the first day he felt so hungry that he left the city, so that he might never see that teacher again!

There is always a meaning to it if the teacher prescribes a fast. In Baghdad there lived a great Sufi who was known for his wonderful attainments. Once he told a young pupil of his to live on a vegetarian diet. The mother of this young man, having heard that since going to that teacher the boy only ate vegetables, went to the teacher's house to tell him what she thought about this. She arrived just when he was at table, and there was chicken in front of him. So the mother said, 'You are teaching your pupils to live on a vegetarian diet and you yourself are enjoying chicken!' Upon this the teacher uncovered the dish, and the chicken flew away; and he said, 'The day when your son too can do this, he may eat chicken!'

There is yet another aspect of self-discipline and that is the habit of thinking and of forgetting. This means on the one hand to be able to think of whatever one wishes to think of, and to continue to do so and to be able to hold that thought; and on the other hand to practise the forgetting of things, so that certain thoughts may not get a hold over one's mind; and in the same way to check thoughts of agitation, anger, depression, prejudice, hatred. This gives moral discipline and by doing so one becomes the master of one's mind.

After one has practised these three aspects of discipline, one is able to arrive at the fourth aspect which is greater still; it is greater because by it one arrives at spiritual experiences. This discipline is practised to free one's consciousness from one's environment. It is the experience of the adepts and they have spent much of their lives arriving at this. In the old school of the Sufis, and even today, there is a custom that when they enter or leave the room of meditation, one among them says, 'Solitude in the crowd.' The suggestion is that even when one is in the midst of the crowd one can still keep one's tranquillity, one's peace, so that one is not disturbed by the surroundings. It is this which enables one to live in the midst of the world and yet progress spiritually; and it is no longer necessary to go into the wilderness, as many souls did in ancient times, in order to develop spiritually.

No doubt this is difficult, but at the same time it is simple; and in a small way everyone experiences it, although unconsciously. A person engaged in something that interests him very much, or that completely occupies his mind, is often not conscious of his environment. A poet, a writer, a composer, a thinker, when he is entirely absorbed in something that he does, is unconscious

of his environment. And it very often happens that one is so
absorbed in something one is doing or thinking about, that one is
not conscious of one's body or one's self. Only what a person is
thinking of exists for him, not even his self. This is the stage
which is termed by Sufis *Fanà*. The word Nirvana about which
so much has been said, is simple to understand in this way. It is
only an experience of the consciousness; in other words it is the
freedom of the soul, reaching a stage where one is not thinking
about oneself, nor about one's environment.

One might ask if these practises are not dangerous in any way.
Everything in this world is dangerous. If we think of the danger
there could be in eating, drinking, going out or coming home,
there could be danger every moment. It is dangerous to go into
the water, but when one can swim that counteracts it. It is even
dangerous to be in the street, but if one can walk and run then
that counteracts the danger. It is in being able to meditate and to
raise one's consciousness above one's environment that the secret
of spiritual development lies.

Once a person is accustomed to the practice of self-discipline
he will find that though in the beginning it may have seemed
difficult, it gradually becomes easier. It does not take long to
experience its wonderful results. Almost everyone complains that
the person who is closest to him does not listen to him. He is
continually saying that the other does not listen to him! But by
self-discipline one rises above this complaint, because one begins
to realize that it is one's own self which does not listen to one.
Then one finds the mischief-maker: it was not the other person,
it was the self; and as one begins to get power over it, one
begins to feel a great mastery. It is a mastery over one's kingdom;
it is a feeling of kingship. And naturally as one begins to experience this phenomenon, everything becomes more and more
easy.

PHYSICAL CONTROL

LIFE HAS two aspects, of which one is known and the other unknown except to a few. This unknown aspect of life may be called the immortal life, the eternal life; and the known aspect may be called mortal life, as it is the experience we have through our physical being which gives us the evidence of life. The immortal life exists but most of us do not know it. This is because of our lack of knowledge, and not because the immortal does not exist. Everything we have in this life, whether an object, a living being, a thought, a condition, a deed, or an experience, breaks up and dies away. Every one of these things has its birth and death; sooner or later what is composed must be decomposed, what is made must break, what is built must be destroyed, and what is visible must disappear.

This shows that there is a struggle between what we call life and the life which is behind it. In Sufi terms we call these two aspects of life *Kazá* and *Kadr*: Kazá, the unlimited aspect of life, and Kadr, the limited aspect in the background. Kadr draws upon the life of Kazá for its existence, and Kazá waits, its mouth open to swallow whatever comes into it. Therefore the adepts and the wise, those who are called mystics or Sufis, have discovered the science of how to withhold the experience of life from the mouth of Kazá, the ever-assimilating aspect of life. If we do not know how to withhold it, it will fall into the mouth of Kazá; for Kazá is always waiting with open mouth, just as an illness awaits the moment when a person is lacking in energy. So in all different forms Kazá is waiting to assimilate everything that comes, which is then merged in it.

The question arises: how can we withhold, how can we keep something from falling into the mouth of Kazá? And the answer is: by controlling our body and our mind. In the East I have seen a man lifting a heavy stone on one finger. One might wonder how that can be possible, but it is the power of will alone which sustains the heavy stone; the finger is only an excuse. I have seen those who experiment in the field of spirit and matter, jumping into the raging fire and coming our safe, cutting the muscles of their body and healing them instantly. It is not a fable that the mystics know how to levitate; it has been seen by thousands of people in India. I do not mean that this power is something which is worth striving for, I only wish to point out what can be accomplished by the power of will.

To establish the reign of will-power over the physical body the first thing necessary is physical control. The scriptures say that the body is the temple of God, but this means that the body is made to be the temple of God; a temple cannot be called a temple of God if God is not brought and placed there. So naturally when a soul feels depressed there is something wrong with the vehicle. When the writer wishes to work and the pen is not in order, it annoys him; there is nothing the matter with the writer; it is the pen which is not right. No discomfort comes from the soul; the soul is happy by nature; the soul is happiness itself. It becomes unhappy when something is the matter with its vehicle, which is its instrument, its tool with which it experiences life. Care of the body, therefore, is the first and the most important principle of religion. Piety without this thought is of little significance. The soul comes into this world in order that it may experience the different phases of manifestation and yet not lose its way, but regain its original freedom with the added experience and knowledge it has gained in this world.

Among the various kinds of physical culture known to the modern world there is nothing that teaches the method or the secret of sustaining an action. For instance to be able to sit in the same posture without moving, to be able to look at the same spot without moving the eyes, to be able to listen to something without being disturbed by something else, to be able to experience hardness, softness, heat, or cold, while keeping one's vibrations even, or to be able to retain the taste of salt, sweet, or sour. Ordinarily these experiences come and go, and man has no control over the extent of his pleasure or joy; he cannot enjoy an experience through any of his senses for as long as he would wish. He depends upon outer things and he does not know how to sustain any experience he may have; he does not realize that the only way of sustaining an experience is by control.

There is another side to this question. Being unconsciously aware that every experience which is pleasant and joyful will soon pass away, man is over-anxious; and instead of trying to retain the experience he hurries it and thereby loses it. For instance the habit of eating hastily or of laughing before an amusing sentence is finished, is caused by the fact that a person fears that the pleasure or joy will pass away. In every experience man loses the power to sustain it because of his anxiety about losing the pleasure it gives. To give another example: the great joy of watching a tragedy in the theatre lies in experiencing it fully, but people are sometimes so thrilled that already at the beginning of the tragedy they begin to shed tears, and then afterwards no tears are left. When once the zenith has been reached, there is no more experience to be had; and so instead of keeping every experience from being swallowed by the mouth of eternal life, man throws it into the life behind him without discovering its secret.

The mystics, therefore, by sitting or standing in different postures have gained control over their muscles and nervous system, and this has an effect on the mind. A person who lacks control over his nervous and his muscular systems has no control over his mind; he eventually loses it. But by having control over one's muscular and nervous systems one gets control over the mind also.

The means by which life draws its power is the breath. With every breath one draws in, one draws the life and power and intelligence from the unseen and unknown life. And when one knows the secret of posture, and draws from the unseen world the energy and power and inspiration, one gets the power of sustaining one's thought, one's word, one's experience, one's pleasure, one's joy. When one asks what is the cause of every tragedy in life, the answer is: limitation. All miseries come from this one thing, limitation. Therefore the mystics have tried by exercises, by practices, and by studies to overcome limitation as much as possible. There is no worse enemy of man than helplessness. When a person feels that he is helpless, this is the end of his joy and happiness.

Furthermore, in order to gain physical control one needs

thought-power as well as both posture and breath. One must get above one's likes and dislikes, for they cause much weakness in life. When one says, 'I cannot stand this', 'I cannot eat this', 'I cannot drink this', 'I cannot bear this', 'I cannot tolerate', 'I cannot endure', all those things show man's weakness. The greater the will-power the more man is able to stand everything that comes along. It does not mean that one has no choice; one can have one's choice, but when one gives in to one's ego then life becomes difficult. There is a false ego in man, which the Sufis call *Nafs*, and this ego feeds on weakness. This ego feels vain when one says, 'I cannot bear it, I do not like it'; it feeds the ego, the vanity. It thinks, 'I am better than others' and thereby this ego becomes strong. But the one who can discriminate, distinguish, choose, while at the same time having everything under control, and who although enjoying sweet things can yet drink a bowl of something bitter, that person has reached mastery.

Also, impulses weaken a person when he gives in helplessly to the impulse. For instance perhaps he has an impulse to go to the park, but instead of waiting till it is the right time to go to the park he quickly puts on his hat and goes along. By following his impulse immediately he loses power over himself. But the one who subordinates his impulse, controlling it, using it for the best purpose, attains mastery. Besides, indulgence in an impulse towards comfort, towards one's own convenience; always looking for the path of least resistance brings weakness. However small the work may be, if a person takes it seriously and finishes it with patience, he gains much power over himself.

Patience is one of the principal things in life, although sometimes patience is as bitter, as hard, as unbearable as death. Sometimes one would prefer death to patience. But it is of the greatest importance for the human race to develop patience in all conditions of life, in all walks of life. Whether we are rich or poor, high or low, this is the one quality that must be developed. Besides it is patience that gives endurance, it is patience that is all-powerful, and by lack of patience one loses much. Very often the answer to one's prayer is within one's reach, the hand of Providence not very far off, and then one loses one's patience and thereby the opportunity. Therefore impatience, in whatever form, is to be avoided. It makes one lose one's equilibrium, and when that is lost nothing can be accomplished. There is no gain to be had from impatience; yet impatience does not necessarily mean sloth, negligence, or laziness.

In conclusion, physical control makes a foundation for the character and the personality, a foundation upon which to build spiritual attainment.

HEALTH

HEALTH is an orderly condition caused by the regular working of the mechanism of the physical body. The regular working of the physical body depends upon the weather, diet, the balance between action and repose, and the condition of the mind.

Many think that it is some deformity of the body, a curve in the spine or a cavity in the brain that affects the mind; few realize that very often the mind produces an irregularity in the spine or in the brain, thereby causing an illness. The ordinary point of view regards an illness as a physical disorder, which can be cured by the means of material remedies. Then there is another point of view: that of people who think more deeply and who say that by not taking notice of an illness or by suggesting to oneself that one is well, one can be restored to health. This point of view can of course be exaggerated, as when some people claim that illness is an illusion, that it has no existence of its own; but the ordinary point of view can also be exaggerated, if one thinks that medicine is the only means of cure and that the mind has little to do with actual illness.

Both these persons, the one who looks at it from the ordinary point of view, and the one who does so from a deeper point of view, will find arguments for and against their idea. Some people go as far as to say that medicine must not be touched by those who have faith, and others affirm that illness is as real as health. In the absence of illness a person can easily call pain an illusion, but when he is suffering, then it is difficult for him to call it an illusion.

If one asks who is the more subject to illness, a spiritual person or a material person, the answer is that a spiritual person who disregards physical laws is just as much subject to illness as a material person who does the same thing. No doubt a spiritually inclined person is supposed to be less likely to fall ill, because his spirit has become harmonious through his spirituality; he creates harmony and he radiates it. He keeps to the realm of nature, in tune with the Infinite. Nevertheless, the life of a spiritual person in the midst of the world is like the life of a fish on the land. The fish is a creature of the water; its sustenance, its joy, its happiness are in the water. A spiritual soul is made for solitude; his joy and happiness are in solitude. A spiritual person set in the midst of the world by destiny feels out of place, and the ever-jarring influences of those around him and the continual impact of impressions which disturb his finer senses, make it more likely that he will become ill than those who push their way in the crowd of the world and are used to being pushed back.

A spiritual soul is an old soul, according to Eastern terminology. Even a young person who is spiritually minded shows the nature of the aged; but at the same time spirituality is perpetual youth. A spiritual person admires all things, appreciates all things, enjoys all things to the full. Therefore, if one says the spiritual person is like an old person it is true; and if one says the spiritual person is like a young person that is true also.

People nowadays have lost the conception of normal health, for the standard of normal health is below the real conception of health. To be healthy is not only to be muscular: to be really healthy is to be able to enjoy and appreciate life fully. To be healthy means to be thoughtful. The one who can feel deeply shows the sign of health. It is not surprising if a material person becomes ill, nor is it amazing if a spiritual person is unwell. The former becomes ill because he has lost his rhythm, the latter because he could not keep to a rhythm which is not his own. Whether one is spiritual or material, one has to live in the midst of the world, and so perforce one shares the conditions of every-one, both far and near; and one is subjected to the influences all around, whether they are desirable or not. One cannot close one's eyes, nor can one close one's heart, to the impressions which continually fall upon one. The best one can do is to keep a careful watch against all that causes irregularity, inharmony, and disorder, to be resigned to all one has to pass through, and to be courageous in order to overcome all that keeps one back from health and perfection.

The Sufi holds that the perfection of life lies in perfecting oneself not only spiritually, but in all the various aspects of life. The man who is not capable of attending to all life's needs is certainly ignorant of the true freedom of life.

Just as for every illness there is a remedy, so for every disaster there is a reconstruction. Any effort, in whatever form and however small, made towards the reconstruction or the betterment of conditions is worth-while. But what we need most to understand is that religion of religions and that philosophy of philosophies which is self-knowledge. We shall not understand the outer life if we do not understand ourselves. It is the knowledge of the self which gives us the knowledge of the world.

What is health? Health is order. And what is order? Order is music. Where there is rhythm, regularity, co-operation, there is harmony and sympathy; and therefore health of mind and health of body depend upon preserving that harmony and keeping intact that sympathy which exist in the mind and in the body. Life in the world, and especially if lived among the crowd, tests and tries our patience every moment of the day; and it is most difficult to preserve that harmony and peace which are at the root of all happiness. Life means struggle with friends and battle with foes; it is all the time giving and taking; and it is very difficult to keep the sympathy and harmony which give health and happiness.

All learning and knowledge are acquired; but this is a divine art, and man has inherited it. Although absorbed in outer learning he has forgotten it, yet it is an art which is known to the soul. It is his own being; it is the deepest knowledge of his heart. No progress, in whatever line, will give a man the satisfaction his soul is craving for except this divine art which is the art of being, the pursuit of his soul. In order to help the reconstruction of the world, the only thing which is both possible and necessary is to learn the art of being, and to become an example before trying to serve humanity.

HARMONY

HARMONY is that which makes beauty, beauty in itself has no meaning. An object which is called beautiful at one time or place may not be beautiful at another. And so it is with thought, speech, and action. That which is called beautiful is only so at a certain time and under certain conditions which make it beautiful; so if one could give a true definition of beauty it is harmony. Harmony in a combination of colours, harmony in the drawing of a design or a line, that is what is called beauty; and a word, a thought, a feeling, or an action which creates harmony is productive of beauty.

Whence comes the tendency towards harmony and whence comes the tendency towards inharmony? The natural tendency of every soul is towards harmony, and the tendency towards inharmony is an unnatural state of mind or affairs; the very fact that it is not natural makes it devoid of beauty. The psychology of man is such that he responds both to harmony and inharmony. He cannot help it, because he is naturally so made; mentally and physically he responds to all that comes to him whether it be harmonious or inharmonious.

The teaching of Christ, 'Resist not evil', is a hint not to respond to inharmony. For instance a word of kindness, of sympathy, or an action of love and affection, finds response, but a word of insult, an action of revolt or of hatred, creates a response too, and that response creates still more inharmony in the world. By giving way to inharmony one allows inharmony to multiply. Where does all the great unrest and discord that one now sees pervading the world come from? It seems that it comes from the ignorance of this fact that inharmony creates inharmony, and that inharmony will multiply. If a person is insulted his natural tendency is to reply by insulting the other person still more. In this way he gets the momentary satisfaction of having given a good answer. But he has responded to that power which came from the other, and these two powers, being negative and positive, create more inharmony.

'Resist not evil' does not mean to take evil into oneself. It only means: do not return the inharmony that comes to you, as a person playing tennis would send back the ball with his racket. But at the same time it does not suggest that one should receive the ball with open hands.

The tendency towards harmony may be likened to a rock in the sea: through wind and storm the rock stands firm; waves come with all their force and yet it still stands bearing it all, letting the waves beat against it. By fighting inharmony one increases it; by not fighting it one refrains from adding fuel to the fire which would otherwise increase and cause destruction. But no doubt the wiser we become, the more difficulties we have to face in life, because every kind of inharmony will be directed towards us for the very reason that we will not fight it. We should realize, however, that all these difficulties have helped to destroy this inharmony which would otherwise have multiplied. This is not without its advantages, for every time we stand firm where there is inharmony we increase our strength, though outwardly it may seem a defeat. But one who is conscious of the increase of his power will never admit that it is a defeat, and after a while the person against whom one has stood firm will realize that it was actually his defeat.

The Sufi avoids all unrhythmic actions; he keeps the rhythm of his speech under the control of patience, not speaking a word before the right time, not giving an answer until the question is finished. A contradictory word he considers to be a discord unless spoken in a debate, and even at such times he tries to resolve it into a consonant chord. A contradictory tendency in a man finally develops into a passion, until he will contradict even his own idea if it happens to be pronounced by another. The Sufi in order to keep harmony even modulates his speech from one key to another; in other words he falls in with another person's idea by looking at the subject from the speaker's point of view instead of his own. He makes a basis for every conversation with an appropriate introduction, thus preparing the ears of the listener for a perfect response. He watches his every movement

and expression, as well as those of others, trying to form a consonant chord of harmony between himself and another.

The attainment of harmony in life takes longer to acquire and
more careful study than does the training of the ear and the cultivation of the voice, although it is acquired in the same manner
as the knowledge of music. To the ear of the Sufi every word
spoken is like a note which is true when harmonious and false
when inharmonious. He makes the scale of his speech either
major, minor, or chromatic, as the occasion demands; and his
words, either sharp, flat, or natural, are in accord with the law of
harmony.

Life in the world has a constantly jarring effect, and the
finer we become the more trying it will be to us. And the time
comes when the more sincere and full of goodwill, the more kind
and sympathetic a person is, the worse life becomes for him. If
he is discouraged by it he goes under, but if he keeps his courage
he will find in the end that it was not disadvantageous, for his
power will some day increase to that stage, to that degree, at
which his presence, his word, and his action will control the
thoughts and feelings and actions of others. Then his rhythm will
become powerful and will cause the rhythm of everybody else to
follow it. This is what is called in the East the quality of the master-
mind. But in order to stand firm against the inharmony that
comes from without, one must first practise standing firm against
all that comes from within, from one's own self. For one's own
self is more difficult to control than other people, and when one is
not able to control oneself and one has failed, it is most difficult
to stand firm against the inharmony outside.

What is it that causes inharmony in oneself? Weakness.
Physical weakness or mental weakness, but it is always weakness.
Very often, therefore, one finds that bodily illness causes disharmony and inharmonious tendencies. Besides there are many
diseases of the mind which the scientists of today have not yet
discovered. Sometimes people are considered sane whose mind
in fact is ill, and as not enough attention is paid to the defects
which are inherent in the diseases of the mind, man has never
had a chance to notice them in himself. He is continually finding
fault with others; whether he works in an office, somewhere in a

good position, at home, or anywhere else, he causes inharmony. Nobody realizes this, for to be treated as insane one must first be recognized as insane.

The cause of every discomfort and of every failure is inharmony; and the most useful thing one could impart in education today is the sense of harmony. To develop harmony in children and to bring it to their notice will not be as difficult as it appears; what is needed is to point out to the young the different aspects of harmony in all the various affairs of life.

BALANCE

WHEN LOOKING at the world with the eyes of the seer, we shall find that the people who are called wise and those who are called foolish are much nearer to each other than they are ordinarily thought to be; their different occupations are much more similar than they generally seem in the unbalanced conditions of life.

Balance is something which is rarely found, among mystics or among others. When we become interested in something, it is our nature to want more and more of it; it makes no difference whether it is spiritual or material. If we become very spiritual we lose the world; and if we were not meant to live in this world we would not have been sent here.

The one who sees the good in others will see more and more good. The one who has a fault-finding tendency will find so many faults that at last the good will seem bad in his eyes. Then the eyes themselves will become bad. There is much more chance of a fall for a person who is running than for one who is walking; the excess of activity brings about the fall.

Sometimes a person has no balance in telling the truth. He says, 'I tell the truth', regardless of whether it is in harmony with his surroundings and whether people are prepared to hear that truth or not. He says, 'I tell the truth, and I don't mind fighting with everybody because I tell the truth!' Therefore the lesson of repose is the most important one to be learnt for this purpose.

Philosophy itself, culminating in the knowledge of God, which is greater and higher than anything else in the world, has often been lost by lack of balance. This is why in the Bible, in the Vedanta, in the Qur'an, even plain truths yet are told in a veiled manner. If the prophets and masters had given the truth in plain words, the world would have gone in the wrong direction. I have often noticed that philosophy, when explained plainly, has been understood quite differently from what was meant.

Activity tends to grow and to keep on growing, and by this

the balance is lost. When we speak we are inclined to speak more and more, and we become so fond of speaking that we like to speak regardless of whether anyone wishes to listen or not. We say what we really do not wish to say; afterwards we wonder why we insulted such and such a person, or why we told him our secret. Sa'di, the great Persian poet, says, 'O, intelligent one, of what use is thy intelligence, if afterwards thou repentest?' Whatever we do, whether good or bad, increases in us more and more. If one day a person thinks for five minutes about music or poetry, the next day that thought will continue for half an hour. If one has a little thought of bitterness, unconsciously the thought will grow until one's mind is full of bitterness. Every sin comes about in this way. Zarathushtra distinguished three kinds of sin: the sin of thought, the sin of speech, and the sin of action. To have the thought of bitterness, the thought of evil, is like doing evil; and to speak evil is also like doing evil. When a person commits an evil action, then it is as it were concrete.

We have gained balance of thought when we can see things not only from our own point of view, with the ideas and the feelings in which we are trained, but from all sides. The one-sided person has no balance. Suppose a man is very patriotic and sees everything from the point of view of patriotism, and he goes to a shop and demands that the shop-keeper sells him some things, for a patriotic purpose, for a very low price. But the shop-keeper may be a poor man, and even for a patriotic purpose he cannot sell his wares at that price. Then too he is a shop-keeper and he thinks of his trade; he cannot be expected to see with the other's patriotic eyes. One person thinks only of patriotism; another only of trade; and a third, who is a musician, says, 'They are crazy; music alone matters!' The poet says, "Poetry is the only thing in the world'. Each of them thinks solely of that with which he is himself engaged. Thus the pious person may exaggerate his piety so much that there is nothing left in him but piety, which at last becomes hypocrisy.

But how, one may ask, can one achieve balance? First there is the balance of activity and repose, of sleeping and waking. If a person believes that by sleeping very much he will become great, and he accustoms himself to do so, he will become a monster instead of a man, because then his body, which is given to him in order to experience the world, is not used. And if one does not sleep at all, in a few days one will have a nervous break-down. If one fasts very much, certainly one will become ethereal; one will be able to see into the other world, into the other planes. If one has learnt the way of inspiration, inspiration will come. But this body, these senses, will become weak, so that one will not be able to experience this world, for which they were given to us.

In India there are mystics called Madzubs who go to the extreme of spirituality. Their external self is forgotten to such an extent that they leave the experience of this world altogether. But extremity in everything is undesirable, whether good or evil. To sleep and wake, to eat and fast, to be active and to be still, to speak and to be silent, that is to have balance.

A disciple was taught by Mohammad a practice by which he experienced ecstasy. After some days he came bringing fruit and flowers which he offered to the Prophet, thanking him greatly and saying, 'The lesson that you taught me has been of such great value to me; it has brought me such joy. My prayers, which used to last a few minutes, now last all day.' Mohammad said, 'I am glad that you liked the lesson, but please, from today, stop the practice!'

The Sufi teaches balance by posture and movement, which includes the control of the actions and the activity of the body; by the practice of Nimaz, Wazifa, and Zikr he teaches the balance of the mind by concentration. To sit at home and close the eyes is not concentration; though the eyes are closed, the thoughts go on. It is important to choose the right object for concentration. By concentration and meditation a person experiences ecstasy; by the control of the self a person experiences the higher world or plane in which all things are one. For this the guidance of a murshid, a teacher, is needed, otherwise the balance will be lost; no one can accomplish this by himself. And if anyone could, he would become so interested in what he experienced there, that he would become absent from this world; absent-mindedness, even lunacy and many other evil consequences would result.

There is no greater happiness or bliss than ecstasy. A person is always thinking, 'I am this which I see; this small amount of flesh and blood and skin is I', but by ecstasy the consciousness is freed from the body, from this confinement, and then it experiences its true existence above all sorrow and pain and trouble. This is the greatest joy. To experience this and to keep control over the body and the senses, through which we experience all the life of this world, this is to have balance, this is the highest state.

ii

It is not only strength or nervous energy that enables man to stand on earth. Besides muscular strength and nervous energy there is balance; it is balance which enables man to stand and walk without falling. One may have muscular strength and nervous energy, but in the absence of balance one will not be able to stand or walk. And when we think of the mind, is it reasoning, is it far-reaching imagination which makes man thoughtful? No, it is balance. There are many whose imagination is so great that they can float in the air for hours together, and there are others whose reason is so powerful that their thoughts go round and round and end nowhere. If there is anything that makes man really thoughtful, it is not great reasoning or far-reaching imagination; it is balance.

It is neither the deep feeling of the heart nor the living in spiritual ecstasy which make a person illuminated. A person can be in ecstasy, see visions, phenomena, and yet not be a spiritual person. A person may have religious ideas, live a pious life, have lofty ideals, yet even then he need not be an illuminated soul. This shows that in order to maintain one's body as it ought to be, and to keep the mind tuned to the right pitch, balance is necessary. When we study nature, we find that the growth of plants and the life of the trees all depend upon balance; and when we think of the cosmos and study the condition of the stars and planets, the main thing we realize is that one heavenly body holds the other. All destruction occurring in nature, such as volcanic eruptions, floods, earthquakes, comes from lack of balance. As long as nature keeps its balance, the abyss in the heart of the earth remains as it is, people can walk over it and not come to any harm.

Storms, famine, all bad conditions, also the plagues that visit mankind, are caused by the upsetting of that balance which secures the well-being of humanity. This teaches us that the secret of the existence of the individual as well as of the whole cosmos resides in balance. It would not be an exaggeration to say that all success and failure are caused by balance or by lack of it. Progress and lack of progress can be explained as coming from balance and lack of balance.

There is another idea connected with balance. Life is movement, and balance is something that controls it; but perfect balance controls movement too much, bringing it to a state of inertia. For instance if the strength of the right hand were equal to the strength of the left hand, if the right leg and the left leg were equal, man would not be able to work or to walk. If each of the two eyes had the same power of sight, a person would not be able to see. Everything is controlled by balance, but too much balance destroys it; for too much balance brings stillness. It is the ordinary balance which is not complete that brings about success. Art comes also from the balance of the sense of line and colour, and genius in science comes from the balance between perception and conception.

The main problem is how to achieve balance, and how to maintain it. In regard to the former I would say that balance is natural, so there is no need to achieve it; the question is only how to maintain balance and not how to attain it. The influence of life in this active world always puts one off one's balance. No matter what direction one takes in life, no matter what one's occupation, one's business in life, there is always difficulty in maintaining balance. The Sufis therefore have found a key to this, and that key is to become isolated within oneself, thereby gaining complete balance within oneself. I have already said that perfect balance means destruction of action; but when one thinks that from morning till evening one's life is nothing but action, one naturally cannot keep this balance. But by devoting a few minutes to meditation, to silence, one can touch that complete balance for a moment; and then in one's active life a balance is maintained in a natural way.

Very often people make the mistake of thinking that by the

help of meditation or silence they can bring about success in activity. If it brings about a successful result, it is only because balance in meditation makes one capable of maintaining the balance necessary for activity. The outer life depends upon the individual's inner condition. Success or failure, progress or standstill, whatever one's state of being, it all comes from the condition that a person is experiencing within himself. A man of common sense will say: for this reason or for that reason you have met with success or failure. A person who is clairvoyant will say that because a spirit or a ghost has said this or that the conditions will be worse or better. The astrologer will say that because this star is in its house or not in its house we are experiencing such and such conditions. But according to the Sufi the condition of the life around one depends absolutely on the condition of one's inner self; so what is needed to change the conditions in the outer life or to tune oneself, is to work on one's inner self to bring about the necessary balance. Once the balance is lost, it is brought back only with great difficulty. In the first place it is often difficult to keep balance in one's everyday life; and once the balance is lost, there is little hope of success, happiness, or progress. It is just like a clock getting out of order; it cannot go until it is put in proper balance again.

It is the same with the condition of the soul. If a person has lost his wealth, has become a spendthrift, has become thoughtless, it is a sign of loss of balance. To be too sad, to be too busy, to be too lazy, all these things show lack of balance. Anything that can be called excessive is always out of balance.

Balance is the state of individual progress and consideration for others. One-sidedness is lack of balance. When we cannot comprehend another person's idea there is lack of balance. At the same time it is difficult to point out exactly where and when there is balance. For instance the features of the Chinese are normal features for China; Greek or Roman features were normal for those times and those people. What we call normal is what is general, what everyone has. Therefore we can say that when it is the season for colds and coughs, colds and coughs are natural.

No doubt life is difficult for many of us, but very often we make it even more difficult for ourselves. When we do not understand the real nature and character of life, we make our own difficulties. In our life only five per cent of our difficulties are caused by the conditions of life, and ninety-five per cent are difficulties caused by ourselves. But in what way, one may ask, are they caused by ourselves? We do not want struggle in life, we dislike strife, we only want harmony and peace. It should be understood that before we can make peace, war is necessary, and that war must be waged with our self. Our worst enemy is our self, our faults, our weaknesses, and our limitations. And our mind is a traitor. It hides our faults even from our own eyes, and points to other people as the reason for all our difficulties. Thus it constantly deludes us, keeping us unaware of the real enemy, and urging us against others, to fight them, making us think that they are our enemies.

But besides this we must turn ourselves towards God. As we rise higher, so our point of view becomes higher, as high as our sight reaches. In this way when a person evolves more and more, his vision becomes wider and wider; and in all he does he will strike the divine note, which is healing and comforting and peace-giving to all souls.

Balance is the security of life; not only of one's own life, but balance helps to maintain all things around one. People in the East have always considered balance to be the chief thing to maintain in life; and the different exercises they have prescribed, whether in the form of religion or in the form of devotion, whether in the philosophical or in the psychic realm, have all been to maintain balance.

STRUGGLE AND RESIGNATION

THERE ARE two distinct paths by which one attains to the spiritual goal, and one is quite contrary to the other. One is the path of resignation; the other is the path of struggle. No doubt in the path of struggle there is also resignation, and in the path of resignation there is also struggle, but generally the one who is treading the path of resignation has only one thought: to be resigned, whereas to the one who strikes the path of struggle, struggle is the main object. Both paths are essential; it is not possible to ignore one of them or to accept only one of them. People often think Sufism means being passive, but it is not so; it is being both active and passive. It is the knowledge of the secret of man's life on earth, of what he needs for his character, for his condition.

When we reflect upon these principles, we find that there are things in life to which we can only be resigned. It is easy to be resigned to things one cannot help, but if one has the power to struggle it is difficult to be resigned. The one who is resigned in easy conditions may not find it difficult, but he does not know what resignation means. For instance a man may have poor relations who want a part of his captial because they are in great need, but in spite of this he cannot resign himself to let them have it; yet when during the night thieves come and break into his house and leave with his whole fortune, he may resign himself very quickly to his loss. This kind of resignation is no virtue. To resign oneself means to do so even when one has the power to resist. All the great ones have recognized the value of resignation and have taught it. Christ said that if someone wants us to walk a certain distance with him, we should walk with him farther still. What does this teach? Resignation. One might think that resignation is unpractical and that this selfish world will take advantage of one. This is true, but the loss is small compared with the gain, if only the heart can sustain the loss. Yet if one is not contented with what has been done, it is better not to be resigned.

If one can be resigned, so much the better; but one should not force one's nature. A man once asked another man to lend him his raincoat. It was immediately given but at the same time the giver was very much annoyed that the other should have asked for it, and when he himself was obliged to go out in the rain he was vexed at having to get wet. It would have been much better for him to have said at once that he was sorry not to be able to lend the coat. Once having given it, however, he should not have grudged it, but should have been glad to get wet having helped the other man; if he gave it he should have done so with his whole heart.

One who is really resigned does not show it. It is not easy. How many people in this world try to learn wonderful spiritual things! But this resignation which is such a simple thing is yet miraculous; this virtue is not only beautiful, it is a miracle. There is resignation in so many little things; we do not always recognize it but it is there. Those around us may ask us to do something which we do not like. Perhaps they say something to us that we do not wish to take in silence; we want to answer back. Then there are the little pin-pricks from all we meet in everyday life. If we were not resigned, we would feel irritated all the time. Therefore to be resigned is not weakness, it is a great strength. As one goes further, one finds that one can be resigned even to cold and heat, to places which are congenial or uncongenial, and all this resignation has a meaning and we benefit by it. We should form a habit of being resigned; not having resigned ourselves to an experience means the loss of an opportunity.

There are also two forces working: the collective power and the individual power. In Sufi terms the one is Kazá; the other Kadr. Very often the individual power will not surrender and consequently it is crushed. For instance if a man is called upon to fight for his country but says that he will not join the army, he is helpless before the might of the whole nation however fine his idealism may be. Here he must resign himself to the condition in which there is a conflict between a lesser and a greater power; here resignation is the only solution.

Of course everything must be understood rightly. Resignation preached foolishly is not profitable. A mureed, who was learning the lesson of resignation from a murshid, was once walking in the middle of the road engrossed in the thought of resignation when a mad elephant came from the other direction. A wise man told him to get out of the way, but he would not because he was trying to resign himself to the elephant, until he was roughly pushed aside by it. They brought him to his murshid who asked him how he came to be injured. He answered that he was practising resignation. The murshid said, 'But did nobody tell you to get out of the way?' 'Yes,' he answered, 'but I would not listen.' 'But', said the murshid, 'why did you not resign yourself to that person?' Often fine principles can be practised to great disadvantage. Nevertheless, resignation has proved to be the path of the saints, because it develops patience in man. And what is patience? It is all the treasure there is. Nothing is more valuable, nothing a greater bliss than patience.

A story is told about the Prophet when he was very ill; he had been suffering for many years. Through his trial his insight became clearer, but his suffering was so great that those around him could not stand it any more, and so he had to seek refuge with God in the forest, to spare them from seeing his pain. As his sight was keen and the ears of his heart were open, he heard a voice coming from the trees, 'I am the medicine for your disease'. The Prophet asked, 'Has the time of my cure come?' The voice answered, 'No.' He said, 'Why should I take you then?' Later he had the same experience. Again he heard the voice. But when he asked if the time of his cure had come, this time the answer was yes. But the Prophet still said, 'Why should I take you?' for he still could not resign himself.

When we think of an extreme ideal, we may wonder if it is not unpractical, especially at this time where there are so many treatments and so many mechanical things. But the thoughtful person will consider how many people have ruined their lives by going from one treatment to another, lacking the patience and resignation in which resides their complete cure. The remedy is not always the answer to the difficulty; often patience is the answer. It seems that man becomes more and more impatient every day owing to this superficial life. There is hardly any resignation to little things, even though it is so much better to be resigned than to worry.

When we throw the mystic light upon this subject, we find that by being resigned we form a harmonious connection with the Infinite. And how should we learn this? Should we do it by being resigned to God? No, that is a still greater lesson to learn. The first lesson to learn is to resign oneself to the little difficulties in life, not to hit out at everything one comes up against. If one were able to manage this one would not need to cultivate great power; even one's presence would be healing. Such a person is more precious than the branch of the rose, for that has many thorns but only few flowers.

Resignation is the outcome of the soul's evolution, for it is the result of either love or wisdom. The truth of this can be seen in the lives of a child and of a grown-up person. As soon as a child becomes attracted to an object, the only thing it knows is that it wants it; and if it is denied this object the child is dissatisfied. Yet as the child grows up and evolves in life it learns resignation. That is the difference between an unripe soul and a soul advanced on the path of wisdom; for the ripened soul shows in its nature the development of the power of resignation. Man certainly has a free will, but its power is very small in comparison with the all-powerful will of God, which manifests in the form of more powerful individuals, of conditions which cannot be changed, and in many other ways. Resignation does not mean giving up something; resignation means being contented to give it up. To be resigned means to find satisfaction in self-denial.

Self-denial cannot be a virtue when it is the result of helplessness and culminates in dissatisfaction. The nature of an unevolved ego is to resent everything that arises in life which hinders the accomplishment of a certain object; but when a person accepts being resigned in the face of a difficulty, and at the same time

feels satisfaction, then even without having accomplished his
object he has risen above it. In this way for the truly resigned soul
even a defeat is really a success.

Resignation is a quality of the saintly souls. It is bitter in
taste but sweet in result. Whatever a man's power and position
in life may be, he has always to meet with a more powerful
will, in whatever form it may manifest. In truth this is the
divine will. By opposing the divine will one may break
oneself; but by resigning oneself to the divine will one
opens up a way. For resignation has the nature of water:
if anything obstructs it it takes another course; and yet it
flows on, making its way so as to meet the ocean in the
end. This is what the saintly souls do who tread the path
of resignation and yet keep their own will alive. That will
has the power to make its way. A person who is resigned
by nature becomes in the end a consolation to himself and
happiness for others.

Resignation is not necessarily weakness or laziness or cowardice
or lack of enthusiasm. Resignation is really the expression of
mastery over one's self. The tendency to submit to the will
of another or to certain conditions does not always work to
the disadvantage of the resigned one. It may sometimes seem
to be unprofitable, but in the end the benefit of such a virtue
is realized. Lack of power of endurance is the cause of souls
not being ready to resign themselves, for they cannot endure
their pain or sustain their loss. Those who are resigned practise
resignation even in the small things of everyday life. They
avoid using their power of will needlessly in every little
thing they do. Resignation is passivity, and sometimes it
seems to be a disadvantage in the life of an active person
who has an object to accomplish. But a continual activity
kept up by power and energy very often results in disaster.
Every activity should be balanced by passivity. One should
be active when it is the time to be active, and become passive
when the conditions ask for passivity. It is in this manner that
success in life is attained and that happiness, which is the quest
of every soul, is gained.

The symbolical meaning of the story of Christ riding on a

donkey on Palm Sunday is that the donkey, which has a cross on its back to indicate that it has to bear all burdens, shows its resignation by submitting to the will of its master. That is the privilege of the one who serves: however humble he will have the privilege of serving God.

RENUNCIATION

RENUNCIATION and asceticism are two different things. The Sufi's moral is renunciation but it is not always the moral of the ascetic. The ascetic does not marry, he does not eat good food, he does not wear fine clothes or do anything that is enjoyable; the Sufi thinks that everything in the world is for him, so that he need not leave the world with a wish unfulfilled. But he does not depend upon these things; he keeps himself free from them. He does not go to the mountains to be in solitude; he lives in the world. He goes to the mountains if he wishes to; still, the mountains cannot hold him there for ever. It is much easier to be religious, to be spiritual, in a cave of the mountains than in the world, but the Sufi has no need to run away from the world, for he has recognized and sees the face of his Beloved, the face of God, everywhere.

If a religious teacher were to say, 'No, you must not hear music, you must not go to see a play, you must not watch dancing, you must not dance yourself', perhaps one in a thousand of his pupils would obey his words and go away into the wilderness. No doubt that pupil would find much more there to help him in his search for spirituality, but he would not have experienced the world and so he would always remain exposed to temptation.

It is much more meritorious and much more difficult to live in the world and yet to be spiritual; to have the responsibilities of life, to give attention to friends and relations, to serve friends and enemies, and yet to remain spiritual. To be troubled by one's surroundings, to be loaded with responsibilities, and to be exposed to opposition, is much harder and greater than to be an ascetic in the jungle. Both courses have their dangers. If one leaves the world, the innate inclination to enjoy and to experience the world may at any moment draw one back; like the Yogi Mahachandra, who was a great saint and had many chelas, and yet was taken away by the Queen Mahila and made a king. He fell in a moment from the great height which he had reached by many years of hard perseverance. The Yogi says that it is better to leave the world; but the Sufi chooses a life in the world with renunciation. He prefers to experience the world in the service of all while at the same time practising renunciation.

Sacrifice is less than renunciation, though a sacrifice is a renunciation just the same; sacrifice is a lesson that the prophets and teachers taught in order that man should learn renunciation. The virtue of the sacrifice lies in the willingness with which it is made. Renunciation, however, is something that does not arise as a principle but as a feeling.

Renunciation has an automatic action on the heart of man, an action which very few realize because very few arrive at that stage where they can renounce. By this action a spiritual spark is kindled in the soul; and when a person has arrived at that stage he has taken the first step on the path of spirituality. The spark produced by this action in the depths of the heart culminates in a flame, a torch in life; and this changes the whole outlook on life. The whole world seems changed, the same world in which one has lived and suffered and enjoyed and learned and unlearned— everything appears to change once renunciation is learned.

Renunciation is in fact denial of the self, and the denial of that which could be of use to one. As all things in this world can be used and abused, so the principle of renunciation can be used and abused; and among the many wrong meanings people attach to self-denial the one that is most common is that it means denying oneself the pleasures and the happiness that the world can offer. If practising renunciation as a principle were a good thing, then there would seem to be no purpose behind the whole of creation. The creation might well never have been manifested if renunciation had been the principle. Therefore renunciation in itself is neither virtue nor sin; it becomes a virtue or a sin according to the use we make of it.

When one considers renunciation from the metaphysical point of view, one finds that this principle serves as a flight of stairs by which to rise above all things. It is the nature of life in the world that all the things we become attracted to in time become not only ties but burdens. Life is an eternal journey, and the more loaded with burdens one is, the harder the journey becomes.

Think how the soul, whose constant desire is to go forward, is daily held back by ties and continually more burdened! As the soul goes on it finds its feet in chains. It wants to go forward, but at every step it is more distracted, so that it becomes more difficult to go on.

That is why all the thinkers and the wise who have come to the realization of life have used renunciation as a remedy. The picture that the sage gives of this is the fable of the dog and the loaf. A dog carrying a loaf in its mouth came to a pool; and when it saw its reflection in the water it thought that it was another dog; it howled and barked and lost its bread. The more we observe our errors in life, our petty desires, the more we find we are not far from the dog in the fable. Think of the national catastrophes of recent times, and how the material things of the world which are forever changing and are not everlasting have been tugged at and fought for! This shows that man is blinded by material life and disregards the secret, hidden things behind that life.

When we try to reason out what we should renounce and how we should practise renunciation, we should remember that no virtue is a virtue if it is forced upon someone who is incapable of it. A person upon whom a virtue is forced, who is forced to renounce, cannot make the right renunciation. No virtue which gives pain is a virtue. If it gives pain how can it be a virtue? A thing is called a virtue because it gives happiness; that which takes away happiness can never be a virtue. Renunciation is only rightly practised by those who understand renunciation and are capable of practising it. For instance, there may be a person with a loaf of bread who is travelling in a train and finds somebody who is hungry and in need of bread. He himself is hungry too, but he has only one piece of bread. If he thinks that it is his Dharma to give it away and be starving, but is unhappy about this, he would do better not to give it away, for then it would be no virtue. If he did this once, he would certainly not do it again another time as he suffered by it and the virtue brought him unhappiness. This virtue would never develop in his character. He alone is capable of renunciation who finds a greater satisfaction in seeing another eat his piece of bread than in eating it himself.

Only he whose heart is full of happiness after an act of renunciation should make a renunciation. This shows that renunciation is not something that can be learned or taught. It comes by itself as the soul develops, when the soul begins to see the true value of things. All that is valuable to others a seer begins to see differently. Thus the value of all the things that we consider precious or not precious, is according to the way we look at them. For one person the renunciation of a penny is too much; for another that of everything he possesses is nothing. It depends on how we look at things. One rises above all that one renounces in life. Man remains the slave of anything which he has not renounced; of that which he has renounced he becomes king. This whole world can become a kingdom to a person who has renounced it.

Renunciation depends upon the evolution of the soul. One who has not evolved spiritually cannot really renounce. Toys so precious to children mean nothing to the grown-up; it is easy to renounce them; and so it is for those who develop spiritually; for them all things are easy to renounce.

How can one progress in this path of renunciation? By becoming able to discriminate between two things. A person with the character of the dog in the fable cannot renounce. He loves both alternatives but life is such that when there are two things before us we have to lose one of them. Man's discrimination must decide what to renounce and for what reason; whether to renounce heaven for the world or the world for heaven, wealth for honour or honour for wealth; whether to renounce things momentarily precious for everlasting things, or everlasting things for things momentarily precious. The nature of life is such that it always shows us two possibilities, and often it is very difficult to choose between them. Frequently one thing is at hand and the other further from our reach, and it is a puzzle which one to renounce or how to get the other. Also, we often lack the will-power to renounce. It requires not only the power to discriminate between two things, but also the will-power to do what we want to do. It is not an easy thing for a man to do in life what he wishes to do; life is difficult. Often we cannot renounce because our own self will not listen to us; and if we cannot even listen to ourselves, then how difficult it must be for others to listen to us!

Renunciation can be learned naturally. We must first train our sense of discrimination, in order to distinguish between what is more valuable and what is less so. We can learn this by testing, just as real gold is tested by imitation gold: that which lasts for a short time and then turns black is imitation; that which always keeps its colour is real. This shows that the value of things can be recognized by their constancy. We might ask if we should not recognize the value of things by their beauty. Indeed, we should recognize them by their beauty; but we must also recognize beauty by its durability. Think of the difference in the price between a flower and a diamond! The flower, with all its fineness, beauty of colour, and fragrance, falls short in comparison with the diamond. The sole reason is that the beauty of the flower will fade next day, while that of the diamond will last. This shows a natural tendency; we do not need to learn it; we are always seeking for beauty, as well as for that which is lasting. If a friendship does not last, however beautiful it may be, what value has it? What value have position and honour that do not last? Man, however, is like a child, running after all that attracts him and always changing: but at the same time his soul seeks constancy.

In learning the lesson of renunciation we can only study our own nature, what our innermost being is yearning for, and try to follow what it tells us. Wisdom comes by this process of renunciation. Wisdom and renunciation go together; by renunciation man becomes wiser, and by being wise he becomes capable of renunciation. The whole trouble in the lives of people in their homes, in the nation, and in the world at large is always man's incapacity for renunciation.

Civilization itself is really only a developed sense of renunciation which manifests itself in our consideration for each other. Every act of courtesy, of politeness, shows renunciation. When a person offers his seat or anything that is good to another, it is renunciation. Civilization in its real sense is renunciation.

The highest and greatest goal that every soul has to reach is God. As everything needs renunciation, that highest goal needs the highest renunciation. But a forced renunciation, even for God, is not a proper nor a true renunciation. Proper renunciation one can only find in those who are capable of it. Think of the story in the Bible of Abraham sacrificing his son. Man today is apt to laugh at some of the ancient stories, reasoning according to his own point of view. But think how many fathers and mothers have given their children as a sacrifice in wartime for their nation, their people, or their honour! This shows that no sacrifice can be too great a sacrifice for one's ideal. There is only the difference of ideal: whether it is a material or a spiritual ideal, whether for earthly gain or for spiritual gain, whether for man or for God.

As long as renunciation is practised for spiritual progress, so long it is the right way. But as soon as renunciation has become a principle, it is abused. Man, in fact, must be the master of life; he must use renunciation, not go under in renunciation. So it is with all virtues. When virtues control a man's life they become idols; and it is not idols that we should worship; it is the ideal behind the idol.

THE DIFFERENCE BETWEEN WILL, WISH, AND DESIRE

WILL IS the development of the wish. When we say that something happened according to the divine will, it means that it was a command; a wish which developed into action. When the wish develops into action it becomes will, it becomes command. One might think it is only one's wish, and indeed it is a wish as long as it is still; although it is there it has not sprung up, it is inactive just like the seed in the ground. But the moment the seed comes out of the ground as a seedling and is in the process of becoming a plant, then it is a will. Therefore wish and will are two different names for the same thing, in its undeveloped state and in the process of its development.

Desire is a weaker or a more primitive stage of the wish. When an idea or a thought that one would like a certain thing is not yet made clear in one's own mind, when one's own mind has not taken a decision, then it is a desire, a fancy. When it is a little more developed then it is a wish; then it stays there and is not dispersed like the clouds. It is tangible, it is there, and yet it is not fulfilled, because for fulfilment it must develop.

There are some people in this world who say that all their lives they have had bad luck; never have their wishes been fulfilled. Also, they very easily imagine that an antagonistic spirit is hindering them, or that God is against them, or the stars, or something else which has prevented their wish from being fulfilled. But generally this is not so. In the first place God wishes the same that we wish; if God wished differently from our wish we could not worship that God who was always against us. Besides there is no benefit in opposing the wish of man, and there is no advantage in opposing the wish of God. It is true that there may be planetary or cosmic conditions which oppose the wish; as it is said: man proposes, God disposes. God is then put in the place of the cosmic forces, but in reality God, with His mercy and compassion, never desires to oppose anyone's wish. And apart from God, even a kind-hearted man would never want to oppose anybody's wish; he would do everything possible to help a person's wish to come true.

What usually happens is that man proves to be the worst enemy of his own desire, for many reasons; and one reason is that he is never sure of what he desires. Among a hundred persons we will find perhaps one who really knows what he desires, while ninety-nine are not sure. One day they think they desire something and the next day they do not, and thus the desire disintegrates in the confusion of the mind.

There is another kind of person: those who have adopted a passive attitude. Such people say it is a sin to desire; and yet they cannot be without some desire. In this passive attitude they decide not to desire; they thwart any desire that was there. And there is a fourth kind: those who desire something but by lack of concentration cannot turn their desire into a wish, and therefore their desires always remain in their primitive stage. Finally there is the fifth kind of person who develops desire into a wish; he goes so far and no further. Thus the desire is not carried through, so to speak, and it never comes to its culmination, which only happens when the wish is developed into a will.

This question is of the greatest importance in the life of everyone. No person can exist in the world without wishing for something. And if there is anyone who has no wish, he should not stay in the world, he should avoid the crowd as he cannot exist there; he should go into the mountains, somewhere away from the world; and even there he should turn into a tree or into a rock in order to exist, because to be a living being without a wish is not possible.

There is a saying in the Gayan, which not everybody is able to understand, 'To repress desire is to suppress a divine impulse'. Those who distinguish between *divine* and *not divine* certainly make the greatest error, as either all is divine or nothing is. The only difference is the same as that between the machine and the engineer. The mind of God is working and at the same time the instrument, the machine of God is working; therefore that which arises as a desire has God as its source and is thus a divine impulse.

The pious man in his ignorance has a false conception of this idea and makes of God a captive in heaven.

Another saying in the Gayan is, 'All that produces longing in the heart deprives it of its freedom.' The truth is that when there is a longing one is tied by a chain, a chain which is stronger than iron. To desire is to be bound; this is not a moral but a philosophical statement. On the other hand, one cannot live without desire; one might just as well be a rock. No doubt if one were free from desire one could have the same freedom as the rock; but even the rock is waiting for the day when it will feel desire. The desire of fulfilment will come with the development of the human form.

The difference between people is according to the wishes they have. One wishes for the earth, the other wishes for heaven. The desire of the one takes him to the height of spiritual progress, and the desire of the other takes him to the depths of the earth. Man is great or small, wise or foolish, on the right road or on the wrong road, according to the desire he has.

According to the Sufis there is Kazá, universal will, universal power; and Kadr, the individual power. Certainly the individual power compared with the universal power is like a drop compared with the sea. It cannot stand against the sweeping waves of the sea that come and destroy it. Nevertheless the drop, being from the same source as the sea, has also a certain amount of strength, and it has the individual will to hold out against opposing forces.

If we want to make this question of the individual will and the universal will more clear, it is in small things that we can do so. A person who is walking in the street and says, 'I feel hungry, I should like to go to a restaurant and have a meal', shows individual will. Another person who goes into the street and sees a poor man says, 'This man seems poor, can I not do something for him? I want to see him looking happier', and as soon as he thinks of the good of another person his will at once becomes the universal will. The reason is that the boundary that limits the will of an individual is the thought of the self; as soon as one has forgotten the thought of self, as soon as one thinks of another, that boundary breaks down and the will becomes stronger. Where did the masters of humanity, those who have been able to do great things in the world, get their will from? It was their own will which was extended by the breaking down of the boundaries of the thought of self. This does not mean that one should entirely give up the thought of self, that one must never think of oneself, never think of one's lunch and dinner. The self is there, one has to think about it. But at the same time in order to expand, in order to let the will grow, the more one forgets oneself the more one is helped.

There are some who take the path of resignation, doing good neither to themselves nor to others. They take the attitude that it will come from somewhere or that somebody will do it, that if they are hungry or in need somebody will come and feed or help them. Their wish is inactive, they do not let their wish become a will, they remain where they are, they are passive. There is no doubt that an intelligent passiveness and resignation can also bring about a wonderful result. But many of these people practise it intellectually. The quality of the saints is to be resigned to all that comes, but then they do not even form a wish. They take all that comes, flowers or thorns; everything that comes they accept. They see thorns, and look upon them as flowers. They are contented with both praise and blame, with both rise and fall; they take life as it is. That is the intelligent way of doing it; the unintelligent way is to say that everything is difficult, and that somebody else will come and do it. This is nothing but a kind of laziness, not passiveness.

In India there is a story of a man who was lying under a cherry-tree, and some ripe cherries were falling near him. But he did not move. When he saw a man coming from a distance, he called out, 'Please come here, will you put this cherry in my mouth?' There are many to be found like this, who give in, who have no enthusiasm, no courage. In this way their will-power is broken down, and in the end they are helpless. There is no comparison between the saintly spirit and the spirit of the helpless, although both become resigned. But the latter is not resigned; he would like the cherry in his mouth, but only if the other gives it to him. The saint does not care if he eats it or not; it is just the same to him.

Then there are others who are over-anxious for their wish to come true. This destroys their wish because they put too great a pressure upon their wish. It is just like guarding a plant against the sun and the rain. If one guards it against the very thing which should help it to grow, then the plant cannot prosper, and it is the same with the wish. If one is too eager about one's wish, and at the same time always afraid that perhaps it will not come true, then one is thinking with doubt and fear and suspicion, and in that way one will destroy one's own wish.

And, again, there is the person who is willing to sacrifice anything or to persevere as much as necessary for even a small wish, which in reality he does not value very much. Yet he gives every thought to it, and he does everything in his power to make that wish come true. That person is taking the same path as the path of the Master. He will meet with success, and it is success which brings further success. If once a person is successful, this success attracts more success; but if once a person fails then this failure attracts further failure. It is the same when one is on the path of accomplishment: each accomplishment gives one a greater power to go forward, and when one is on the downward path then every step leads one downward.

The question arises as to which desire and wish one should give up, and which one should nourish. One must have discrimination; if there is no discrimination, then one will take a wrong path. It may lead to success but it will be a wrong kind of success. If one fostered every desire and wish, and believed they should all be accomplished, then it might sometimes be right and sometimes not. The sense of discrimination should first be developed in order to understand what leads one to a lasting happiness, a greater peace, a higher attainment. But once a person has discrimination and has chosen a wish, then he should not analyse it too much. Many have formed a habit of analysing everything all day long. If a person holds a wish for ten years and analyses it every day in his mind, he acts against it; he looks at it every time from a new point of view and tries to find what is wrong with his own wish, and thus in the end he crushes it in every possible way. In ten years time his wish, which should have come true, will be broken to pieces. There are many intellectual people, people who doubt, people with analytical minds, who are the greatest enemies of their own wishes.

Some think that it is wrong for a person to express his wish in prayer since God knows everything. Why should one tell God that something should happen? God knows the secret of every heart. Besides is it not selfish to bring our wish before God? If it is a good wish it must come true of itself! The answer is that prayer is a reminder to God, prayer is a song before God, who enjoys it, who hears it, who is reminded about something. But how can our prayer, our insignificant voice, reach God? It reaches God through our ears. God is within us. If our soul can hear our voice God can hear it too. Prayer is the best way, because then the wish is put in a beautiful form which harmonizes with God, and which brings about a closer relationship between God and man.

Furthermore, one can never think too often or too much of the wish one has. One should dream about it, imagine it, think about it, keep it continually in mind, and do everything possible towards its fulfilment; but one should do this with poise, with tranquillity, with patience, with confidence, with ease, and not by thinking hard about it. The one who thinks hard about his wish destroys it; it is just like overheating something or giving too much water to a plant. It is destroyed by the very thing which should help it. If a person worries about his wish he certainly either has no patience, or he has some fear or some doubt; all these things destroy the wish. A wish must be cherished easily, with comfort, with hope, with confidence, and with patience. Doubt is like rust to the wish: it eats into it; and fear is still worse: it destroys it. And when a person has no discrimination, and is not sure whether it is a right wish or a wrong wish, whether it should come true or not, one day he will say, 'I should so much like it to come true', another day he says, 'I do not care if it comes true or not', after a week he says, 'I wish it would happen now', and after a month, 'I do not care any more.' It is just like making a fire and then putting it out; every time one extinguishes the fire it is gone, and one will have to make it anew.

The question whether a wish is desirable or not depends upon our stage of evolution. A person whose evolution is such that he has no wish other than for the needs of his daily life, must not think that he should wish for something higher. If his heart is inclined to that kind of wish he should not worry about it. But if he feels in his heart, 'No, I really cannot wish for this, I can think of something much higher', then he must accept the consequences. And the consequences will be that he will have to go through tests and trials; and if he does not mind this, so much the better.

There are many things in this world which we want and which we need, and yet we do not necessarily think about them. If they come it is all right, and if they do not come we may feel uncomfortable for a time, but that feeling passes. We cannot give our mind and thought to them if we are evolved and are thinking of something higher and greater than what we need in everyday life, and that slips from our grasp. This is why great poets, thinkers, and saints very often lacked the things of everyday life. With the power they had, they could command everything, even gold to come to their house, or the army to come or to go—they had only to command. Yet they could not give their mind to it, they could only wish for something which was in accordance with their particular evolution.

So each person can only wish for something equal to his evolution; he could not properly wish for something which is beneath his evolution, even if he were told to do so. Very often to help a person in a certain situation I have said to him, 'Now concentrate on this particular object.' But being more evolved, he thought with his brain; his heart was somewhere else and so it never came true. One can give one's heart and mind and whole being to something which is on a par with one's evolution, but if it is not on a par one cannot give one's whole being to it, maybe only one's thought. What is thought? Thought without feeling has no power; if the soul and the spirit are not at the back of it, there is no power.

It must be understood that our higher wish should be apart from what we need in everyday life. We should never mix it, but always think of what we need in everyday life as being something practical, though if it really is our wish, then it is all right. But we should cherish and maintain our higher wish as something sacred, something given to us by God to cherish, to bring to fulfilment. For it is in the fulfilment of one's highest and best and deepest wish that the purpose of life lies.

PART II

THE LAW OF ATTRACTION

IN NATURE the two great principles are the attraction of like to like and the attraction of opposites.

Looking at nature we see that if there is one speck of dust on the wall, more dust will collect there. It is sometimes hard to find one fly in the room, but if there is one fly we shall see that there are other flies near it. Where there is one ant or one sparrow, there will be other ants or sparrows near. In the jungle, where there is one parrot there will be a great many parrots in the same part of the forest. However much dogs may quarrel and fight, they enjoy being together best. The rabbit does not care to be among sparrows, nor does the donkey want to consort with serpents. Where there is one grain of wheat, more wheat grows; and where one finds one small rose-bush, there will be many roses.

This shows us that like is drawn to like, to what it has affinity with. It is for this reason that the nations and races have their particular characteristics and attributes; because for centuries people of like character and like qualities have collected together, forming groups. The French are unlike the English, who again are different from the Swedes; the Swedes differ from the Germans. It is not difficult for a person whose intelligence is trained in this direction, to distinguish at a glance a Belgian from a Frenchman, a German from an Italian, even in a crowd.

Families also have their likenesses, which come from the same principle. In India, where great attention is paid to heredity, this goes to great lengths. There every province, every district, has its peculiar character. A Gujarati will always like to be with another Gujarati, and where there are two or three Marathas they are happy; they do not want a Panjabi in their company. It is the same with Bengalis and Madrassis. Why? Because each rejoices in his own element.

The first reason for the attraction of like to like is the blood-relationship. At the present time relationship is much less thought of; we hardly know who our relations are any more. It is however a great bond; when the blood is the same, then the form is made of the same element.

There is a story of a young man who became a wrestler at the court of the King of Persia. No one knew anything about his ancestry except the king, who had brought him up with great care. This wrestler, whose name was Kushtam, became the champion of his country, and was trying to become a world champion. But the king would not allow him to meet foreigners or even to talk to them. He wrestled with many wrestlers and every time he won, but the custom of the time was that the one who was defeated had to acknowledge his defeat or be killed.

One day there arrived a great wrestler from another country, and it was arranged that this young man should fight with him. The match took place, and in the end the wrestler threw Kushtam; but the young man was very proud and would not acknowledge his defeat, so the wrestler had to kill him. And as he felt the thrust of the knife, while he still had enough strength left, he said, 'You have killed me, but certainly one day you will meet my father and he will kill you'. The other asked what his name was. And when he heard him answer, 'Kushtam', he clutched his head and wept; he went mad, realizing that he had killed his own son.

An attraction comes silently to the mind, but it is not always clear because it is acting through matter. The difference between spirit and matter is that when the divine intelligence is pouring out directly it is spirit, and when it is radiating through a dense medium it is matter. Thus in both spirit and matter there is divine intelligence.

There is a great attraction between twins. Twins are meant to be united, although they are not always as united as one might expect them to be. If twins are twins in the real sense of the word, that is if two twin souls have started on the journey together and have managed to come to the earth together, they are the most united. There have been twins who were so united than when one fell ill the other would fall ill too; if one was happy the other would be happy even though they might be separated. But there can also be twins who are like two people out in the rain who happen to find shelter in the same place; and that is another matter.

There may also be two souls born in different countries, and brought up by different parents, who will attract one another and support one another all their lives. They may be good friends, they may be partners, they may be in the position of master and servant. One may call them twin souls, and they resemble each other as do children of the same parents, and yet not quite as brothers or sisters. They are unselfish towards each other, and they attract each other's thoughts and ideas, sometimes even showing similarity in their work.

The second reason for the attraction of like to like is the affinity resulting from having the same kind of occupation. A farmer who has been tilling the soil all day, will want to be with other farmers in the evening with whom he can talk about the crops. He does not want to sit among literary people. A soldier prefers to be with other soldiers. A sportsman wishes to be with sportsmen; he will not want to be among the learned in whose society he feels out of place. A man with a taste for literature always seeks other literary people. A musician likes the society of musicians. I have experienced this myself when sometimes there were Indians in my audience, even people from my own province, who proved to be less appreciative than the Western musicians who were there. The latter did not perhaps understand the words I was singing, but because they were musicians their interest in the music made them akin to its being.

The third reason is the similarity of qualities. A brave person will like to be with other brave people; he will not like to be with cowards. A kind person will seek other kind-hearted people. The affectionate are drawn to the affectionate, not to the cold-hearted. A quarrelsome person will seek out another quarrelsome person to fight with. Like is always recognized by like. If there are two thieves in a company, they will at once recognize each other. If a thief goes from Paris to New York it will be very easy for him to find a brother there; someone else might take a very long time to find such a person, but he knows at once, 'This is a thief, this is my brother!' A cruel man attracts the cruelty of others. If we deceive another ever so little we shall at once find those who deceive us, even if deceit does not really belong to our nature. This is the explanation of what we call the punishment of our sins. It is not that God gives us a certain punishment, but that by our wickedness, by our evil thoughts, we attract towards us the same wickedness, the same evil thoughts from others. The evil we do brings the same evil upon us from others. A little kindness in us attracts their kindness. A kind person meets with kindness where-ever he goes, even among the cruel. The smallest generosity on our part attracts the generosity of the generous. By the repetition of the name of God, by impressing upon our soul the kindness, the mercy, the infinite goodness of God, we create those qualities in our soul, and we draw to us that mercy, that kindness, that goodness, in whatever form and name it may come.

Besides the attraction of like to like there is the attraction of each to its opposite. There are the two great forces in nature, the creative force and the force that answers it, the receptive force; one can also call them the active and the passive forces, or Jelal and Jemal.

This can be understood by the law of rhythm. In every rhythm there is the stronger beat and the weaker beat. In two-four time, for instance, we count *one*-two, *one*-two, the strong beat and the beat that only has just enough force to counterbalance the other. We see the same in form, where convexity counterbalances concavity.

The representatives of these two forces in nature are the male and the female. But while in every man some qualities are male and some are female, and in every woman some of the qualities are female and some male, yet everywhere it is the strength, the creative power that rules, and it is the responsive power that is ruled. Man has the creative power, and when we observe woman we see that in all aspects of life she is responsive. Occasionally a woman may be so creative that the man becomes responsive. and this makes him her slave; but normally it is the man who has the creative power, and this makes him dominate her.

One may say that this is not just; but all the same it is man who has many more magnetic qualities who should rule, while woman who has the responsive qualities should be ruled. This is the philosophical aspect of this question; as to the moral aspect, one should realize that what is responsive needs far greater care, and that the creative power should pay much more attention to it. Until more attention is paid to a woman's life we cannot say that we are really civilized. And as to the social aspect, I have heard many complaints coming from all sides in the West; but the East too has a great deal to learn in the treatment of women.

We know that the ears are the receivers of sound; they do not create. The eyes are creative. The nose perceives the odour; it cannot create. The lips and the mouth create, and they are attracted to each other. When the ears hear a sound the eyes at once want to see what it is and from whence it comes. The nose can tell us the flavour of something much sooner and more exactly than the palate. The nose at once wants to interfere with what the mouth does. It says, 'Do not chew that any longer; I don't want it.' Or it says, 'Do justice to that; I like it.' We also find that when our right hand takes hold of something the left hand wants to help it; when our right foot comes forward the left foot at once wishes to join it; when we fold one arm the other arm wants to be folded too. One leg is inclined to cross the other, even in spite of the superstition which exists in India that it brings bad luck to sleep with the legs crossed. Everyone knows it, but it is most difficult for anyone to get out of this habit because it is so natural.

Often a person would rather be with his opposite than with one who is nearer his own level. When two who are nearly of equal strength meet, they do not readily harmonize. Students of breath will easily understand this. They know that there is a more active breath and a less active breath, and that when they both become equally active there is a clash. If one person is a great singer and another is teaching voice-production they can agree together; there is no competition between them. The one wants to be heard, the other does not. But if two great opera-singers come together they will rarely agree; there will be a rivalry between them.

A wise man would rather have a foolish servant than a half-wise one who will question his orders. There is a story of a servant who when he was sent to fetch the doctor went first to the undertaker. If a wise person cannot be among the wise he would rather be among the foolish than among the half-wise.

I have often seen that those with simple faith can be inspired and become illuminated, while the intellectual is always reasoning and does not advance one step. This is why scientists and mystics are hardly ever in harmony. The scientists will always say, 'If you know something, I know something too. If you are something, I am something too.'

It sometimes happens that there is repulsion between two people at first sight which later turns into a fast friendship; but it is not often so. Those who are to be friends are generally friends at first sight. In the former case there may be something which has a repellent influence, but after some time, when one has got over it and has become accustomed to it, one can bear it more easily; then one may find something interesting in the other person, and may even become friends. It is like becoming accustomed to poison.

There will always be some society, some association that we like, and some that we do not like; and always some that do not like us and some that appreciate us; for we always prefer our own element. There is nothing surprising in this and nothing to blame; it is simply the law of attraction. But the Sufi makes himself harmonious with all; he makes himself the element of all. He creates the element that is active within, and that element is love. We can learn this from the Bible which says that God is love. This is the only way in which the union of mankind, universal brotherhood, can be brought about. The differences and distinctions are external, but man is so trained from the beginning to see differences that he does not see the underlying unity.

People have said that by strong rule they would unite the world. What a mistake! What happens when we try to rule our family with a strong hand? It will never be united. It is love alone that can unite the world.

People have said, 'We are of this race, we are superior and you are inferior; our religion is superior, yours is inferior; our nation is great, yours is less.' The cause of the First World War was that the nations of Europe had all reached the same level. If one of them made a good aircraft or a good submarine another made a better still. One was strong, but the other wanted to be still stronger.

PAIRS OF OPPOSITES

IN RELIGIOUS terminology one often makes use of pairs of opposites, such as God and devil, heaven and hell, sin and virtue. Man begins acquiring knowledge by learning about pairs of opposites, and he cannot at once rise to that level where he comprehends life without these. In one way the idea is not correct; it is not right to conceive of God, who is all-powerful, as having another personality, an opposite power which one calls the devil. But at the same time it would puzzle a believer who considers God to be all goodness and all beauty if he were told that God also contains everything that is bad and evil. A devotee whose object is to raise his ideal of God as high as he can by devotion and worship, is hindered by being made to see that all that he considers wicked and ugly is also a part of God.

However this idea diminishes God, making Him limited, and producing a power, if not equal, yet all the same opposite to God. But whichever means the wise of the world have used to guide humanity, whether this limited idea of God being opposed by another power, Satan, or the other idea that God is all-powerful, their wisdom has always been used to help them to understand life more perfectly. Certainly when we imagine a power for wrong and evil, and picture it as a personality, calling it devil, we limit the power of the One whom we always call the Almighty. Nevertheless, it gives a picture, it is more comprehensible and tangible to distinguish between the God of good and the Lord of evil. It is not we who begin by contrasting the two; we do not need to begin in this way, because life itself does it for us. And if we did not distinguish between the two, if we arrived directly at the conception of unity, we would be missing a great deal in life. It is only after having distinguished between them that we can come to the idea of unity which raises us above it all. For instance, when a person says he will not look at anyone else's faults and closes his eyes, he has missed a great deal. But the one who has seen them and yet risen above them is the person who deserves to close his eyes from all that is evil.

The purpose of our life on earth is to look at all the distinctions and differences without being overwhelmed by them, as this may bring us down. We should go on, rising above them all, and at the same time experiencing them all. For instance a man may say, 'I have never given a thought to anyone who has done me a good turn, and I have never bothered about any harm that has ever come to me from anyone. I have always had just that one idea before me and I have always followed it.' He may be advanced, he may be spiritual, he may be pious, and yet he has missed a great deal. But the one who has received all the good that has come to him with grateful thanks and who has felt it, and at the same time has also felt the harm done to him and has forgiven and pardoned it all, he is the one who has seen the world and who will go beyond it.

Heaven and hell are two places which have been invented for our understanding; one where a person is exalted, where he is happy and is rewarded, the other where he is punished. It makes things more clear to us; yet where do we experience all the unhappiness and sorrow and discomfort, and where do we experience all the pleasure and happiness and joy? It is on the same earth, it is under the same sun. We were told about these two different places because we are capable only of seeing them as two different places; and the wise at any time of the world's civilization could not do better than try to make the subtle ideas of life as simple and comprehensible to man as possible. For instance, if I were to say that the world of thought and the world of action are different, it would be true; and yet both belong to the same world in which we live. It is not only how it is said, but it is also how we look at it.

There is a saying in the Gayan, 'I would have either heaven or hell, but not purgatory'. This is a metaphysical expression; but at the same time one can find a philosophical truth in it: that life means pain or pleasure, and that the absence of pain or pleasure is death. This idea is expressed in all scriptures. Both heaven and hell have either pain or pleasure; what is devoid of pain or pleasure cannot, in the ordinary sense of the word, be called life.

It is the understanding of all things from every point of view which enlightens when one neither refuses to believe them, nor believes them in a blind way. Cannot one's own mind, and also one's situation in life, be turned from hell to heaven and from heaven to hell? This is where one sees the difference between the two, and at the same time their oneness.

This brings us to the question of sin and virtue. It may be said that sin and virtue are standards of good and evil made by the teachers of religion, that by these standards of morals the world is kept in order, and that it is the breaking of this order which causes the decline of religion, with wars, famines, and disasters as a result. Messengers are sent from time to time to uphold this order, and spiritual controllers are appointed in every part of the earth. In all ages people have decided that one particular thing is sin, and another virtue. And whenever the wise have done this they have been right, and yet they differ from one another. This is because if a greater light is thrown on this subject, although it is still possible to look at sin in the light of sin, and at virtue in the light of virtue, yet very often one can also see that under the cover of virtue there was a sin, and under the cover of sin there was a virtue.

As the people of different races, nations, and religions each have their own standards of right and wrong, their own conception of good and evil, and their own ideas about sin and virtue, it is difficult to discern the law governing these opposites. It becomes clear, however, when one understands the law of vibrations. Every thing and every being seem separate from one another on the surface of existence, but beneath the surface on every plane they are nearer to each other, while on the innermost plane they all become one. Thus every disturbance to the peace of the smallest part of existence on the surface, affects the whole inwardly. Therefore any thought, speech, or action that disturbs peace is wrong, evil, and a sin; but if it brings about peace it is right, good, and a virtue. Life being like a dome, its nature is also dome-like. Disturbance of the slightest part of life disturbs the whole and returns as a curse upon the person who caused it; any peace produced on the surface comforts the whole, and thence returns as peace to the producer. This is the philosophy underlying the idea of the reward of good deeds and the punishment of bad deeds given by the higher powers.

When people came to Christ accusing a person of doing wrong, the Master could not think of anything else but forgiveness. For he did not see in the wrong-doer what the others saw. To distinguish between right and wrong is not the work of an ordinary mind, and the curious thing is that the more ignorant a person is, the more ready he is to do so. Very often it is the angle from which we view a thing which makes it right or wrong, and if we were able to see it from different angles, the very thing we called wrong we should at the same time call right. Neither can people when they say that they judge from the results they see be sure that there was not a reward in the punishment, or a punishment in the reward.

This shows us that life is a puzzle of duality. The idea of opposites keeps us in an illusion. Seeing this to be the nature and character of life, the Sufi says that it is not very important to distinguish between two opposites; what is most important is to recognize that One which is hidden behind it all. Naturally when he comes to this realization, the Sufi climbs upward on that ladder which leads him to unity, to the idea of unity which comes through the synthesis of life, by seeing the One in all things and in all beings. One may believe that the world, that humanity, has always evolved, or one may believe that it has advanced and gone back again, or that it is going round and round in circles, or one may have some other belief; but in whatever age the wise were born, they have always believed the same thing: that behind all life is oneness, and that wisdom lies in the understanding of that oneness. When a person awakens to the spirit of unity and sees the oneness behind all things, his point of view becomes different, and his attitude changes thereby. He no longer says to his friend, 'I love you because you are my friend.' He says, 'I love you because you are myself.' He says, as a mystic would say, 'Whether you have done wrong or whether I have done wrong does not matter. What matters is to right the wrong.'

It seems that some persons are quite happy in committing sin, but sin can never make one really happy. Even if there were a certain pleasure in it for the moment, it would re-echo, and the echo of a false note is never pleasing to the musical ear. If a person were really happy in his sin, we could be assured that it was really his virtue, and that it was only to us, from our point of view, that his action seemed sinful. Therefore the Sufi attends to his own journey and does not judge others. If there is only a comparative difference between good and evil, sin and virtue, why, then, should there be punishment for evil and reward for good? The effect of good is itself a reward for good, and the effect of evil is itself a punishment, but from our limited point of view we attribute these effects to a third person, to a divine ideal.

The miseries and wickedness of humanity do not come from good, but good comes out of wickedness and miseries. If it were not for wickedness and miseries and wrong we would never have appreciated what good and right mean. It is the idea of these two opposite poles which makes us able to distinguish between the two qualities. If we had recognized only one, we would have called it goodness or wickedness, and it would have remained just one. Calling it by two different names helps us to distinguish between them.

One might wonder if souls can deliberately kill their spirituality by evil-doing and evil living, and so perish. But it is not so; it only covers them with clouds of ignorance which cause discomfort. The soul is not meant to perish.

Many have been resentful towards God for having sent them misery in their lives, but misery is always part of life's experience. Some may become very angry and say, 'This is not just', or 'This is not right, for how could God who is just and good allow unjust things to happen?' But our sight is very limited, and our conception of right and wrong and good and evil is only our own, and not according to God's plan. It is true that as long as we see it as such, it is so for us and for those who look at it from our point of view; but when it comes to God the whole dimension is changed, the whole point of view is changed.

It is for this reason that the wise in all ages, instead of trying to judge the action of God, have so to speak put aside their sense of justice for the time being; and they have tried to learn one thing only, and that was resignation to the will of God. By doing this they have reached a stage at which they could see from God's point of view. But if they tried to express that point of view to the world, the world would call them mad. Therefore they have called themselves *Muni*, which means those who keep silent.

People often ask why those who do evil and act wrongly so
often succeed, while there are others who do right but never
succeed. But this is not the rule. The rule is that the one who
succeeds through wrong will only succeed through wrong; by
doing right he will meet with failure. And the one who succeeds
by doing right will always succeed by doing right; he will fail
if he does wrong. Furthermore, for the one who ascends, both
right and wrong become like steps by which to ascend; while for
the one who descends, both good and evil become steps by which
to descend. There is no man in this world who can say, 'I am
faultless', but that does not mean that he is not destined to reach
his goal.

It is a great pity if a person does right or good because he wants
to progress or become spiritual. For what is goodness after all?
It is a very small price to pay for spirituality; and the man who
depends upon his goodness to attain spirituality may just as well
wait a thousand years. For it is just like a man who is collecting
all the sand he can to make a hill so that he may climb to heaven.
If one is not good for the love of goodness, if one does not do
right for one's love of justice, for one's own satisfaction, there is
no meaning in doing right, there is no virtue in doing good. To
be spiritual is to become nothing; to become good is to become
something. And to be something is like being nothing, while to
be nothing is like being all things. The claim to spirituality hinders
the natural perfection; self-effacement is a return to the Garden of
Eden.

There is no risk that a person endeavouring to become selfless will become a prey to all the conditions in life, quite the
contrary, for all strength and wisdom resides in perfection. The
absence of perfection is the tragedy of life. The person who holds
on to himself is a burden even to the earth. The earth can easily
bear mountains upon its back, but the person who is egotistic
is heavier. And what happens in the end? Even his own soul
cannot bear him, and this is why many commit suicide. Committing suicide is just like breaking apart two things which are
connected with one another. It is wilfully separating what is
meant to be connected. It was the scheme of nature to accomplish

something, and by separating the two parts these have been deprived of the privilege of that which the scheme of nature wished to accomplish. But the claim of the self has become so heavy upon the soul that the soul wants to rid itself of it. A hint was given about this by Jesus Christ, when he said, 'Blessed are the poor in spirit.' What does poor in spirit mean? It means the ego that is effaced.

RESIST NOT EVIL

OFTEN ONE wonders at the phrase in the Bible, 'Resist not evil', and it is not always given the right interpretation. To interpret it one should first explain what evil means. Is there any particular action or thing which one can point out as being evil? No doubt man is always apt to do so, but nothing can be evil according to a fixed principle. Then what is it? It is something which is devoid of harmony, it is something which lacks beauty and love, and above all it is something which does not fit into the accommodation of life. What fits into the accommodation that life offers cannot be evil.

Evil may be likened to fire. The nature of fire is to destroy everything that lies in its path, but although the power of evil is as great as the power of fire, yet evil is also as weak as fire. For as fire does not endure, so evil does not last. As fire destroys itself, so evil is its own destruction. Why is it said, do not resist evil? Because resistance gives life to evil; non-resistance lets it burn itself out. In the form of anger, passion, greed, or stubbornness one sees evil, and also in the form of deceit and treachery. But the root of evil is always one and the same: selfishness. In one person the evil is perhaps manifest on the surface, in another person it is hidden in the depths of the heart.

There is a saying in the East, 'Do not invoke the name of Satan, or else he will rise from his grave'. An inconsiderate or thoughtless person often falls into the error of awakening that devil even if he is asleep, for he does not know the music of life. In order to live in the world one should become a musician of life. Every person therein is a note; and when one feels that way, then one has an instrument in one's hand. The whole world is like an orchestra by which a symphony is to be played.

Even in small things one can observe the same law. Very often the greatest trouble that one has in life is not because of the difficulties others make, but because of one's own lack of comprehension of human nature. If one knew human nature one would realize that the first and the last lesson to learn is not to resist evil. For resistance becomes fuel to the fire. If we say to someone, 'Do not do that', if we ask someone, 'Why did you do it?' if we re-reproach someone, saying, 'You have done such and such a thing', in all these ways we only make the evil stronger, we only fix him firmer in his fault.

Everyone in this world can be a kind of teacher, but not a real teacher, for a real teacher is the one who always teaches himself; and the more he teaches himself, the more he realizes that there is so much to be learnt that a whole lifetime would not be enough. And the more one learns the more one overlooks the evil in others. It does not mean that the evil is greater or less in others, it only means that one has realized that the enemy which one saw in others is really in oneself. The worst enemy one was faced with in outer life one finds to be in one's own heart. It makes one feel humiliated, but it teaches the true lesson: of finding in oneself the same element which one wished to resist in another.

Life is a place where it is necessary to move gently. Whether it be in thought, speech, or action, the rhythm must be controlled; the law of harmony must be observed in all that one does. One should know that even walking barefoot on thorns will not make one free from accusation: the thorns will accuse one of having trampled upon them. If living in this world is as delicate as that, can anyone say he has gained sufficient wisdom? Or can anyone think he can afford to live in this world without giving a thought to this problem?

I was once asked how anyone at the head of a business or institution could possibly keep to the rule of not resisting evil. I said that I had seen people at the head of certain factories who had won the hearts of everyone working there, while there were other directors against whom every worker in the factory was speaking. It may be that the latter made a greater profit than the former, yet in the end they would find the gain of the former to be more enduring than their own. The ways of wisdom and tenderness cannot be made into a restricted principle for people to follow. A brush can never take the place of a knife, and therefore we all have to use every method and activity according to the circumstances. Nevertheless, the thought of not resisting evil should always be in the background.

The problem of evil is great. Many cannot bear even to hear it mentioned, although they are faced with it every moment of their lives, and to leave this problem unsolved does not help. Everyone is ready to judge, to observe, or to take notice of the evil in another, not realizing that sometimes the surface of a thing is quite different from its depth. Perhaps that which seems evil has something good underneath; or what appears good may contain a spark of evil. And by what standard can we determine evil and good, and who can judge the evil and good of anyone else? If one can judge at all, it is one's own evil and good. No one except God has the power to judge another. The sense of justice that is given to man is in order that he may judge his own actions; it is for this purpose that the sense of justice has been given to him.

When we look at life we shall see that it is nothing but a struggle both individually and collectively. And it seems that if there is anything worth while in this life it is that which is other than this struggle, the give and take of kindness and love, and the doing of any action of selflessness. However well qualified a person may be in the things of the world, his qualifications reach only to a certain point; they do not go beyond it. But what is really required is qualification in the understanding of life, the understanding of the law which is working behind it. It is this qualification alone which will diminish man's continual struggle, for it will give him less to resist. It will make him more tolerant of the natural condition of human beings. As soon as one realizes that one cannot expect from anyone something of which he is not capable, one becomes tolerant.

The difficulty is that everyone demands more of another person in the way of thought and consideration, of kindness and love, than he does of himself. Man wants more justice and fairness on the part of another than he is himself prepared to give; and his standard may be so high that another person cannot keep up to it, which in turn makes him disappointed. What generally happens is that one does not just remain quiet after being disappointed but one resists, and so the struggle of life continues. One should not expect the pear-tree to bear roses, nor the rose-bush to produce jasmine. Every person is like a certain plant, but not the same plant. We may be fond of roses, but every plant does not bear roses; if we want roses we should seek only the plant on which roses grow, and we must not be disappointed if what we find is not the rose plant. In this way we can correct our own deception.

When people say that someone is bad it really means that the surface has become bad. The depth cannot be bad, however bad a person may seem. For goodness is life itself; and a person who would be all bad could not live. The very fact that he is living shows that there is a spark of goodness in him. Besides just as there are various objects so there are various persons; some show softness outside, hardness inside; some show hardness outside and softness inside; some are very good in the depth and evil on the surface; and some are evil on the surface and good in the depth, for there are as many different varieties as there are souls.

What education, what point of view, what attitude in life is the best and will give the greatest happiness? It is the attitude of overlooking evil instead of resisting it. There are three ways of living one's life, which can be compared with struggling in the sea whose waves are rising and falling all the time. The first will struggle as long as life will permit; but the rising and the falling of the waves in the sea continue for ever and ever, and in the end he will be drowned. And so it is with man. Man struggling on, intoxicated by his struggle, will go on as long as his energy will permit it. In this struggle he may seem powerful, he may seem to have conquered others, he may seem to have done greater things than others, but what does it amount to? In the end he will be drowned. But there is another person who knows how to move smoothly through the water, and he understands the rhythm of moving his arms and legs; he swims with the rising and falling of the waves. He is not struggling. This man may hope to arrive at the port if it is near. If his ideal is not too far distant, then he is the one to fulfil it. And the third person is the one who walks on the water. It is this which is the meaning of Christ's walking upon the waters.

Life is just like waves, it is making its way continually. The one who allows himself to be disturbed by it will be more and more disturbed every day; the one who does not take any notice of it will keep inwardly serene. The one who sees all things and yet rises above them is the one who will walk over the sea. No one can reach the highest summits of life, of wisdom, in a moment; even a whole lifetime is too short. Yet hope is necessary, for the one who hopes and sees the possibilities climbs towards the summit, but the one who has no hope has no legs to ascend the hill of wisdom, the summit of which is the desired goal.

JUDGING

MAN IS generally very ready to pass judgment without any restraint and to express his opinion instantly. He will not stop to think whether he himself has arrived at the same stage as the one whom he is judging or whether he has any right to judge him. Jesus Christ said about judging that he who was without fault should throw the first stone; it teaches a great lesson.

For the Sufi who sees in every form the divine form, in every heart the divine shrine, to judge anyone, whatever be his position, his action, his condition, is altogether against his religion; and in this way he develops the philosophy which he has first learnt intellectually.

Not blaming others is principally a question of self-restraint or self-control, of politeness, kindness, sympathy, and graciousness; of an attitude of worship towards God, the Creator of all beings, and of realizing that all are His children, good or bad. If someone's child happens to be plain in appearance, would it be polite to say before the parents, 'This child is plain'?

The Father and Mother of all beings is there, comprehending and knowing what is going on in every person's heart. He sees all faults and merits before we do, and when we judge so readily it is before that Artist who has made everything, and not behind His back; it is in His presence. If we realized this it would not be difficult to feel the personality of God everywhere.

There comes a time after we have continually practised the virtue of not judging, when we see the reason behind every fault we notice in anyone we meet. Then we become more tolerant, more forgiving. When a person who is ill makes a fuss by moaning and wailing, it disturbs us at first. We say how wrong it is, how annoying, what a bad nature he has. But the understanding of the reason behind it, that it is not his bad nature but the illness, will make us more tolerant; when we see no reason it makes us not only severe with that person, but blind to the light of God, blind to that forgiveness, that unique essence of God which can be found in the human heart.

The difference that exists between man's justice and God's justice can be seen in the following simile. When children are quarrelling over their toys, they each have a reason. The one thinks a certain toy most attractive; why should he not possess it? The other says the toy was given to him and why should he not keep it? Both have their reason and both are right. But the father's justice is different; the father knows what is the nature of each child and what he wants to bring out in the nature of that child. That is why he gave the toys to the children, to bring out something in their nature. The child does not know this and if older would have accused the father of ignoring his wishes. He does not understand the justice of the father; he has to grow to another stage to do that. It is the same with the justice of God and man. Man's justice is obscured by his preconceived ideas of favour and disfavour and by his learning, which is nothing compared to the knowledge of God.

If one ever gets a glimpse of divine justice it is only by constantly believing in the justice of God in spite of all the proofs which seem to contradict His justice. Judging by these one might come to the conclusion that there is no justice, that everything just works mechanically. Ideas such as those of Karma and reincarnation may seem satisfactory, but the fact remains that they have their root in God who is behind all. God could not be all-powerful if every individual were powerful enough to work out his own Karma. And even if everything were working mechanically, there would still have to be an engineer; and is he subjected to his machine? If God is limited He can no more be God. God is perfect in His justice, in His wisdom, in His power. But if we question the cause of all those happenings which do not seem to us to be justified, we then come to another question: can a composer give a definite justification for every note that he has written in his composition? He cannot. He can only say, 'It is a stream which has come from my heart. I have tried to keep to certain rules of composition; but I am not concerned with every note. I am concerned with the effort by which the whole was produced.'

There is the law but there is also love; law is a habit and love is being; law has been created but love has never been created. So love is predominant. As God is beyond the law, so love is above the law. Therefore, if we would find a solution to our ever-recurring question of why it is so, it is not by the study of the law. The study of the law will only give an immense appetite; it will never bring satisfaction. If there is anything that will bring satisfaction it is diving deep into love, and then we shall realize that there is nothing which is not just; we shall never again say that anything is unjust. This is the point the wise reach, and they call it the culmination of wisdom.

There is a saying that God forgives more than He judges, but how do we know that God forgives? In the first place justice is born, and love has never been born; it always has been and will always be. Justice is born of a certain sense in man, the sense of fairness; as this sense matures it begins to seek for evenness, and what is not even it does not like. In order to develop this sense we need inspiration from all that has existed before; justice is the outcome of what we see, but this is not so with love which is spontaneous and always present. As it is said in the Bible, God is love; and therefore, while justice is God's nature, love is God's very being. He forgives because He is forgiveness Himself; He judges because it is His nature to judge.

Justice comes from God's intelligence, and the expression of God's intelligence in this world of illusion is limited. When judging limited things our intelligence becomes limited also; we are as limited as the objects before us. The greater the object, the greater becomes our vision.

There is only one thing that is truly just, and that is to say, 'I must not do this.' When one says this to another person one may be very wrong. The mystic develops his mind in this manner, purifying it by pure thought, feeling, and action, free from all sense of separateness, only following this one line of thought. Whatever differences in principles of what is right and wrong the various religious faiths may show, no two individuals will ever differ in this one natural principle: that every soul seeks after beauty, and that every virtue, righteousness, good action, is nothing but a glimpse of beauty.

HSM

When once he has made this moral his own, the Sufi does not need to follow a particular belief or faith to restrict himself in a particular path. He can follow the Hindu way, the Muslim way, the way of any church or faith, provided he treads this royal road: that the whole universe is but an immanence of beauty. We are born with the tendency to admire it in every form, and we should not blind ourselves by being dependent on one particular line of beauty.

Forgiveness does not judge; there is only the feeling of love, and therefore, whatever be the other's fault, once a person has forgiven, the resulting happiness and joy are shared by both. Justice does not give that joy. The one who judges too much is unhappy himself, and he makes the one whom he judges unhappy too. The one who forgives is happy; he does not keep any grudge in his heart; he makes his heart pure and free from it. God's greatest attribute is forgivingness.

Man accuses God of having done many things wrong; it is often only out of respect and because of his reverent attitude that he says nothing, but if he felt free he would make a thousand accusations. There is no one who could be accused so often and for so many things as God. The reason is that it is our limited self which judges, though it is quite unable to understand.

THE PRIVILEGE OF BEING HUMAN

MANKIND is so absorbed in life's pleasures and pains that a man has hardly a moment to think what a privilege it is to be human. Life in the world no doubt contains more pain than pleasure; and that which one considers to be pleasure costs so much that when it is weighed against the pain it costs it too becomes pain, and since man is so absorbed in his worldly life he finds nothing but pain and grievance in life. Thus until he changes his outlook he cannot understand the privilege of being human.

Yet however unhappy a person may be in life, if he were asked if he would prefer to be a rock rather than a human being, his answer would be that he would rather suffer and be a human being than be a rock. Whatever the condition of a man's life, should he be asked if he would rather be a tree than a man, he would choose to be a human being. And although the life of the birds and beasts is so free from care and troubles and so free in the forest, yet if a man were asked whether he would prefer to be one of them and be in the forest, he would surely prefer to be a man. This shows that when human life is compared with the various other aspects of life, it reveals its greatness and its privilege; but when it is not compared with those other forms of life, then man is discontented and his eyes are closed to the privilege of being human.

Another thing is that man is mostly selfish, and what interests him is that which concerns his own life; not knowing the troubles of the lives of others, he feels the burden of his own life even more than the burden of the whole world. If only man in his poverty could realize that there are others whose sufferings are perhaps greater than his; in his troubles that there are others whose difficulties are perhaps greater than his! Self-pity is the worst poverty. It overwhelms a man, and he sees nothing but his own troubles and pains; and then it seems to him that he is the most unhappy person, more so than anyone in the world.

Sometimes we find satisfaction in self-pity. The reason is that

it is our nature to find satisfaction in love; and when we are
confined to ourselves we begin to love ourselves, and then self-
pity arises because we feel our limitation. But the love of self
always brings dissatisfaction, for the self is not made to be loved;
the self is made to love. The first condition of love is to forget oneself. One cannot love another and oneself at the same time, and
if one says, 'If you give me something I will give you something
in return', that is another kind of love, it is more like business.

Man's ego is the false ego, God's ego is the true ego. But what
is the ego? Ego is part of a line: one end of the line is God's ego,
the other end is man's ego; and the latter is false because man has
covered it by his illusion, calling it himself. Therefore, when that
ego is broken by love or by wisdom or by meditation, then the
clouds that cover it are dispersed and the true ego, the ego of
God, manifests itself.

Sa'di writes in the account of his life, 'Once I had no shoes and
I had to walk barefoot in the hot sand, and I thought how very
miserable I was; and then I met a man who was lame, for whom
walking was very difficult. I bowed down at once to heaven
and offered thanks that I was much better off than he, who had
not even feet to walk upon.' This shows that it is not a man's
situation in life, but his attitude towards life that makes him
happy or unhappy; and this attitude can even make such a
difference that one man would be unhappy in a palace while
another would be very happy in a humble cottage.

The difference is only in the horizon that one sees. There is one
person who looks only at the circumstances of his own life; there
is another who looks at the lives of many other people: it is a
difference of horizon.

Besides, it is the impulse that comes from within which has
an influence on one's affairs. If there is an influence always working from within, if there is discontent and dissatisfaction in life,
one finds its effect in one's affairs. For instance a person impressed
by an illness can never be cured by a physician or medicines. A
person impressed by poverty will never get on in life. A person
who thinks that everybody is against him, everybody ill-treats
him, and everybody has a poor opinion of him, will always find
that it is so wherever he goes. There are many people in the world,

in business, in professions, whose first thought before they go to their work is that perhaps they will not be successful. The masters of humanity, at whatever period they came to the world, always taught faith as man's first lesson; faith in success, faith in love, faith in kindness, and faith in God. And this faith cannot be developed unless man is self-confident, and it is essential that man should learn to trust others. If he does not trust anyone, life will be hard for him. If he doubts, if he suspects everyone he meets, then he will not trust the people nearest to him, even his closest relations; and he will soon develop such a state of distrust that he will even distrust himself.

The trust of someone who trusts another but does not trust himself is profitless. But someone who trusts another because he trusts himself has the real trust; and by this trust in himself he can make his life happy whatever his conditions may be.

In the Hindu traditions there is a very well-known concept, that of the tree of the fulfilment of desires. There is a story in India of a man who was told that there was a tree of the fulfilment of desires, and he went in search of it; and after going through forests and across mountains he arrived at last at a place where he lay down and slept under a tree without knowing that it was the tree of the fulfilment of desires. Before he went to sleep he was so tired that he thought, 'What a good thing it would be if I had a soft bed to rest upon and a beautiful house with a courtyard around it and a fountain, and people waiting upon me!' And with this thought he went to sleep. And when he opened his eyes he saw that he was lying in a soft bed and there was a beautiful house and a courtyard and a fountain, and there were people waiting upon him; and he was very much astonished, for he remembered that before going to sleep he had thought of all this. But as he went further on his journey and thought deeply about his experience, he realized that he had actually slept under the tree he was looking for, and that the miracle of that tree had been accomplished.

The interpretation of this legend is a philosophy in itself. It is man himself who is the tree of fulfilment of his desire, and the root of this tree is in the heart of man. The trees and plants with their fruits and flowers, the beasts with their strength and power, and the birds with their wings, are unable to arrive at the stage which man can reach; and it is for this reason that he is called 'man', which in Sanskrit has the same root as the word 'mind'.

The trees in the forest await that blessing, that freedom, that liberation, in stillness and quiet; and the mountains and the whole of nature seem to await the unfoldment, the privilege of which is given to man. That is why the traditions tell us that man is made in the image of God. Thus one may say that the most fitting instrument for God to work with is the human being; but from the mystical point of view one may also say that the Creator takes the heart of man through which to experience the whole of creation. This shows that no being on earth is more capable of happiness, of satisfaction, of joy, of peace, than man. It is a pity when man is not aware of this privilege of being human, for every moment in life that he passes in this error of unawareness is wasted and is his great loss.

Man's greatest privilege is to become a suitable instrument of God, and until he knows this he has not realized his true purpose. The whole tragedy in the life of man is his ignorance of this fact. From the moment that a man realizes this he lives the real life, the life of harmony between God and man. When Jesus Christ said, 'Seek ye first the kingdom of God, and all these things shall be added unto you', this teaching was in answer to the cry of humanity; some were crying, 'I have no wealth'; others, 'I have no rest', or, 'My situation in life is difficult', or, 'My friends are troubling me', or, 'I want a higher position'. And the answer to them all is what Christ said.

One may ask how we can understand this from a practical, a scientific point of view. The answer is that external things are not in direct connection with us, and so they are often unattainable by us. We can sometimes attain our wish, although frequently we fail; but in seeking the kingdom of heaven we seek the centre of all, both within and without, for all that is in heaven or on earth is directly connected with the centre. In this way we are able to reach all that is on earth and in heaven from the centre; but whatever we seek which is not at the centre may be snatched away from us.

In the Qur'an it is written that God is the light of the heavens and of the earth. Besides the desire to obtain the things of the earth there is that innermost desire, working unconsciously every moment of life, to come into touch with the infinite. When a painter is painting, or when a musician is singing or playing, if he thinks, 'It is my painting, my playing, my music', he may have a certain satisfaction, but it is like a drop in the ocean. If, however, he connects his painting or his music with the consciousness of God, if he thinks, 'It is Thy painting, Thy music, not mine', then he connects himself with the centre, and his life becomes the life of God.

There is much in life that one can call good, there is much to be contented with, and there is much that one can admire, if one can only adopt this attitude; this is what can make a man contented and give him a happy life. God is the painter of all this beautiful creation, and if we do not connect ourselves with the painter we cannot admire his painting. When one goes to the house of a friend whom one likes and admires every little thing is so pleasant; but when one goes to the house of an enemy everything is disagreeable. Our devotion, our love, our friendship for God can make the whole of creation a source of happiness. In the house of a dear friend a loaf of bread, a glass of milk, is most delicious; but in the house of someone we dislike even the best dishes are tasteless. And as soon as one begins to realize that the mansions in the house of the Father are in this world with its many religions, races, and nations, which yet are all in the house of God, then, however humble and difficult the situation in life, it must sooner or later become happier and better; for we feel that we are in the house of the one we love and admire, and all that we meet with we accept with love and gratitude because it comes from the one we love.

For all his claims to civilization and progress, man seems to have fallen into the greatest error. For centuries the world has not been in such a state as it is now, one nation hating the other, looking with contempt on another. What do we call it? Is it progress or is it a standstill? Or is it worse than that? Is this not the time when thoughtful souls should awake from sleep, and devote themselves to doing whatever good they can to humanity in order to better the conditions of the world, instead of each one thinking only of his own interests?

OUR GOD PART AND OUR MAN PART

NOT ONLY in this age but also in past ages, the first thing realized by man has been his own limited existence formed of matter, which he called 'I'. This is not his fault; it is because religions have been interpreted with the intention of dominating the people, of holding them in the grasp of those who understood their meaning. The priests have only allowed people to understand very little, and all the rest they have kept for themselves. They have said, 'You are ordinary beings. God is much too high for you to understand. We can communicate with Him, we can understand Him, but you must stay where you are.'

All his life Buddha fought hard against this. When someone spoke to him of a spirit, of God, or made a show of a holy, a spiritual life, he said, 'I do not believe in it.' But this was very extreme, for it led people into another error; it led them to say that there was no God, no spirit.

Another reason for this separation was that it has always been the tendency of those who had the same way of thought, the same belief or faith, to come together in one group, in one society, in order to have the encouragement of each other's thought. By this they separated themselves from the rest of humanity.

The mystic has never believed with a blind belief. In fact he does not believe, he experiences. He experiences that he is himself the whole Being. There is a verse of a Hindustani poet, which says:

> Behind the human face God was hiding,
>   I did not know.
> I veiled my eyes and was separated from Truth,
>   I did not know.

It is a very beautiful verse, and it has a deep meaning.

All of us have our God part and our man part. Man is made of two things, spirit and substance. The spirit is the finer part and the substance is the grosser part; the finer part, the spirit, has turned into the grosser part. One part is the external, limited self that we see, and the other is the unlimited being. .

Man's external self is composed of the five elements, but in reality man is much larger and extends much further than we generally believe. For instance, when someone stands before an audience he appears to be of a certain size; but when he speaks he is as large as the area to which his voice carries. Although a friend or a beloved may be thousands of miles away he will feel our attachment, our affection. The feeling originates here, but manifests over there; this shows that in our feelings we are larger still.

The breath goes still further; by the breath we can send our thoughts wherever we wish, and we are able to know the thought and the condition of every being. The thought of someone who wishes to accomplish a certain thing reaches out in order to prepare it. Man is like a telescope: at one end there is the man part, the limited existence; and at the other end there is the God part, the unlimited Being. At one end we are so small; at the other we are so vast that we are the whole Being.

If each of us is so great, as great as the whole Being, we might ask how there can be room for so many of us. Are there then several whole Beings? There are not. Through our ignorance we see many and make distinctions, saying: 'This is I, that is you, this is a friend, that is an enemy, I like this one, that one I do not like.' But in the hereafter all are connected; there we are all the same.

Man has two natures: *Farishtagi*, the angelic, and *Hayvanat*, the animal. Hayvanat means man's body and that part of his nature which needs food and drink and sleep and the satisfaction of all its passions. His anger and his jealousy are animal, also his fear of one who is stronger than himself and his envy of someone who is better than himself. In all these man is the same as the animals.

Farishtagi is the part of his nature that goes back to its source. It is not man's intelligence; the animals also have intelligence, though the animals cannot ask, 'From whence have I come? For what purpose am I here?' When man knows this, when he recognizes his origin, then he is a divine being. This angelic nature is his kindness, his love, his sympathy, and his desire for knowledge. A great Hindustani poet has said, 'We created man for feeling; if not, for our praise the angels were enough in Heaven.'

In his worship man, thinking that he glorifies God, in reality reduces God. We take a part and call it 'I'. We occupy this part and thereby deduct this part from God. I remember that my murshid when he met with any difficulty used to say with a deep sigh, 'Bandagi becharegi', which means, 'By coming here, He has become helpless'.

What connection is there between Allah and Bandeh, between God and man, and what connection is there between man and God? What we call 'I' is formed by the impressions of the external world, of the world of illusion, which have fallen upon the soul. An infant will never say, 'I'. If it has something in its hand and one takes it away, it does not care. It does not distinguish between old and young. Whoever comes near to it, friend or enemy, is the same to the infant. The intellect that recognizes things by their distinctions and differences has deluded the soul.

We can see that that which we call 'I' is not the true nature of our soul because we are never really happy. Whatever we do, whatever we have, whatever power we possess, we can never be happy. We say that this or that makes us unhappy, but it is only the distance that makes us so; the soul is unhappy in its separation.

A person sees that his coat is worn and poor, and he says, 'I am poor'. He sees that his coat is grand and he thinks: 'I am grand'. It is not he who is grand, it is his coat. Whatever is before the soul, the soul recognizes as 'I'. But what is 'I'? The coat is not I, because when the coat is taken off, the self remains. When we are not experiencing through the senses the consciousness still remains.

The Sufi, by the inactivity of the senses, by different postures and practices, produces stillness; and then by the repetition of the name of God he merges his consciousness in the whole Consciousness, in God. This has been understood by the Greek philosophers; it has also been understood by the Vedantists. The Sufi keeps to the adoration, the reverence that he has for God; he bows and prostrates himself before God. And he gives the beautiful name of Beloved to God. He understands that by saying, 'This too is God', he glorifies God; he does not reduce Him.

With all his humility, with all his devotion, he realizes his one-ness with the highest Being.

It is difficult to separate God from man; in reality there is no separation. God's action and man's action are the same; only, God's action is perfect and man's action is imperfect. We upon earth are dependent upon so many things. First of all we must eat. If he did not need to eat, man would not have to work; he could sit with his friends and think of God or of something else. Then he must sleep; and there are so many other necessities.

There is a verse of Zahir which says, 'The seekers have lost themselves before they sought Thee.' And the great poet Amir says, 'Do not say that man is God for he is not God. And do not say that man is separate from God, for he is not separate.'

It is not difficult to have occult or psychic powers; to be virtuous is not difficult, nor to keep our life pure. But to be merciful, to be compassionate, to be human, is difficult. God has many names: the Great, the Almighty, the Sovereign, but He is mostly called the Merciful and the Compassionate. In these qualities we are never perfect, and we never shall be. One should go into one's room at night and repent of what one has done, of all the thousand bad thoughts one has had of friends and enemies. A Persian poet says, 'The whole secret of the two worlds is in these two words: with thy friends be loving, with thy enemies courteous.'

If we have understood this then this world is nothing; and if we have recognized that it is a passing thing, why not let others enjoy themselves while we look on? Why not let others put on a beau-tiful dress, while we look at it? Why not let others eat a good dinner, while we watch or stay in the kitchen and cook it? Why not let others sit in the carriage, and we pull it, instead of sitting in it ourselves and making others draw it? Keeping our life noble means being merciful and compassionate. But it is the tendency of every man to take what is best from another; even in friendship there is that tendency. All are seeking their own enjoyment and want to leave the worst to another; but if one is a seeker of God one should take the opposite way, even if it is contrary to all the world.

There are three courses: the first is renunciation; this is the way of the saints and the sages. It means following in the ideal and accepting whatever troubles and sorrows and ill-treatment may result. The second is selfishness, which means being more selfish than the rest of the world. The third is the greatest and the most difficult. It means having all the responsibilities, all the cares of life, friends and everything, and being as unselfish, as good as possible and yet just selfish enough not to be trampled upon.

If a person is turning round in a circle, the first time he goes slowly, the second time he goes faster, the fourth time he goes faster still, and the fifth, sixth, seventh, or eighth time he will fall down. The first time he experiences the joy of turning, the second and third and fourth times he experiences it more and more, till at last he is drunk with it and falls down and experiences it to the full. This is what the universe has been doing, night and day, from the creation till now. In every activity there is an intoxication. Whatever we do we wish to do more and more, whatever the action may be. If a man is a patriot he will be more and more patriotic. A singer will sing more and more songs until he loses his voice. If a person gambles he will want to do it more and more. If a person has been drunk or drugged he will want more and more of whatever the drink or drugs may be.

Hafiz says, 'Before sunrise the wine was poured out. The wine was borrowed from the eyes of Saki, the wine-giver.' Saki is the manifestation, which so intoxicates us that we believe that this is all that exists until we have become so enslaved by it that we cannot free ourselves any more.

MAN, THE SEED OF GOD

THERE ARE various ideas and beliefs as to the relationship between God and man; and it is natural that there should be various beliefs, because every man has his own conception of God. There is no comparison between God and man: for man, being limited, can be compared with another being, but God, being perfect, is beyond comparison. The prophets and masters in all ages have tried their best to give man some idea of God's being; but it has always been difficult, for it is impossible to define God in words. It is like trying to put the ocean into a bottle. However large the bottle, it can never accommodate the ocean. The words that we use in our everyday language are the names of limited forms, and we give God, who is above name and form, a name for our convenience. If there is any possibility of understanding God and His being, it is only possible through finding the relationship between man and God. The reason for calling man the seed of God, is that this picture gives, to some extent, an idea of the relationship which exists between man and God.

There is a root, there is a stem, there are branches, there are leaves, and there comes a flower; but in the heart of the flower there is something which tells the history of the whole plant. One might say that it is for the sake of the flower that the plant was created, but in point of fact it is the seed in the heart of the flower which continues the species of that plant. That seed is the secret of the plant, and it is its source and goal. It is that seed which was the beginning, it is from out of that seed that the root came; then the seedling emerged, and so it became a plant. After that the seed disappeared; but after the coming of the leaves and branches and the flowers it appeared again. It appeared again, not as one seed, but as many seeds, in multiplicity, and yet it was the same. And towards what goal, for what result did this happen? In order that the seed should come again as the result of the whole plant.

To the man of simple belief, who believes only in his particular idea, there is no relationship between God and man; but for the man who wishes to understand this relationship, the proof of it is to be found in everything. This is the idea which is spoken of in the Bible, where it is said that God created man in His own image. It is the same as if the seed out of which the plant comes were to say, 'Out of my own image I have created the seed which will come forth from the heart of the flower. I shall appear as many, although in the beginning I am one grain.'

This idea again explains to us why it is said that man was created in God's image, when the whole of manifestation, the whole of creation has come from God. The leaf, the branch, and the stem have all come out of the seed, but they are not the image of the seed. The image of the seed is the seed itself. Not only this: the essence of the seed is in the seed. Of course there is some energy, some power, some colour, some fragrance in the flower, in the leaves, and in the stem; but at the same time all the properties that belong to the stem, flower, petals, and leaves are to be found in the seed.

This shows us that man is the culmination of the whole of creation, and that in him the whole universe is manifested. The mineral kingdom, the vegetable kingdom, and the animal kingdom are all to be found in the being, in the spirit of man. It not only means that the different properties such as mineral and vegetable are to be found in the physical body that is made for man, but his mind and his heart also show all the different qualities. The heart is like either a fertile soil or a barren desert: it shows love or lack of love, the productive faculty or destructiveness.

There are different kinds of stones; there are precious stones and there are pebbles and rocks, but among human hearts there is a still greater variety. Think of those whose thoughts, whose feelings, have proved to be more precious than anything that the world can offer: the poets, the artists, the inventors, the thinkers, the philosophers, the servants of humanity, the inspirers of man, the benefactors of mankind. No wealth, no precious stone, whether diamond or ruby, can be compared with these; and yet it has the same quality. And then there are rock-like hearts: one may knock against them and break oneself, and still they will not move. There is a wax-like quality in the heart, or there is the quality of the stone. There are melting hearts and there are hearts which will never melt. Is there anything in nature which is not found in man? Is there not in his feeling, in his thoughts, in his qualities, the aspect of running water, of a fertile soil, and of fruitful trees? Is there not in the heart of man the image of the plant and of fragrant flowers? But the flowers that come from the human heart live longer; their fragrance will spread through the whole world, and their colour will be seen by all people. How delicious are the fruits that human hearts can bear; they immortalize souls and lift them up!

There are on the other hand mentalities in which nothing springs up except the desire to hurt and harm their fellow-men, producing poison through their fruits and flowers, hurting others by thought, speech, or action; and they can hurt more than thorns. There are some whose feelings and thoughts are like gold and silver, and there are others whose thoughts are just like iron and steel. And the variety that one can see in human nature is so vast that all the objects that one can obtain from this earth cannot equal it.

Man not only shows in his nature, in his qualities, in his body, in his thought and feeling, the heritage of this earth, but also that of heaven. Man is subjected to the influence of the planets, of the sun, of the moon, of heat and cold, of air and water and fire, and of all the different elements of which this whole cosmic system is composed. All these elements are to be found in his thoughts, in his feelings, in his body. One can find a person with warmth representing fire; another person who is cold represents water. There are human beings who in their thought and feeling represent the air element; their quickness, their restlessness, show the air element in them.

Does not man represent the sun and moon in his positive and negative character? Does not duality of sex show this? In every man and in every woman there are both the sun quality and the moon quality, and it is these two opposite qualities which give balance to the character. When one quality is predominant and the other is completely missing then there is a lack of balance somewhere.

And if one pursues the thought of mysticism still further, one finds that not only all visible manifestation is present in man, but also all that is invisible. If the angels, the fairies, or the ghosts, elementals, or any other of man's imaginings can be found anywhere, it is in human nature. Angels at all times have been pictured in the image of man.

If all that exists in the world and in heaven is to be found in man, then what remains? God Himself has said in the scriptures, that He has made man in His own image. In other words, 'If you wish to see Me, I am to be found in man'. How thoughtless then on the part of man when, absorbed in his high ideals, he begins to condemn man, to look down upon man! However low and weak and sinful a man may be, there is yet the possibility of his rising higher than anything else in the whole of manifestation, whether on earth or in heaven; nothing else can reach the height which man is destined to reach. Therefore the point of view of the mystics and the thinkers of all ages has always been reflected in their manner, which was a respectful attitude to all men.

In the example of the life of Jesus Christ one can see what compassion, what forgiveness, what tolerance, what understanding the Master showed when a sinner was brought before him. A man who shows contempt towards his fellow-men may be called religious or pious, but he can never be called truly spiritual or wise, whatever be his condition. The man who has no respect for mankind has no attitude of worship towards God. The one who has not recognized the image of God in man, has not seen the Artist who has made this creation; he has deprived himself of this vision which is most sacred and most holy. A person who thinks that man is earthly does not know where his soul comes from. The soul comes from above; it is in the soul of man that God is reflected. A man who feels hatred and contempt, whatever be his belief, faith, or religion, has not understood the secret of all religions which is in the heart of man. And certainly, however good, however virtuous a person may be, however tolerant or forgiving, if at the same time he does not recognize God in man, he has not touched religion.

There is, however, another side to the question. As man evolves, so he finds the limitations, the errors, and the infirmities of human nature; and so it becomes difficult for him to live in the world and to face all that comes. Also, it becomes very difficult for man to be fine, to be good and kind and sensitive, and yet at the same time to be tolerant. Then the tendency comes to push everything away, and to keep himself away from everybody else. But the purpose of being born on earth is not that. It is to find that perfection which is within oneself. However good and kind a man may be, if he has not found the purpose for which he was born on earth, he has not fulfilled the object of his life.

There are as many different aspects of that purpose as there are people in the world; but behind all of them there is one purpose, which may be called the purpose of the whole of creation. And that purpose is accomplished when the inventor looks at his invention working, when the architect builds a house which he has designed, and he enters it and sees how well it is made; the purpose is accomplished when a play is produced, and the producer watches it, that is the fulfilment of his purpose. Every man seems to have his own purpose, but all these purposes are nothing but steps to the one and only purpose which is the purpose of God. If our small desires are granted today, tomorrow there is another wish; and whatever be the desire, when it is granted there is next day another desire. This shows that the whole of humanity is directed towards one desire, the desire which is God's object: the fuller experience of life within and without, the fuller knowledge of life above and below. It is the widening of the outlook: that it may become so wide that in the soul, which is vaster than the world, all may be reflected; that the sight may become so keen that it may probe the depths of the earth and the highest of the heavens. In this lies the fulfilment of the soul; and the soul who will not make every possible effort and every sacrifice for its attainment, has not understood religion. What is the Sufi Message? It is the esoteric training, practising and working throughout life towards that attainment which is the fulfilment of the purpose of God.

EVOLUTION

THERE ARE two aspects of the question of the evolution of man through the different kingdoms of creation. One is the biological aspect. One sees that from the vegetable kingdom the animal kingdom is born in the form of germs, worms, and insects. As matter evolves, it is used by higher entities, and thus it evolves still more. But the law of evolution is difficult. Matter as a whole is evolving towards a much better and fresher condition.

Then there is primitive man. Modern science has not been able to find the link between man and monkey, but there have been many races which have come and have died out; even now several races still live in regions where science has not yet discovered them. But if the missing link is not yet found it does not matter. It is after all a mystical conception as well as a scientific one. The difference is that science speaks about it plainly, although it cannot get any exact proof, while mysticism mentions it vaguely in the beautiful form of legends and poetry; for instance in the story of Rama and the monkey army, where the word 'monkey' is used because there is no other term for that missing link.

But this is not the only process which goes on. Every aspect of a question must be looked at from a different point of view; unless one does so from at least two points of view, one will always have difficulty in understanding it fully. If one watches the work of the potter one sees that he kneads the clay, colours it, and then moulds it into the different vessels he wants to make. As long as he has enough different clays and colours at hand he does not begin his work every time by again fetching clay and then kneading and colouring it. In the same way one sees that vegetable matter comes from the vegetable kingdom and that man comes from man.

By looking at this question from both these aspects one comes to understand that both processes are needed. For instance there is the work of the colour-merchant and that of the artist. The task of the colour-merchant is to have different substances and to mix

them and produce the desired colour. The artist does not need
to go through that process; he gets his colours ready-made from
the colour-merchant. In other words, it is not necessary for every
person to pass through all the mineral, vegetable, and other
aspects of creation, so there is no reason for distress!

God grants us our wishes at two different times. One is when
our heart is free from every thought and feeling and maintained
in a most peaceful and tranquil condition. At that time every
wish we may have is just like a seed sown in the right season.
And if we have the patience and strength to wait and trust in the
great power of God, whatever the wish may be it will certainly be
granted. The other time is when we are satisfied, when we are
very happy. Whatever wish we have during that period will be
granted, just as the rain coming from above at the proper time will
bring with it fruit and flowers.

If one of our objects is what our soul is seeking and the other
is life's necessities, it is preferable to sacrifice the necessities and
keep to the object which the soul is seeking. But another point
of view is that in order to become spiritual we need not become
unwordly; we can just as well live in the world but yet not be of
the world.

Everything in creation has an opposite. There is the sun and
there is the moon. There is man and there is woman. There is
night and there is day. The colours are distinguished by their
variety and so are the forms. To distinguish anything there
must be opposites; where there is no opposite one cannot distinguish. There must be health to distinguish it from illness.

In ancient times many have tried to help the imagination of
those who sought goodness by teaching them belief in Satan,
saying that God is all goodness and Satan all badness. This was in
order to explain to those who could not understand where
badness came from. In reality badness is only the shadow of
goodness; and as a shadow is non-existent so evil is non-
existent. Good is always going forward; what is left behind
is less good, and what is gained on the journey forward is more
good. But when we compare things then we call one thing
evil and the other good. Therefore people have called the devil,
on whom we should turn our back, all evil; and God, to whom

we should give our faith, all goodness. It was simply a method
of teaching the people of ancient times. In reality God is beyond
comparison, though of course we compare God with something
when we call Him good, as many do. What is our own goodness?
It is very small; it is not something to judge God by.

There is a stage in the evolution of a man's life when every
question is answered by the life around him. He may have a
living being before him, or be surrounded by nature; he may
be awake or asleep, but the answer to his question comes as an
echo of the question itself. Just as certain things become an
accommodation for the air, turning it into a sound, so everything
becomes an accommodation for each thought of the sage, helping
it to resound; and in this resonance there is an answer. In point of
fact the answer is contained in the question itself. A question has
no existence without an answer. It is man's limited vision that
makes him see only the question without the answer.

While all things have their opposites, it is also true that in each
the spirit of the opposite exists. In man the quality of woman
exists; in woman the spirit of man. In the sun the form of the
moon exists, in the moon the light of the sun. The closer one
approaches reality, the nearer one comes to unity. The evidence
of this realization is that no sooner has a question arisen in the
heart, than the answer comes as its echo either within or without.
If we look in front of ourselves, the answer is before us; if we
look behind the answer is behind; if we look up the answer
awaits us in the sky; if we look down the answer is engraved for
us on the earth; and if we close our eyes we will find the answer
within us. It is like climbing a mountain, a mountain whose
name is *Why?* When we have climbed it, then we are face to
face with our ideal. It is not study which brings us to this realization; it is reached by rising above all that hinders our faith in
truth.

SPIRITUAL CIRCULATION THROUGH THE VEINS OF NATURE

WHEN ONE observes keenly the nature of this life of variety, one finds that behind the veil of variety there is only one life, the source and goal of all things. It is this life which may be called the blood of the universe, circulating through the veins of nature. It may be called either substance or spirit, it is something out of which all that is seen and all intelligence is moulded and kept alive and in working order. It is this life which we know as intelligence.

Intelligence, which is often confused with intellect, is something which is to be found even in the lower creation. It can be traced in plant life, and sensed even in the heart of the rock. People often think that the intellect is a development which manifests as mind in the life of man, and that the lower animals have no mind, that mind is a development of matter depending upon the brain. But the mystics of all times, the prophets and all meditative souls, say that what was is and will be, and that as it is all the same substance life is not subject to change, nor does it develop. It is a different grade of evolution which makes us capable of understanding, and which gives us the feeling that mind is a development proceeding from matter. The great ones, the meditative souls who dwelt in the wilderness and the forests and communicated with the life around them, realized this truth; and very often they experienced a greater harmony and peace and upliftment where there was no visible life. Life is intelligence, everywhere, and the more one communicates with life, the more one feels that even the rock is not without life, that through it pulses the blood of the universe. And when we look at life from this point of view, we see that there is no place, no object which is not sacred; that even in a rock one may find the source and goal of all things in that particular form.

Many who are experienced in plant life know how responsive plants are to the sympathy of the person who lives with them and looks after them. It has been proved that plants breathe; and if breath is to be found in plant life, certainly there is intelligence too. I once happened to see a stone whose owner called it a magic stone, but in reality it was quite ordinary; only it often changed its colour and shade, especially when a particular person held it. So even a stone can respond to a person's mind, and this teaches us that there is a great deal to explore in the mineral kingdom. This is not a discovery of today; it was known to the people of ancient times. We read in the Persian poems of Jelal-ud-Din Rumi that God slept in the mineral kingdom, dreamed in the vegetable, became conscious in the animal, and realized Himself in the human being.

But this one life is to be seen in a more pronounced form in human beings, in the intellect they show, in the work they do, in the magnetizing of the atmosphere, in the thought-power they exercise, in the influence of healing. Although one person is separated from another, although there may be no outer connection, yet even at a distance the influence of thoughts and feelings is felt. There were many instances of this during the war when mothers and wives of soldiers, in times of pain, illness, or death, were conscious of their distress without any other source of communication. How often when people are in close touch do they perceive each other's condition, not only by thought-waves, but in the realm of feeling also; this shows that there is one body, and that in that body there is one life which continually circulates as the blood does in our veins.

This gives a logical explanation of the law of cause and effect. A wrong-doer may escape earthly witnesses, but he cannot escape this one life in which he lives and moves and has his being. A person who has done good to another may never see that other again; yet the good must return to him as there is only one body and one life. Just as with the circulation in the physical body the essence of all we eat is absorbed in the blood, so our every thought, word, and action affects the one life.

Often people question or ridicule certain superstitions; they ask for instance how past, present, and future can be read from cards. But this, and also the science of astrology and crystal-gazing, may be explained by the fact that there is one life in which the circulation is always pulsing; one music, one rhythm; a person only needs to be acquainted with the theme of the music to be able to read and understand it.

Not only by cards and crystal-gazing can one read the past, present, and future, but by many other means; if we are able to communicate with even one vein of this one life, then we are in touch with all the veins of the universe. Some means are better, some are worse, but through any medium we can reach understanding, thus proving that there is one life behind all. Man may be taught to do good, he may learn righteousness, but this is virtue forced upon him as the result of a certain teaching; real virtue only comes by understanding the oneness of life, thus binding man to friend and enemy alike. Jesus Christ teaches, 'Love your enemies', and while it is often difficult to love our friends, we are not able to love our enemies unless we realize the secret of the one life behind everything, in spite of the world of variety which is continually creating illusion.

If by religion, philosophy, or mysticism this realization is attained, then one touches the secret of life, and a mighty power is gained without any wonder-working. This lesson is easy to learn intellectually, this truth can be consumed like food in a moment, but this is not enough; to digest it the whole of one's life is not sufficient, for truth is mixed with facts, and when truth becomes a fact it loses its importance. Absorbed in the world of variety we are apt to forget truth, for we are always engrossed in facts. That is why people who spend much time in meditation try to think of the oneness of being, and try to meditate on the ultimate truth of being. It works like the winding of a clock: it only takes a minute to wind but it goes on all day long. So in meditation the same thought goes on, and in everything one does or says one uses the same truth.

How much harm is caused by the lack of understanding of this truth! All such disasters as wars, floods, earthquakes, famines, all the dire events that cannot be controlled by man, come from disorder in the body of the universe; when the blood is disordered everything goes wrong, and though sometimes it seems that what is harmful to one part is helpful to another, yet in the long run one sees that every part suffers. The after-effect is felt by the whole world as strain and pain and all kinds of suffering.

If one raised one's eyes from this world of illusion and looked up, and asked God to tell one the secret and the mystery of His creation, one would hear in answer that every thing and being is put in its own place, and each is busy carrying out that work which has to be done in the whole scheme of nature. Life is a symphony; and the action of every person in this symphony is the playing of his particular part in the music.

When the war was going on all the people were called to arms, and were placed, regardless of their profession, qualifications, or moral standards, where they were most needed; the reason was that the 'call of the purpose' was to be the first consideration. If there is anything which will bring peace to the thinker, it is the understanding of this idea. The thought that one is suffering now because of one's sins in a past life may bring an answer to the enquiring and reasoning of the mind and stop it from rebelling for the moment, but will it take away the irritation that the misery is causing in the heart? Will that mind ever excuse God for having judged him so severely? He may own to his past mistakes, but will he ever believe in God as a God of love and compassion, as a God of mercy, or as a God of forgiveness?

If God were separate from man, and if He rejoiced in the suffering of man, then one might blame Him. But as the Sufi realizes, He is the sufferer and the suffering; yet at the same time He is beyond all suffering. This fact can be understood by not merely believing in God, but by knowing Him. Suppose our hands dropped a heavy weight on our feet and hurt them, are our hands to be blamed? No, for they share the pain with the feet, and although the feet seem to be hurt, yet that which feels the hurt is our being, our absolute being, and therefore the hand shares the hurt with the foot.

So it is with God: all our lives are His and He takes part in every feeling of joy and pain which we feel, but at the same time His perfect being keeps Him above all earthly joys and pains, where as our imperfection limits us, so that we become subject to all joys and pains, however small they are.

People often ask why should man suffer and make sacrifices for God. When his suffering and sacrifice is over he will find that though he began to do so for God, in the end it proved to be for himself. It is the foolishly selfish man who is selfish; the wisely selfish man proves to be selfless. This consciousness is attained by self-realization; first man must realize himself and find out of what he is composed. He is composed of spirit and matter. He consists, in himself, of the mineral, vegetable, and animal worlds, the jinn and the angel; and it is his task to balance all these, knowing that he has been created neither to be as spiritual as an angel, nor to be as material as an animal. When he strikes the happy medium he will certainly tread the path which is meant for a human being to tread, the path which leads straight to the goal. 'Strait is the gate, and narrow is the way', narrow because any step taken on either side will lead to some other path. Balance is the keynote of spiritual attainment.

The soul of the whole of creation is one, the life behind all these ever-moving phantoms is one. Meditation on this truth and the awakening to it will harmonize the condition of the world. And when the soul begins to see the truth it is born again; to such a soul all that seems truth to an average person appears false, and what seems truth to this soul means nothing to the average person; all that seems to the average person to be important and precious in life, has no value nor importance at all for this soul. Thus he naturally finds himself alone in a crowd which lives in a world quite different from that in which he lives. Imagine living in a world where nobody speaks our language! Yet he can live in the world, for he knows its language, although life in the world is as unprofitable to him as the world of children playing with their toys is to a grown-up person.

Prophets and great mystics have come to the world from time to time, as the physician comes to help the patient whose health is disordered; and when the great ones have come they have brought a new life to the world, given to the organism of the universe to help it to run smoothly. The Sufis have always existed as mystics, and their lives have been devoted to meditation and spiritual practices. What have they learnt from these meditations? They have learnt the essence of everything, the oneness or unity; and it is by thinking about unity, by realizing it, and by living it that man fulfils the purpose of life.

DESTINY AND FREE WILL

VERY OFTEN those who believe in destiny do not believe in free will. There are some who have had some success in their work and have recognized it as the outcome of that work. Then they think that if anything exists it must be free will; that they have achieved results according to what they have done. And there are others who have tried and not succeeded. In that case they feel that there is something holding them back from getting results, and then they think that there must be such a thing as destiny, and it is that which is holding them back. Many people think that it is a form of laziness to be a fatalist and they call destiny a superstition; and there are others who admit that free will is a conception, an idea, but that in reality all is governed by destiny.

The idea of free will has its meaning, and belief in it has its peculiar benefit in life. At the same time the idea of destiny is very profound; whether a person believes in it or not, there is always an attraction about it. The one who reads the future will always attract both the one who believes in destiny and the one who does not. The believer bows to him with faith; the unbeliever goes his way with a smile. Both are attracted because it is the greatest mystery there is. One's own life in which one is most interested always remains a secret and a mystery, and this mystery is greater than any other in the world. No one can say, 'I have no interest in knowing about my life, in knowing why I have had that past, why I have this present, and what future I shall have'. To know about it is one's greatest desire.

When one thinks about destiny the question arises whether there is a plan drawn up, and whether every occurrence in life must happen according to that plan; and, if it is drawn up, on what grounds, and by whom? If it is God who has drawn it up, how far can He be called just for making one happy and another miserable, one great and another small; letting one enjoy himself and at the same time making another suffer, though living under the same sun and walking on the same earth? And if it is not destiny but man's action, is it then the action of the past which brings about the action of the present, and if it is so, to what degree is man responsible for it? These questions take one to the depths of life's mystery, and once they are solved a great philosophical problem is solved.

The mystic finds the secret of life by knowing how to make a plan according to what he wishes. However, he arrives at this stage by first giving up his plan. For a person who has no power over his plan, it is better to give it up into the hands of God. The more one depends upon the Maker of the plan, the more one is able to make it oneself. It is just like the mother who, as long as her little child cannot walk by itself and depends on holding her hand, does not allow the child to go alone. And even when she allows it to walk alone she holds her hands round it so that it may not fall. When a man takes his own responsibility into his hands, calling it free will, he loses, so to speak, that dependence on God which holds him and which makes God responsible. Therefore it is a saintly person who arrives at resigning himself to the will of God; and afterwards this may develop into his free will, which will then be the will of God. This is what marks the difference between the saintly character and the character of the master: the character of the saint is to be resigned fully to the will of God; and the character of the master is to find the will of God in his own free will.

Very often we ask why, if there is a God and if God is love and is kind and merciful, there should be so much suffering as if people were being punished. But that is our small way of looking at it. In reality if our eyes were open and we could see deeper into life, we would realize that there is no such thing as punishment. In all things there is the mercy of God, but we only call that God's mercy which we can perceive and understand; that which we cannot see and understand we think of as a punishment from God. Whether the parents scold the child or whether they caress it, in both there is their love and nothing else. As Tagore says, 'When Thou tunest me to a higher pitch, then I feel pain. But I know, Lord, that pain is to attune me to the right pitch.'

When we arrive at stilling our agitation and becoming peaceful, resigning our will to the will of God, then we begin to see the love of God in all things, and never again think that God can be anything other than love. That is why the Sufi does not always think of God as a Creator, as a King, or as a Judge; but as a Beloved, as a Lover, and as Love itself.

Most people have a preconceived idea and keep this idea like a wall before them; they do not try to think any further and are content with what they know about it. There is no doubt that a man is born with a plan which is to be accomplished in life; not only of what his instincts or merits or gifts will be, but also the whole plan of how his life will turn out. There is a saying in the East that you can read the life of an infant by looking at its feet. Even the little feet of the infant show the sign of the plan that it is to follow through life.

There is a story that throws some light upon the relation between destiny and free will. There was a seer working as a porter in a rich man's house. Now there is a belief in the East that no sooner is a child born than angels come and write on its forehead the whole plan of its destiny. This porter was a wonderful man. At the door, as soon as the angels came, he said, 'Stop, where are you going? I am master here, you cannot go in unless you promise to tell me about the plan.' So the angels told him. And again the next time that a child was born in that house, the porter took down notes of what was going to happen.

After some time the parents passed away. They had been rich, but they lost their money for some reason or other, and the children had to leave their home and were without a refuge. Then this old porter took upon his shoulders the burden of looking after them, but as soon as they were a few years older the children each went to different countries. One day the porter thought that it was his duty to go and see how they were getting on. Also for a seer it is most interesting to observe the material phenomena of something he has seen inwardly as a vision; it is a satisfaction to him, a delight, when all that he has felt inwardly becomes materialized and he sees it happening on the outer plane. It gives him the greatest pleasure.

So the porter went and saw one of the children working as a

horse groom, and he was very sorry about this. He went to the young man and said, 'It could not be avoided, it was meant that you should be what you are. But I want to give you some advice, because it makes me sad to think that you, at whose house there were so many horses, have to work as a horse groom. Here is a little money, take it and go to another city and try to work there as a horse trainer. The horses of the rich men will be given to you to train; and I am sure you will be successful.' The young man asked, 'Can I do anything else?' He said, 'No, that is the only way. You would have been a groom all your life if I had not told you this. There is nothing else you can do; this is the only door open for you. Do it, and then you will have success.' The young man did as he was told and was very successful.

The porter went to the other son and asked, 'What are your circumstances?' He said, 'My circumstances? I wander about in the forest and catch birds and sell them in the city; but I make hardly enough money to live.' In those days there was a fashion among kings to keep a certain bird as a pet; that bird was called Shabaz, the king's bird. And the porter said, 'You must not look for game birds, you must look only for this bird Shabaz.' The boy said, 'But if I cannot find it, then I shall starve and die!' The old man said, 'Do you know what your father was, and what you are?' 'Yes,' he said, 'I know, I have had bad luck.' The man said, 'You will have better luck if you will only listen to me. You need not change; your profession is still catching birds. But catch Shabaz. You can sell it for millions. That is the bird you ought to catch.'

This story makes us realize what the seer does. A definite plan was made for those two young men; at the same time there was scope for free will to work, but within that plan. And if they had not realized that scope they would have had to continue leading a miserable life. It is a great lesson and those who can understand this lesson can benefit immensely by it.

Sa'di, the great poet of Persia, has said, 'Every soul is born for a certain purpose and the light of that purpose is kindled in that soul.'

The Hindus believe a person is born with what they call Karma; some action of the past or an impression he has brought with him to the earth as a good influence or a bad influence or as something that he has to pay back. No doubt there is some truth in this idea, and we can see the proof of that truth very often; for instance when a person is placed in a situation where he has to serve, as if he has to pay a debt to someone. He may not have the slightest desire to do so; but at the same time it falls on his shoulders, he cannot help it. It is as if the highest Power has determined that it should be so; whether he does it willingly or unwillingly he must give his time, his thought, his sympathy, and his service to someone else.

Then one sees a person receiving money, comfort, love, and sympathy from someone else, regardless of whether he deserves it all or not. This shows that although from one's birth there is a relation between give and take, yet man is born with certain obligations. It also shows that however powerful and great a person may be, however good the circumstances might seem, when there is to be a difficulty, one cannot help it; the difficulty comes. And then at other times in life, in spite of all obstacles, a way opens; we do not have to do much and everything goes smoothly. This also shows that there is a plan, that it is not only qualifications and cleverness that make us successful. But there are times where we are meant to have an easy life, success, and all we wish; and there are other times when we have to do without it, we cannot help it.

Is it something a person is born with, or is it the effect of a person's action on the earth? Both. Suppose an artist first thought out a design for a certain picture, and while he was making that picture he became so inspired that it suggested to him that he should change the design. And as he went on he changed it to such an extent that it became quite different from the picture he had originally conceived. To the same extent life may be changed by action. A right action, a good action, is productive of power and is creative and it can help far more than man imagines.

The question is to what extent can man help himself. Man has two aspects in him. One aspect is his mechanical being, where he is but a machine controlled by conditions, by his impressions, by outer influences, by cosmic influences, and by his actions; everything working mechanically turns his life accordingly. He has no power over conditions, he is just a tool of influences. The more pronounced this aspect is in man, the less evolved he is. It is the sign of a lesser evolution. But there is another aspect in man which is creative, in which he shows he is not only part of God but linked with God, because his innermost self is God. Be not surprised therefore if you hear stories of sages, masters, saints, and prophets whose command affected the cosmos and by whose will whole peoples moved as they wished them to move. It is nothing to be surprised at. Outwardly every man is about the same size; no man is as tall as a camel or as large as an elephant. Outwardly men vary only a little. But inwardly there is no comparison in the size of the spirit; no comparison between the understanding of one man and of another. One walks, one runs, one flies, and one creeps; yet all walk on the same earth, all live under the same sun, and they are all called men. Nevertheless there is no man who has not a spark of this power, who has not the possibility of changing conditions by his free will, if only he can realize what it is. It is the absence of this realization which make a man a machine.

As to man's destiny, it is not only his own action but also the thought of another that can change a man's life. I have seen for instance many cases where a loving mother was not pleased with her growing child who did not satisfy her. This will always make it suffer in some way or another. The child may become a qualified man, a capable man, but if he has not satisfied his mother that is quite enough for him to have bad luck. A keen study will make one understand how these things work; but from childhood we have been so absorbed in our own life and our own interests that we do not think very much about how we are affected by the thought and feeling of those around us.

A rich man, if he is displeased with his servant and speaks roughly to him or insults him, may not realize it at the time, but perhaps the feeling of this servant who is dependent on him and who is bound to that particular place is hurt. And when this rich man goes to his office, to his affairs, he may get back that pinprick which he gave. He does not know it; he believes he has given a pinprick to a servant who could not return it; but someone else returns it without his realizing that this is the answer to what he

has done. The more we think about this the more we shall understand how God works through all beings, even through animals
and birds. And then when we are able to believe this, we cannot
help believing what Buddha has said: that the essence of religion
is harmlessness. Harmlessness does not only mean to refrain from
killing. Many are killed without killing; in order to kill a person
one does not need to murder him. A glance, a word, a thought can
kill a person and that is worse than death.

It is this experience that I had in mind when I said in the
Gayan, 'My bare feet! Step gently on life's path, lest the thorns
lying on the way should murmur at being trampled upon by
you.'

There is no end to consideration, once a person begins to think
about it. If there is any religion it is in consideration, considering
that feeling which can be hurt by a moment's thoughtlessness.
If there is any abode of God, it is in the heart of man. If the heart
is touched wrongly it has an effect upon destiny. One does not
realize to what extent destiny can be changed by the feeling of
another person; it can change it more than our own feeling. One
always wishes good for oneself; no one wishes to be unhappy.

There are also planetary influences. What are these planetary
influences and what relation do they have to us? The answer is
that man is a planet also; and as one planet is related to the other,
so in the same way the planets are related to mankind. Naturally
a change in the condition of a planet and the effect produced by
that planet have an influence upon man's life. One might ask if
man is really so small as to be under the influence of a planet.
Yes, outwardly; outwardly man is as small as a drop in the ocean.
If the planet is an ocean, then the individual is a drop. But
inwardly the planet is a drop in the ocean of man; that is the
heart of man. Asif, the great philosopher, says, 'My ignorance,
the day you depart my heart will be open, and this whole
universe will become a bubble in the ocean of my heart.'

Limitation, smallness, and imperfection are the outcome
of ignorance. But when the heart is open the whole universe is
in it, and the source of destiny, its secret and its mystery are in the
hand of man. What, then, is the way in which to believe in
destiny and free will? The best way of believing in destiny is to

think that all the disagreeable things we have gone through are part of destiny and belong to the past; to think that we are free from it. And the best way of looking at free will is to keep in mind that all that is to come, all that is before us, is the outcome of free will. To keep before us as a concentration that nothing wrong will touch us, that all that is good for us lies before us. It is wrong to think that worse things are in store for us because destiny has preserved our Karma and ordained that we must suffer, and that one has to pay according to one's Karma. For the one who is conscious of Karma will have to pay a high interest; the more conscious he is of it, the higher the interest he will have to pay.

In conclusion one comes to understand that there are two aspects of will working through all things in life. One is the individual will, the other is the divine will. When a person goes along ignoring the divine will, naturally the human will fails and he finds difficulty, for he is swimming against the tide. The moment a person works in consonance, in harmony, with the divine will, things become smooth.

One may object that life has not been smooth for great personalities such as Christ. From childhood there were difficulties; his parents had to flee to the desert, and when the young Jesus was brought among people there were still greater difficulties. And all the great saints and sages had great difficulties all through life; things were not all smooth for them. Did they work against destiny, against the will of God? This question makes us realize that the will of God meets with difficulty on the material plane. In the Bible we read, 'Thy will be done in earth, as it is in heaven', but it is not as easy for His will to be done on earth as it is in heaven.

This suggestion teaches us a great lesson, and that lesson is that there is a conscious will working and that there is an unconscious will working. But conscious working is divine working. It may be that the divine will has difficulty, but at the same time this difficulty has a meaning in it. In other words, success or failure of God and of God's power means nothing because ultimately both are success; but success and failure of man means nothing because in the end both are failure.

If a man succeeds in collecting much wealth or in attaining a high position, what is the end of it? It will belong to someone else who will snatch it from his hand. Therefore whether we have success or failure in life, if it is individual in the end it will be failure. But in the case of godly things, whether it is failure or success, it is always success in the end. It cannot be otherwise; it is the only gain there is. As Nanak says, 'The grain that takes refuge near the centre of the grinding mill is saved'. So is the man who keeps close to God. He draws his power and inspiration from God, and when his life is directed by that power and inspiration, whether he has difficulties or not, the way is always smooth and the end is what it ought to be.

DIVINE IMPULSE

THE FIRST question that arises when one reflects upon the subject of divine impulse is, where does every impulse come from? Every movement, every vibration, every motion has one source. The Bible hints at this when it says, 'The Word was God'. The Word means vibration, and vibration means movement.

Vibration was the first or original aspect of Brahma, the Creator. Every impulse, every action on any plane of its existence has its origin in the one source. In the Qur'an it is said, 'God is all power; there is no power but God's.' All that is done is done by His power.

If all the scriptures state this, then where does Satan come in? What is the meaning behind the power of Satan? Another power is suggested besides the power of God, and sometimes the power attributed to Satan seems mightier than the power attributed to God; this is a puzzle to many. The explanation is to be found in the understanding of metaphysics and of the laws of nature. There is one law which is the natural law; all that happens and is directed by nature's law is harmonious. The gardens made by man may seem superficially to be an improvement upon the wild country-side, but eventually, on closer examination, the garden with its artificial layout appears limited in beauty and harmony. The inspiration one can get in the woods, in the countryside, is much greater than in the man-made garden, for there man has limited the possibilities of inspiration, as the life he radiates is limited. Man makes a law and finds he cannot keep it, so he makes another law, and is never satisfied; for he does not take into account nature's laws of peace and harmony.

It is said that nature is cruel; yes, but man is far more cruel than the animals. Animals have never destroyed lives on the scale that man has. All the apparent cruelty of nature cannot compare with the cruelty, ignorance, and injustice of man. Jesus Christ said, 'Thy will be done'. There is much for us to learn from this. Man makes the world in which he lives different from the plan of God and the laws of nature, and so the will of God is not done; this prayer teaches man that he must find out what is the will of God. It is not necessary for animals and birds to find out the will of God, for they are directed by nature's impulse; they are closer to nature than man, but man's life is so far removed from the life of nature that every movement is difficult. At the present time we do not realize this; with all our knowledge we make life more and more complicated, and so the strife becomes greater and greater. For every person, old or young, rich or poor, life is a difficult struggle, for we go further and further from the impulse which comes direct from the source from whence every impulse comes.

From the metaphysical point of view there are different rhythms describing the condition of man, and these are called in the Vedanta Satva, Rajas, and Tammas. Tammas is a rhythm which is chaotic, destructive, and every impulse that comes to man while he is in this chaotic rhythm is followed by destructive results. Any impulse coming from a person who is in the rhythm of Rajas will be accomplished, but the impulse that comes when he is in the rhythm of Satva is inspired and is in harmony with the rhythm of the universe.

The active life of man gives little time for concentration, and for getting mind and body into the state in which he can experience the rhythm which gives inspiration and meets with the will of God. This experience comes in answer to the prayer of Christ already mentioned, 'Thy will be done on earth as it is in heaven'. By producing that condition of mind and body, one tunes oneself to a certain pitch which is harmonious and heavenly, and in which the divine will is as easily done as it is in heaven. It is in this rhythm alone that the will of God can be done.

It was not because of any prejudice against the world that the great ones left the world and went into the forests and caves; they went in order to tune themselves to that rhythm in which they could experience heaven. Heaven is not a country or a continent, it is a state, a condition within oneself, only experienced when the rhythm is in perfect working order. If one knows this one realizes that happiness is man's own property. Man is his own enemy; he seeks for happiness in the wrong direction and never finds it. It is a continual illusion. Man thinks, 'If I only had this or that, I should be happy for ever', and he never arrives at it because he pursues an illusion instead of the truth. Happiness is only to be found within; and when man tunes himself he finds everything which his soul yearns for within himself.

The nature of every impulse is that it goes through three stages; and having done so it is realized as a result, whether right or wrong, beneficent or harmful, as soon as the impulse springs from within. There is no impulse which in its beginning is wrong or purposeless or out of harmony, for in the sum total of all things every impulse has its purpose. It is our limited outlook that judges. The justice which is behind everything is so perfect that in the ultimate result everything fits into its proper place. It is during the process through which the impulse passes that it becomes right or wrong, but not at the beginning or the end; for the beginning has a purpose, and the end has answered the demand. This is a question of metaphysics, and one must study it from different points of view or one will be very much confused. Man with so little knowledge is ready to condemn or to admire, and thousands of times he fails to judge rightly. All great souls who have attained illumination have realized this. Christ says, 'Judge not'. Then tolerance comes, and when one realizes what is behind the impulse one says very little.

An impulse first rises in the region of feeling, and in this region it is either strengthened or destroyed. The feeling may be love or hatred, kindness or bitterness; but whatever the feeling may be, the impulse which has risen either gains strength to go forward or is destroyed. For instance a person may have a great feeling of kindness; then the impulse of revenge rises but it is destroyed before it can materialize. Another person has a great feeling of bitterness, but while the impulse is to forgive, it will be destroyed before it ever touches the reason; he will not have to call on his thought to judge, for his feeling will destroy it. Or a person has a great feeling of bitterness and the impulse rises to do a kind service, but it is destroyed before it reaches the realm of thought, which is the second region through which the impulse rises. Or if the impulse rises till it reaches that realm of thought one may reason, 'Why should I help? Why should I serve? Does he deserve it? Will he benefit by it? Is it right?' All these problems are settled in this region. Then thirdly comes the realm of action. If the mind consumes it, it goes no further; but if the mind allows it, it comes into the region of action and is realized as a result.

One may ask how sages and thinkers have distinguished the divine impulse among the different impulses that arise in the heart of man. First we must understand what the word 'divine' means. Divine means a state of perfection. This state is experienced by God through man; in other words, when a man has risen to the stage of development where he can be the perfect instrument of God, when nothing of his own being stands in the way of the direct impulse that comes from within, that spirit may be called perfect. That which is most precious, that which is the purpose of man's life is to arrive at that state of perfection where he can be the perfect instrument of God.

When a man has reached this stage, he at first begins to realize God only at certain moments; then as he develops he does it for a longer time; and those who develop still further pass most of their time in that realization. Then their feeling and thought no longer hinder the divine impulse, for it rises freely and reveals the divine purpose. The message of the prophets and teachers of all times has been to teach man how to make peace with God. The fulfilment of life's purpose is in harmonizing with God, and this is done by distinguishing the divine impulse.

One can distinguish a divine impulse from others just as in music one can distinguish the true note from the false, the harmony from the discord. It is only a matter of training the ear. When the ear is trained one can distinguish the slightest discord; the greater the musician, the more capable he is of distinguishing harmony and discord, the true and the false note. Many think that what we call right or wrong, good or bad, is something we learn or acquire. That is true when it is man-made right or wrong; but every child has a sense of what is naturally right and wrong. The child feels the wrong vibration at once. The infant feels whether its surroundings are harmonious or not; but man confuses himself so that he can no longer distinguish clearly. For man to learn to know for himself is a great advance along the spiritual path. When a man is clear as to the feeling he gets from every impulse, he has advanced far. There are some who say after a bad result, 'I am sorry', but then it is too late, it was not true 'ear-training'.

The divine impulse is an impulse full of love; it gives happiness, it creates peace. The difficulty is that not every man observes the beginning of the impulse; most men only observe the result. They are like an intoxicated person, and so in time, as with a drunken man, they become confused and depressed, and there is struggle and strife. But man was not born for this; he was born for happiness. Peace, love, kindness, and harmony are parts of his own being, and when a person is unhappy it means that he has lost himself, that he does not know where he is.

Man is seeking for phenomena; he wants miracles, communication with ghosts or spirits, he is looking for something complex; and yet the simplest thing and the most valuable thing in life is to find one's true self.

THE LAW OF LIFE

ALL THAT comes to a person, in reality he arrives at. By this
I do not mean to say that a person cannot make something,
create it, earn it, deserve it, or that it does not come to him by
chance. What comes may come in any of the above five ways,
but at the same time in reality it is he who arrives at it. These
five ways are realms through which a certain thing comes, but
what brings this about is man himself. This subtle idea remains
hidden until a person has insight into the law of life and observes
its inner working clearly. For instance, if one said that someone
had gained a certain position or rank or wealth or fame by working for it, outwardly it might be true; but many work and do
not achieve it. Besides one might say that all the blessings of
Providence come to one if one deserves them; but one can see
so much in life which is contrary to this principle, for there are
many who do not deserve and yet they attain. With every
appearance of free will there yet seems to be helplessness in all
aspects of life. And as to what man calls chance, there is much to
be said against this idea too; for a deep insight into life will prove
that what seems to be chance in reality is not chance at all; it
only seems to be so, for illusion is the nature of life.

Every soul is, so to speak, continually making its way towards something, sometimes consciously and sometimes unconsciously. What a person does outwardly is an appearance of
action, an action having no connection with his inner activity
which is like a journey. Not everyone knows whither he is
making his way, and yet everyone is making his way; whether
it is towards the goal one desires, or whether it is towards quite
the opposite goal which one has never desired, one does not
know. But when the goal is realized on the physical plane, then
a person becomes conscious and says, 'I have not worked for it, I
have not created it, I have not deserved it, I have not earned it;
how is it possible that it has come?' If it is an object which had
been desired by him then perhaps he gives himself the credit for

it; he tries to believe that he has made it in some way. And if it is not desirable then he wants to attribute it to someone else, or to suppose that for some reason or other it has happened like that. But in reality it is a destination at which one has arrived at the end of one's journey; one cannot say definitely that one has created it or made it or deserved it, or that it has happened by accident. What can be said is that one has journeyed towards it, either consciously or unconsciously, and has arrived at it. That is why in point of fact no one, whatever his experiences, has ever left the way towards his destined goal.

Nevertheless, what is most necessary is to connect the outward action with the inward journey, as the harmony of that journey will certainly prove to be a source of ease and comfort. It is this which is meant when it is said that one must have harmony within oneself; and once this harmony is established one begins to see the cause of all things much more clearly.

One might ask in what way harmony can be established between the inner journey and the outward action. What generally happens is that a person is so much absorbed in his outward action that his inner attitude becomes obscured from his view. And the first thing necessary is to remove that screen which hides the inner attitude from one's sight. Everyone is conscious of what he does, but not always conscious of his inner attitude; in other words everyone knows what he is doing, but not everyone necessarily knows where he is going.

No doubt the more one is conscious of one's action, the less it becomes. For although thought controls action, it only gives a rhythm, a balance to life. Compared with a person who is capable of running but does not know where he is going, the one who is walking slowly but knows where he is going is better off.

There are two distinct aspects of one's action: there is an action of the inner life and there is an action of the outer life, the inner being and the outer being. The outer being is our physical action and the inner action is our attitude. Both may be actions of free will, but in a certain way they both prove to be mechanical or automatic actions. The inner action has great power and influence upon the outer action. A person may be busy all day doing a certain thing, but at the same time, if his attitude is working against him he can never have success in his work. A person may deserve a great reward for his outer action, although he may not deserve it for his inner action; therefore if these two actions are contrary to one another nothing constructive is done and the desired results are not attained. The true result, the result that is desirable, comes through harmony between these two activities.

There is another metaphysical side to this question. There are two kinds of experience in life: sensation and exaltation. Action is connected with sensation, and repose with exaltation. Both have their place in life, although our everyday pursuits and our interest cause us to become engrossed in what we call sensation. By sensation I mean every experience we have through the senses: looking at beautiful things, listening to music, enjoying line and colour, smelling perfume, and experiencing life through touch— the softness, hardness, warmth, and coldness of objects. Our recreations, amusements, means of comfort and convenience, our sports and all activities from morning till evening are all connected with sensation. And that most important experience of all, exaltation, is left out. The only means of exaltation we know is by resting and sleeping; and we only rest and sleep because we cannot do any more. Many people would like not to rest at all if they could help it. Once a very busy friend of mine in New York told me he would be very glad if instead of twenty-four hours he had forty-eight hours in the day, because there was so much to do! Those who rest do not do it for the sake of resting, and it is the same with sleep: we do not call upon sleep; we cannot help it coming to us.

We never think about this most important subject in life: exaltation; and that is because sensation is movement, action, and that is what we prefer; whereas exaltation is lack of movement, lack of action. Sensation is created by a rhythm; it is rapidity of rhythm which brings about sensation. Exaltation is quite different; it means ease, repose, relaxation. One is not interested in it unless one knows what it brings about, yet all the prophets, teachers, and masters of every age have taught this art of relaxation, this art of repose, in different forms, whether in religious ceremonials, occult practices, or in the form of prayer or silence.

MANIFESTATION, GRAVITATION, ASSIMILA-TION, AND PERFECTION

THE ABSOLUTE in both its manifested and unmanifested condition is intelligence. And it is the manifestation of this intelligence which may be called light, life, and love. It is the dense form of intelligence which is light. And as the sun is not only the source of the moon, the planets, and the stars, but also of fire, of flame, of glow, and of every aspect of light, so the supreme Spirit is the source of all aspects of manifestation. The sun is the centralization of the all-pervading radiance.

The light which was spread all around began to function in one spot; there it became more radiant, more glowing, more power-ful than the radiance that was left in space. This light again functioned in the moon, and its different currents functioned in different planets and stars. This is an accurate picture of the origin of the creation. The all-pervading light of intelligence first centralized itself, thus making itself the spirit of the whole universe; and from there it began to manifest. So the omniscient spirit, by centralizing in one spot, has become the source of both the seen and the unseen manifestation. This is why in all ages the wise have worshipped the sun as the symbol of God, although the sun is only the outward symbol of God.

A close study of the formation of the sun and of its influence on everything in life will help us to understand the divine Spirit. Heat, gas-light, electric light, the coal fire, the wood fire, the candle, the flame of the oil-lamp, all these different manifesta-tions of light have their source in the sun; it is the sun which is showing itself in all these different forms, although we generally consider the sun to be separate from all other aspects of light. In the same way the supreme Spirit is manifested in all forms, in all things and beings, in the seen and unseen worlds; and yet it stands remote, as the sun stands remote from all other forms of light. The Qur'an says, 'God is the light of heaven and of earth'; and in reality all forms, however dense they may be, are to some degree the radiance of that spirit which is all light. All the different colours are different degrees of that same light.

The supreme Spirit, the source of all things, has two aspects, audible and visible. In its audible aspect the Spirit is the Word, as the Bible calls sound; the Hindus call it *Nada*. In its physical aspect the supreme Spirit is the light; in its finer aspect the light of intelligence, in its dense aspect the radiance of all objects. Manifestation is the phenomenon of the light playing in three directions; this is the real meaning of the Trinity. One direction is the light that sees, the other is the light that is seen, and the third is the light that shows all things. In other words, the eyes which see, the object that is seen, and the light that enables the eyes to see the object, are all one and the same light playing in three different ways. There is a sura of the Qur'an where it says, 'I have made your light, and by your light I create the universe.' In other words, the all-pervading Spirit says to the centralized aspect of itself, 'I made you first, and out of you I have made the whole universe'. This is the key to the whole of creation.

The process of manifestation is like the projecting of rays from the sun. Why does the sun shoot out its rays? Because it is its nature. And the same answer applies to the question of why the supreme Spirit manifests. Because it is its nature. No sooner has the all-pervading light become centralized in one spot and formed the sun, than the rays begin to shoot out. In the same way, the omniscient light, as soon as it centralized itself in one spot, began to shoot out its rays; and just as there are many rays of the sun, so there are many rays of the spirit of intelligence, in other words of God, the real Self. And each of these rays is a soul. Thus the ray is the manifestation of the sun, and man is the manifestation of God. The rays spread forth and reach far, and yet they remain connected with the sun.

As these rays go forward the first plane they strike is the angelic plane. The second plane they strike is the plane of the jinns; and the third is the physical plane. But have these rays left the supreme spirit in order to come to the angelic plane; have they left the angelic plane in order to come to the plane of the jinns; have they left the jinn plane in order to come to the physical plane? No, they have passed through all three, and while passing through they have received all that can be received from each place, learned all that is to be learned, gathered all that is to be gathered; but they still exist on those planes although they do not know it. They are only conscious of that plane where their ray has opened its eyes; in other words, we are sitting in this room, but we only see what is before our eyes and not what is behind our back. Thus every soul has at the back of it the angelic plane and the jinn plane, but before its eyes there is only this physical plane. Therefore it is only conscious of the physical plane and is unconscious of the planes from which it has turned its eyes, though even after manifesting on earth it is still connected with the higher spheres. It lives in all spheres, but mostly knows only one sphere, unaware of the others on which it has turned its back. Thus the soul, deprived of the heavenly bliss, becomes conscious of the troubles and limitations of life on earth. It was not that Adam was driven out of the Garden of Eden; he only turned his back on it, and that made him an exile from heaven.

The souls which have opened their eyes fully to the angelic plane and become interested in it have remained there; and it is the inhabitants of that plane that may be called angels. The souls which did not open their eyes fully on that plane only passed through it, and if they became interested in the jinn plane they remained there. Souls which went still further towards manifestation, and reached on the physical plane the ultimate call of their destiny, have opened their eyes there and have become human beings, which is the most wide awake state of all.

One speaks of these planes as if they were places. In point of fact they are conditions, but what we call a place is also a condition. It is only because it is rigid in its physical appearance that we think of it as a place, but in reality it is a condition. That is why those who have understood this have called it an illusion.

A person who has left America for Europe, and who has gone from Europe to the Orient, has brought something of America with him to Europe, and has taken something of Europe to the Orient. And so every soul that has come to the earth has brought with it something of the angelic plane and something of the plane of the jinn; and it shows in its life on the physical plane that which it has brought from these two planes of existence. Innocence, love of beauty, deep sympathy, love of song, a tendency towards solitude, love of harmony, all these belong to the angelic plane. Inventive genius, intellectuality, reasoning, law, justice, love of poetry and science, all these belong to the plane of the jinns. That is why one says of those who show any of these qualities, 'Here is an angelic person', or 'Here is a genius'.

The soul has put on an inner garb and an outer garb; and it is these garbs that shape the soul, completely as a human being belonging to the physical plane. One garb is hidden beneath another. One might think that the garb of the jinn plane would be smaller in size than the physical one, and the garb of the angelic plane smaller still as it is covered by that of the jinn plane; but this is not necessarily so. To our physical eyes everything must have a certain rate of vibration to be visible; and it is the physical vibrations of matter that make it visible to our eyes. The vibrations of the garb of the jinn plane are so subtle that our physical eyes cannot see it, and it is as much an inner garb as an outer garb. Its size need not to be as small as that of the physical body; in fact it is incomparably larger.

It is the same with the garb that the soul has adopted from the angelic plane, which is not necessarily so small that it can be covered by the two garbs just described, but on the contrary is even larger and finer. Only, the eyes of this plane cannot see it; it vibrates more quickly, and we see things according to their vibration rate. If they are invisible it is not because they are invisible by nature, but because they are invisible to our sight. Since we are dependent upon our physical eyes in order to see, that which the physical eyes cannot see, we naturally say is unseen. It is only unseen because we cannot see it as a form, so it is not an exaggeration to say that man is at the same time a jinn and an angel, for man passes through these two planes. He does not know it, but he shows the qualities of each of these planes. The love quality in man, the sense of beauty, joy, aspiration, all these tendencies, besides the innocence of human nature, come from the angelic plane. The purity in the face of an infant gives us proof of its having just arrived from that plane. The infant's smile, its friendliness, and its readiness to appreciate everything beautiful, its love of life, all these things are signs of the angelic spheres.

As a soul remains longer on earth, it loses the angelic qualities and adopts new qualities. Thus, while an infant shows the angelic quality, a child shows the quality of the jinn by wanting to know all about names and forms, and by asking its mother and other people with great curiosity about them. And when a man has passed that stage he seems to become full of miseries, worries, and helplessness.

In some people we see the angelic quality predominating; they are good and kind and innocent, forgiving, pure-hearted, righteous, virtuous, lovers of beauty, always inclined to high aspirations. If we studied human nature more keenly we would find a great many examples of the angelic nature. And again there are poets, composers, and intellectual people, writers and inventors who show the quality of the jinn.

Why do souls come to the earth? Why has this creation taken place? What is the purpose of this manifestation? These questions may be answered in one word: satisfaction—for the satisfaction of God. Why is God not satisfied without it? Because God is the only Being, and the desire of being is to become conscious of being. This consciousness experiences life through various channels, names, and forms, and in man this consciousness of being reaches its culmination. To put it simply, it is through man that God experiences life in its highest perfection. If anyone asks what man's duty is if that is the purpose, the answer is: his most sacred duty is to attain to that perfect consciousness which is his Dharma, his true religion. In order to perform his duty he may have to struggle with himself, he may have to go through suffering and pain, he may have to pass many tests and trials. But by making many sacrifices, and practising renunciation, he will attain to that consciousness which is God-consciousness, in which resides all perfection.

As we have seen, if we studied human nature more keenly we would find a great many examples of people with an angelic nature, and also of those who show jinn qualities; however, there are more people who show human qualities. These can again be divided into three classes: there is the human quality, there is the animal quality, and there is the devilish quality, depending on the rate of vibrations and the rhythm. Intense rhythm produces the devilish quality; moderate rhythm shows the animal quality; an even rhythm shows the human quality. The form of this rhythm may be described thus: that the human quality is mobile, the animal quality is uneven, and the devilish quality is zigzag.

The gravitation known to science is the material gravitation, which means that all that belongs to the dense earth is attracted to the dense earth. But in exactly the same way all that belongs to the spirit is attracted to the spirit. Therefore man is pulled from both sides, and he is pulled more than any other creature, for he is closer to the spirit. On one side the earth demands his body, on the other side the spirit asks for his soul. If man gives in to the attraction of the earth, then the body drags the soul towards the earth. If man gives himself over to the attraction of the spirit, then the spirit drags the body to the spirit. In this way man is subject to the law of gravity from both sides, from the earth and from heaven.

The law of gravity is similar to the law which governs the relation between the sun and the ray. The ray never leaves the sun; its tendency is to reach out and then to withdraw and to return towards the sun, in other words to merge into the sun. The inclination of the soul is the same. However much the body depends upon the dense earth, and however much the mind revels in the intellectual spheres, the soul's continual inclination is to withdraw itself to its origin. But since the physical manifestation speaks loudest, and the mind makes its own sound, the gentle cry of the soul remains unheard.

We have seen above that as the soul passed through these different planes it borrowed from each of them the things that belong to that plane: qualities, tendencies, ideas, thoughts, feelings, impressions, flesh, skin, bone, and blood. But what the soul has borrowed it must give back when it has done its work; it was borrowed for a certain time and for a certain purpose. When the purpose is fulfilled and when the time has come, then every plane asks for that which the soul has borrowed from it. And one cannot help but give it back. It is this process which is called assimilation. Since man is born greedy and selfish he has taken all that was given to him willingly, even enthusiastically; but he gives it back grudgingly, calling it death.

Assimilation, therefore, is to give back to the earth the physical matter which one has used on this physical plane. It becomes assimilated by the earth, and the soul becomes free of that burden which it once carried, and begins to experience a greater liberty and a greater ease. For death is only releasing the soul from limitation and from a great captivity.

Death is nothing but the taking off of one garb and giving it back to that plane from which it was borrowed. For one cannot take the garb of the lower plane to the higher plane. The soul is only released when it is willing or compelled to give its garb to the plane it has borrowed it from; it is this which releases the soul to continue on its journey. And as it proceeds after its stay there, it must again give back its garb and be purified from it in order to go further.

If people knew this they would look at life from a different point of view. They would understand the meaning of the moral that we cannot retain anything that does not really belong to us. And we come to realize after the study of this philosophy that even our body does not belong to us. It is a borrowed property and it must be returned one day. Therefore the wise disown it before they are obliged to give it up. All the spiritual exercises given by teachers are practised for this purpose: that we may begin to disown our body from today, that we may not have the pain of having lost something we thought to be most precious.

This knowledge also throws light upon the question of death. Death is not really death; it is only a passing phase, it is only a change, like changing our clothes. Perhaps we might wonder whether we become less by dying; but it is not so. We become more by dying, not less. For once the physical garb has been discarded the soul enjoys a greater freedom, a greater liberation, because the limitation of the physical body is greater. The physical body weighs heavily on the soul, and the day when this burden is removed, the soul feels lighter; its faculties, tendencies, inspiration, powers, all manifest more freely. Therefore death is no loss.

What is it that brings about death? Either the body, owing to weakness, is not capable of serving the soul properly; or the soul has finished its mission on that plane and does not want the body any more. The body clings to the soul and the soul holds the body; that is the position. When the body is too feeble, it naturally loses its grip on the soul, and generally it loses it more and more till it can no longer hold the soul. Or the soul holds the body as long as it has to accomplish something; and when the soul sees no further purpose then it loses its hold upon the body, and so gradually the body drops out of the hands of the soul.

It is by this process that death is brought about, whereas birth is the contrary process. Human bodies are the clay that is needed to make a body for the soul. The soul has to knock at the door of the physical plane and the body is given to it. This idea, this philosophy, is symbolized by Cupid.

Life on the plane of the jinn is longer than life on the physical plane. It is this life which may be called the life in the hereafter. But here too there comes a time when all that was borrowed from the jinn plane has to be given back to that plane, for it did not belong to the soul either. Thus no one can take anything with him beyond the substance of another plane; each plane has its own substance, and that substance must be returned to it. That is the only way the soul can be freed from that plane in order to rise above it. When the soul soars higher it must give up even the angelic qualities. They must be assimilated in the angelic plane before the soul can dissolve into the great Ocean, the supreme Spirit. That dissolving is called the merging into the real self.

There is one most important thing that can be learned from this process: every soul which is coming from the source towards manifestation gives what it brings from the source to the returning souls it meets, and these give back all they have collected. It is this exchange which is the cause of the various conditions of life into which man is born on coming to earth. One is intelligent, another is simple, one is born in a rich family, another in poor surroundings, one is healthy, the other weak, one will have a great purpose, the other does not know what he should do. It is all determined. By what? By the fact that a soul coming from the source has collected all kinds of things on its way from souls returning to the source.

There is a give and take on the planes through which the soul has to pass, and this give and take is between those souls which are going from the source towards manifestation and the souls which are returning from manifestation to the source. As a traveller coming from Asia to America and a traveller going from America to Asia may meet in Europe and may exchange money or thoughts, taking upon themselves one another's debts, knowledge, happiness, or misery, in the same way we experience our life on earth. One soul takes a route, sometimes without knowing it, which leads to riches, to success; and another soul takes a route which leads him to failure, to committing errors. It all depends on what route one has taken from the beginning. Hafiz explains this idea poetically, saying that each person has his own wine, and his love is according to the wine he possesses. Whether it be the wine of happiness, the wine of joy, or of sorrow, the wine of misery, of courage, of fear, of trust, of distrust, of faith, or of disbelief, it is in the intoxication of this wine that he acts, showing the effect of the wine to the world.

In this exchange between souls going from the source to manifestation and coming back from manifestation to the source, one takes the wine of selfishness, another that of unselfishness. A Persian poet, Bedil, says, 'Before dawn the wine was poured out, the wine which was taken from the eyes of the Beloved.' By dawn the poet means birth, the time when the soul begins its journey from the angelic plane, and the eyes of the Beloved mean this most deceiving world. The first cup that the soul drinks determines its life afterwards.

Many believe that man, when he attains to a higher evolution, becomes richer in knowledge. Certainly, higher evolution is itself a knowledge; but the knowledge man gains from earthly sources is not a coin which is current on other planes. Man makes much of the coin of this plane, small and limited though the world is. It always amuses me when a person comes and says, 'I have read so many books on occult science; I think I am quite ready to be initiated'. Imagine how reading about occult science should entitle one to spirituality! The language of that country is different, and intellectual knowledge is not current there; the learning there consists of unlearning what we have learned here.

The question of spiritual attainment is quite different, and it must be dealt with from a totally different point of view.

The condition of the soul may be likened to a mirror. It reflects the object which is before it, but that object is not engraved in the mirror; it only occupies it during the time it veils it. In the same way the soul is veiled by experiences; in other words, our experiences may delude the soul, may cover it or bury it, but they cannot penetrate it. Also, what is called individuality is only a temporary state, and as soon as the soul has awakened it no longer attaches much importance to individuality, which is something made up of garbs borrowed from the different planes. It is like a doll made of rags. When we understand this we give all importance to the soul, the soul which is real, which comes from the real, and which seeks after the real.

The final question is: what can be the purpose of the creation of man? Is anything gained by it? Yes, the realization attained by the experience of life. And it is a divine realization when the experience has led the soul to that height where it is no longer only an individual soul, but where it is conscious of all planes of existence, not only of the source but of all the planes of limitation. And when all the inspiration and power latent in man are within his reach, then that realization is called perfection. It is that perfection of which Jesus Christ spoke, 'Be ye perfect even as your Father in heaven is perfect.'

KÁRMA AND REINCARNATION

i

MUCH MORE emphasis is placed on the doctrine of Karma in Hindu theology than in the religions of Beni Israel. By Hindu theology I do not mean only the Vedantic or Brahmin, but also the Buddhist; by the religion of Beni Israel I do not mean the Judaic only, but also the Christian and Muslim. The whole of Hindu philosophy is based upon the doctrine of Karma, but the moral of the religions of Beni Israel is also based upon Karma; the only difference is that in the one case the philosophy is based on Karma, and in the other it is the morals.

The meaning of the word Karma is action. It is quite evident that what one sows one reaps; the present is the echo of the past, the future is the reflection of the present; and therefore it is logical that the past should make the present and the present make the future. Nevertheless, in the Sufi school little is said upon this subject, and very often people interested in the doctrine of Karma begin to wonder if Sufism is opposed to it. It is not at all opposed to it, but because of the way a Sufi looks at it he cannot but close his lips.

In the first place what a person calls right or wrong is only according to his own knowledge. He calls something right which he knows as right, which he has learned to call right; he calls something wrong which he has learned to call wrong. And in this way there may be various nations, communities, and races, differing in their conceptions of right and wrong. A person accuses another of wrongdoing only on such grounds as he knows to be wrong. And how does he know a thing to be wrong? Because he has learned it, he has read it in a book, or he has been told so. People have looked with horror, with hatred, with prejudice at the doings of one another, individuals, communities, nations, and races; and yet there is no label, there is no stamp, there is no seal upon actions which points them out as being right or wrong. This is one aspect of this question.

There is also another way of looking at it. At every step of
evolution man's conception of good and bad, of right and wrong,
changes. How does it change? Does he see more wrong or does
he see less wrong as he evolves? One might naturally think that
by virtue of one's evolution one would see more wrong, but
that is not the case; the more one evolves the less wrong one sees,
for then it is not always the action itself which counts, it is the
motive behind it. Sometimes an action, apparently right, may
be made wrong by the motive behind it. Sometimes an action,
apparently wrong, may be right on account of its motive.
Therefore although the ignorant are ready to form an opinion
of another person's action, for the wise it is most difficult to form
an opinion of the action of another.

Seen from the religious point of view, if a man evolves spiritually he sees less and less wrong at every stage of his evolution.
How can God be counting the minor faults of human beings who
know so little about life? We read in the Bible, 'God is love';
but what does love mean? Love means forgiveness, love does
not mean judging. When people make of God a cruel judge,
sitting in the seat of judgment, getting hold of every person
and asking him about his faults, judging him for his actions,
sentencing him to be cast out of the heavens, then where is the
God of love?

Some people believe that accidents are prepared by their
Karma. In a way this is true, but one should not emphasize this.
If one asks why there is a drum or a trumpet in the orchestra, the
answer is: In order that the music may be played as the composer
wished it to be played. Perhaps to our mind it is disagreeable;
but the composer wrote music which required a drum or a
trumpet. In the same way all that seems to us useless is there for
some purpose, all making the divine symphony. We say, 'Why
is this?' but it is our limited mind which says that. In reality
everything has its place and purpose. Someone asked the Prophet
in jest why mosquitoes were created, and the Prophet answered,
'That you might not sleep all night, but might devote some hours
of the night to your prayers.'

Coming to the philosophical point of view one may ask
whether man is a machine or an engineer. If he is a machine, then

he must go on for years and years under a kind of mechanical action of his evil deeds, in which case he is not responsible for his actions. But if he is an engineer then he is responsible for his actions; and if he is responsible for his actions, then he is the master of his destiny, and makes his destiny what he wishes it to be.

The difference between the human and the divine is the difference between the two ends of the same line. One represents limitation, the other the unlimited. One end represents imperfection, the other perfection. And when we consider the human beings of this world, we see that they do not all stand at the same end; they fill the gap between one extreme and the other. Although just now the world is going through a phase of exalting the idea of equality, it happens that the nobility of the soul, even its divinity, is ignored. In every phase of life one notices this. There is one vote for everybody in the state, and also in the home; it is the same everywhere. But when we come to understand the spiritual life of things we shall realize that just as on the piano all the notes are not the same, so all the souls are not alike. Man starts his life as a mechanism, a machine, but he can develop to the stage where he is an engineer. The restriction of Karma is only for the machine.

No doubt every soul has to be a machine first in order to become an engineer later; and one does not turn at once into an engineer. One does this gradually; that is why the influence of Karma is not the same upon every soul. The law of Karma is different for each individual. A thing can be sin for one person and a virtue for another; it can be right for the one and wrong for the other. According to this law each individual has his own Karma to meet with.

Speaking from this point of view, the Sufi says, 'It is true that if things go wrong with me, it is the effect of my actions. But that does not mean that I should submit to it. I should be resigned to it because it results from my past actions; but I must make my destiny because I am the engineer.' That is the difference. I have heard a person say, 'I have been ill for so many years, but I have been resigned to it. I bear it easily because it is my Karma, I am paying back.' By that he may prolong the paying, which was intended perhaps for ten years, for the rest of his life. The Sufi in this case acts not only as a patient but also as a doctor to himself. He says, 'Is my condition bad? Is it the effect of the past? I am going to cure it. The past has brought the present, but out of this present I will make the future.' It only means that he does not allow past influences to overwhelm his life; he wants to produce now the influence that will make his life better later.

Besides there is something still more essential connected with this subject. Before a person takes upon himself the responsibility of paying back for his past, does he ask himself, 'What was I in the past?' If he does not know this, why must he hold himself responsible for it? We can only be responsible for something with which our conscience is tainted; and that is quite a sufficient load to carry in life. Why add to it a load of the unknown past?

When we look at our selves philosophically, what do we see? The keener our sight becomes, the less of our self can we find. The more conscious of reality we become the less conscious we are of our small self. So all this burden of past actions is carried by man without his ever having been invited to take it up. He could just as well have ignored it. It does not benefit him; it only gives him a brief satisfaction to think that his troubles are just; but this idea of justice fortifies his discomfort. The pain that could have been stopped continues because he has fortified the pain.

The main object of esoteric work is to put away the thought of oneself: what one was, what one is, and what one will be. One would be much better occupied in thinking about life as a whole: what it is, what it should have been, what it will be. This idea produces a kind of synthetic point of view and unites instead of dispersing. It is constructive, and the secret of spiritual liberation is to be found in it. Brahmins, Vedantists, and Buddhists, who hold Karma to be the foremost doctrine, rise above the idea of Karma as soon as they touch the idea of the goal that is to be attained by spirituality, which they call *Mukti* or *Nirvana*. For it is a condition that unless a person has risen above that idea he does not touch Nirvana.

ii

The religious argument for reincarnation is that since not every man is worthy to be merged directly into God, he reincarnates an indefinite number of times in order to become purified until he reaches the final destination; thus he is bound to pay all penalties before he reaches the presence of God. The answer to this is that if even man, with his limited sense of justice, never punishes anybody without telling him for what fault, then how could God, the most merciful and just, make a soul reincarnate on earth as a penalty without making him aware of his fault?

The scientific argument for reincarnation tells us that a seed goes into the earth and produces other seeds, and this goes on thousands of times, always producing seed again; in this way there is a possibility of reincarnation. So if the seed has sufficient strength to return as a seed, why should not man's soul re-adorn itself with a human body? The answer is that even the seed, until it reaches the innermost culmination, is never able to spring up again as a seed. Besides even then it cannot be called a reincarnation of the seed, but rather a regeneration; also, one seed produces many seeds, and for that reason it cannot be called an incarnation, as the nature of incarnation would be one coming from one and not one turning into many.

The same is the case with the soul, which experiences life independently through the five elements and goes back to its own source, carrying the impressions of the outer world and discarding them at each step it takes towards its own essence, the universal Spirit. The earth-substance passes into the earth; the water returns to water; the fire takes its own element into itself; the air takes away its own property; and the ether does the same. When the frame of the five elements, which, just like the sunglass, was able to receive the reflection of the spirit, is dispersed, then the soul makes its own way to its original source. After the body and astral frame are broken up there is no possibility of individuality, because there is none left but the only Being.

Reincarnation of a person in someone's thought while awake, or in his dream while asleep, can be recognized; for all beings besides his own self produced in such a way, are produced out of his own mind; therefore they may be called reincarnations. Yet this would not be perfectly justified, because every thought and dream has a birth, life, and death. So even they can be taken as individualities, and as a world produced from a single being.

There are some who pretend, or at least imagine, that they can recollect their past incarnations; but in many cases they say so in order to create a sensation and for the sake of notoriety; or it may be just in order to give expression to their whims and delusions. In India one will not find much talk about reincarnation; people there will speak more about Karma. The Yogis, who are among the principal exponents of the idea of reincarnation, do not for one moment believe that reincarnation is for them. If one asks a Yogi he will say, 'No, I am striving for *Mukti*, salvation. It is you who want to be born again, and therefore you will be born again; you would be very disappointed if you were not.' This, however, needs to be seen from a subtle point of view; the Yogi applies 'you' to what he knows to be the self in the person he addresses. This theory opens up a vast field of interest and curiosity for the imagination of those who can see the objective world. But, again, there are some who always seek for something new. This desire grows to such an extent that even if a new God were produced, they would still seek for another.

It may appear by observing the world's evolution, that it is the soul which owing to its previous experience in life enables itself to manifest in a better condition than in the past; but in reality it is not so. The evolution of the world does not depend upon the soul's previous experience; the reason why the world progresses at each step of evolution is that the soul partakes of the improved conditions on its way towards manifestation, thus helping manifestation to progress towards perfection.

The doctrine of reincarnation's claim to truth rests chiefly on the law of action, and this at once appeals to the intellect. It means that if a man is a genius in music it is because of his past experience of it; if a person is lame or blind from birth, it is the penalty for past bad actions; if a person is wise and spiritual, wealthy and powerful, it is because of his good actions in the past; thus every soul doing good or evil reaps the results through its reincarnation until it arrives at its destiny.

Against this doctrine it may be argued that it is not through any fault of the legs that they have to bear the weight of the body, nor was it because the head had done better in the past that it was made the crown of the whole form. The world is the embodiment of one Being, one God. The explanation of this can be found in what a Persian dervish once said, 'Man lives in the joy of his belief in God, not knowing whether He is his friend or foe. It is as if when the ocean makes its waves leap up joyfully, a twig floating upon them thinks that it is for it alone that the ocean has caused the rising and falling'.

Such is the case with all conditions in life. An individual may think he has done something in the past and that is why he is like this now. But it is the rule of God's justice, and he is mistaken here. The ocean-like God has many to think of and to judge; and therefore the rise and fall are either caused by Kazá, the waves of the ocean of existence, or by that which a soul has gathered, either of good or evil, while on the way towards manifestation.

The thinkers who have taught the doctrine of reincarnation have never meant it to be understood as it is by people in general. The reincarnation meant by them was the partaking by the fresh soul descending towards manifestation of the attributes of the souls which are ascending towards their original source, which give their load of impressions to the willing souls met with on the way. The soul having once manifested in the body, never has sufficient power to manifest again. The idea of the soul reincarnating in another form has but little truth in it. If it were true that the soul reincarnates as a matter of course, why does it not reincarnate in its original form, which it could easily have collected again?

The truth of the reincarnation theory can be understood in this way: that the selfsame proportion of Consciousness which has once been a soul *might* happen to form again as a soul; but in general there is no such possibility. It would be as rare as a bubble forming the selfsame bubble again; for generally either half, a quarter, or even a hundredth part of the first bubble would be produced, or a bubble perhaps a hundred times as large as the first one. In any case the soul has to merge into the Consciousness before it is sufficiently alive to manifest again. That is why we cannot call it the same soul, for it is quite purified from its previous

conditions. It is just like a drop of ink: when it falls into the ocean
the water merges into water and its inky substance sinks to the
bottom. It can never remain as a distinct drop of ink, but becomes
the pure water of the ocean. If it were again taken out of the water
it would no longer show its previous substance. Such is the nature
of the soul when merged again in the ocean of Consciousness.

iii

There are three ways of knowing about life in the hereafter:
to know intellectually, by theory; to know by the process of
meditation, or 'dying before death', that is attaining the state one
experiences after death during one's lifetime; and to die oneself.

Those who seek this knowledge are of three kinds. First there
is the student who studies it from authentic sources, in order to
discover some theory that his reason can accept intellectually.
Then there is the adept. His way is the way of meditation; by
meditation he develops that state in which he is as though dead;
in which he can rise above the life of the material body, even if
only for a moment; and in that way he experiences life after
death, which is the beginning of the knowledge of immortality.
And thirdly there is the person who wishes to communicate with
spirits so as to know about their condition. If he is himself capable
of communicating with spirits he can, to a certain extent, get the
knowledge from them.

A person of the first kind, who tries intellectually to discover
a doctrine which will fit in with his reason, will readily agree with
the doctrine of reincarnation, because that doctrine explains life
intellectually in a way that satisfies the reason. When I have been
asked what the Sufi has to say about reincarnation, my silence at
times, and my yes or no at other times, have left it vague. Some
perhaps thought that I did not believe in it; and that if I did not
believe in it then naturally the Sufis in general would not believe
in it. This is not the case. Every Sufi is free to believe whatever
he feels is right and whatever he is able to understand. He is not
nailed to any particular belief.

Instead of troubling about these beliefs the Sufi wants to go
straight to the central idea; and when he stands there he sees the

truth of all things. For the mystery of life is that whenever you take the divine lantern in the hand, all things become clear to you. Therefore Sufism gives freedom to everyone to believe for himself and to find out things for himself.

For my yes there was a reason, and for my no there was a reason; not for myself but for the one who asked me the question. People in the world want to make everything rigid, even things which are of the finest nature and which words cannot explain. It is just like wanting to weigh the soul or photograph the spirit when someone describes the hereafter. They should not depend upon my words; self-realization is the aim. Belief in doctrines is a pill to cure sick people. Actually all things are true up to a certain point, but when compared with the ultimate truth they fail to prove their existence. Things appear different from the various planes from which one looks at them; and when a person standing in the valley asks another standing on top of a mountain what he sees there, he cannot tell much. The questioner must come to the top of the mountain and see for himself; there can be no common ground of conversation between the two until then. The Sufi's method is quietude and silent progress, arriving by this way at the stage where one can see for oneself. One might say that much patience is needed. It is so; but then the spiritual path is for the patient; patience is the most difficult thing there is.

If someone asked me why I do not say plainly what happens in the hereafter, whether we come back to earth or whether we go on somewhere else, I would answer, 'What you consider yourself to be I do not consider you to be; what you are in your view, you are not in mine. If I speak according to my view it will confuse you just now; you must develop to that plane where I see you. The way in which you consider yourself is an elementary way; now it is a reality to you, but there will come a time when you will realize it was nothing but imagination.' How can I give my opinion to someone to whom it is incomprehensible? Therefore the way of the Sufi is silence.

Sufism is not against reincarnation nor against any particular doctrine. Why should it be, since it is a religion which has come to reconcile religions? It is not the idea of a Sufi to oppose any doctrine. I have never spoken against this doctrine of reincarnation, as I do not see the wrong of it; but neither do I see the right of it. When the purpose is the realization of the unity of life, of the unity of God, then the idea of reincarnation, which is based upon the false ego, is not fruitful. Sufism wants to teach man what he is; as soon as man has solved that question he need no longer ask, 'What will my actions do for me?' It is the question of what one is that Sufism wants to solve. At the same time what is apparent is different from what is hidden. Is a man who is born in a palace being rewarded, or is the man who is perhaps starving in the street being punished?

What has Christ brought? Salvation. What has Mohammad brought? Najat, salvation. What have the Avatars of the Hindus brought? Mukti, salvation. One always finds the same thing, salvation. That is why it is preferable to keep away from the doctrine of reincarnation and to hold before our vision the ideal of unity, the ideal in which we are united and in which lies the fulfilment of life.

Can we then, one may ask, reach salvation in this life? Evolution is different for every soul, but man can generally reach salvation if he sincerely and earnestly wishes it and pursues it. Not only is God all-powerful, but man has a part of this power too. Salvation is in the hand of God, but also in the hand of man. In the wish of man there is the wish of God; the courage of man is the courage of God, and in the confidence of man there is the confidence of God. When we say, as it is written in the Bible, 'Thy Will be done', and at the same time we realize that our wish and our will are not apart from the divine Will, then our will will be done too. But if we do not wish for salvation just now, we will not reach it; for it is necessary as it is said in the Bible to knock at the door; then the answer comes. There is nothing in the world that is unattainable for man, who is made the Khalif, the ruler, of the kingdom of God; there is nothing that is impossible. No doubt there are things which are difficult, and yet there is no difficulty which cannot be overcome. If man only had the courage, he would reach that source where his origin is.

PART III

LIFE IN THE HEREAFTER

IT IS difficult to explain what life in the spirit-world consists of, and difficult to put into words, but one may get some idea by observing the life of the birds which can fly over seas and forests, over hills and dales, and which feel in tune with nature and express their joy in song. There is also the life of the deer dwelling in the woods or in the mountains, drinking water at the natural springs, moving about in the open spaces, looking at the horizon from morning till evening, the sun as their time-keeper, and the moon serving as their torch. And then imagine our lives, the lives of human beings in crowded cities, days in factories and nights indoors, away from God, away from nature, even away from our self—a life completely absorbed in the struggle for existence, an ever-increasing struggle to which there is no end!

What is purgatory? In Sufi terms it is called *Nazá*, which means suspension of activity. If there is any death it is stillness and inactivity. It is like a clock which has stopped for a time; it needs winding, and a little movement sets it going. In the same way there comes the impulse of life, which, breaking through this cloud of mortality, makes the soul see the daylight after the darkness of the night. And what does the soul see in this bright daylight? It sees itself living as before, having the same name and form, yet now progressing. The soul finds a greater freedom in this sphere and less limitation than it previously experienced in its life on the earth. Before the soul now is a world which is not strange to it, but which it has made during its life on earth. That which the soul has known as mind, that very mind is now a world to the soul; that which the soul called imagination while on earth, is now a reality before it. If this world is artistic, it is the art produced by the soul. If there is absence of beauty, that is also caused by the neglect of beauty by the soul while on earth.

The picture of *Jannat*, paradise, the ideas about heaven, and the conception of the infernal regions are an actual experience to the soul now; the soul is not sent to the one or the other place to be among the many who are rejoicing there, or suffering for their sins. These are the kingdoms that the soul has made while on earth, just as some creatures build nests to live in during the winter. The immediate hereafter is the winter of the soul. It passes this winter in the world which it has made either agreeable or disagreeable for itself. One might wonder if the soul lives a solitary life in this world that it has made. It does not; how can it be solitary? The mind, the secret of which is known to so few in the world, this mind can be as large as the world, and larger still. This mind can contain all that exists in the world, and even all that the universe contains within itself. The understanding of the mind widens one's outlook on life. When one arrives at this point, at first bewilderment is produced; but then the nature of God which is a phenomenon in itself is revealed.

People often wonder what connection there is between the soul which has passed from the earth and those who are still on the earth. No doubt there is now a wall which divides those on this earth from those on the other plane; yet the connection of the heart is still intact and it remains unbroken as long as the link of sympathy is there. But why, one may ask, do the lovers of those who have passed away from the earth not know anything about the condition of their beloveds on the other side? They know it in their souls, but the veils of the illusion of the physical world cover their hearts; that is why they cannot receive clear reflections. Besides it is not only the link of love and sympathy; it is the belief in the hereafter, to the extent of conviction, which raises those still on earth to the knowledge about their beloved ones who have passed to the other side. Those who deny the hereafter, deny themselves that knowledge which is the essence of all learning. It is easier for those who have passed from the earth to the other side to get into touch with those on the earth, for they have one veil the less.

The soul is on a continual journey. On whatever plane it is, it is journeying all the time; and on this journey it has a purpose to accomplish: many purposes contained and hidden in one purpose.

When there are objects which remain unfulfilled in one's lifetime on earth, they are accomplished on the further journey in the spirit-world, for nothing that the human heart has once desired remains unfulfilled. If it is not fulfilled here, it is accomplished in the hereafter. The desire of the soul is the wish of God; small or great, right or wrong, it has a moment of fulfilment. If that moment does not come while the soul is on the earth plane, it comes to the soul in the spirit world.

The soul proves its divine origin on all planes of existence in creating for itself all that it desires, in producing for itself the fulfilment of the wish of the heart, in attracting and drawing to itself all that it wants. The source of the soul is perfect, and so is its goal; therefore even in its limitation the soul has the spark of perfection. The nature of perfection is that no desire remains. Even in the limitation that the soul experiences on the earth, where it lives the life of limitation, its one desire is still perfection. So every want is supplied, for the reason that the Perfect One, even in the world of variety, does everything possible to experience perfection.

The condition of the next world is mostly like the condition of the dream world. In dreams one does not see oneself as very different from what one appears in everyday life, except in some cases and at some times; and for that there are reasons. Nevertheless, the power of the soul in the next world is much greater than that which it has in this world of limitation. The soul in the other world so to speak matures, and finds within itself the power of which it was ignorant during life on earth, the power of creating and producing all that it wishes; and its movements not being so much hindered by time and space, it is capable of accomplishing and of doing for itself things which were difficult for it to do on the earth plane.

In regard to the idea of reincarnation, when in ancient times the Hindus said to a wicked person, 'Next time you are born, you will come as a dog or monkey', it was in order to tell this man, who did not know anything of life beyond himself, that his animal qualities would come again as the heritage of the animal world, so that he would not appear again to his human friends as a man, but as an animal. When they said to a good person, 'Your good actions will bring you back as a better person', they were explaining to the man who did not know the two extreme poles of his soul, that no good action could be lost; and for the man who did not know what to hope for in the hereafter, and who only knew about life as it is lived on the earth, it was a consolation to know that all the good he had done would come again, and in that sense the theory which was thus explained was true.

It is only a difference of words; the soul which comes from above has neither name nor form, nor any particular identity; it makes no difference to the soul what it is called. Since it has no name, it might just as well adopt the name of the coat which was put on it, and such is the nature of life. The robe of justice put on a person makes him a judge, and the uniform of the policeman makes him a constable; but the judge was not born a judge, nor the constable a policeman; they were born on earth nameless, though not formless. Distinctions and differences belong to the lower world, not to the higher; therefore the Sufi does not argue against the idea of reincarnation. The difference is only in words; and it is necessary as a precaution to keep the door open for souls who wish to enter the kingdom of God, so that they may not feel bound by a dogma which teaches that they will have to be dragged back, after having left the earth plane, by their Karma. The soul of man is the spark of God, and though God is helpless on the earth, He is all-powerful in heaven; and by teaching the prayer, 'Thy kingdom come, Thy will be done on earth as it is in heaven', the Master has given a key to open that door behind which is the secret of that almighty power and perfect wisdom which raises the soul above all limitations.

The soul eventually rises to the standard which was the standard of its ideal; then it accomplishes or finishes the work which was its desire when on the earth. There are difficulties in doing and in accomplishing something in the spirit-world also, though not as many as here on the earth. The laws of that world are different from the laws of this world of limitations, and there the souls will find in abundance all that is scarce here.

A beautiful picture of the spirit-world is to be found in the story of Krishna. The Gopis of Brindaban all asked the young Krishna to dance with them. Krishna smiled, and told each one that in the night of the full moon he would do so. All the Gopis gathered in the valley of Brindaban, and then a miracle happened:

however many Gopis there happened to be, everyone of them had a dance with Krishna; they all had their desire fulfilled. This is a symbolical teaching which explains that the divine Being may be found in every soul.

The spirit-world is incomprehensible to the mind which is only acquainted with the laws of the physical world. An individual who is a limited being here, is like a world there; a soul is a person here and a planet there. When one considers the helplessness of this plane, one cannot for a single moment imagine the greatness, the facility, the convenience, the comfort, and the possibilities of the next world; and it is human nature that that which is unknown to man, means nothing to him. A pessimist came to Hazrat Ali and said, 'Is there really a hereafter for which you are preparing us by telling us to refrain from things that we desire, and to live a life of goodness and piety? What if there is no such thing as a hereafter?' Ali answered, 'If there is no such thing as a hereafter, I shall be in the same situation as you are; but if there is a hereafter, then I shall be the gainer, and you will be the loser!' Life lives and death dies; the one who lives will live, must live; there is no alternative.

The manifestation is an interesting dream, an illusion caused by cover upon cover; the soul is covered by a thousand veils. These covers do not give happiness to the soul but intoxication. The further the soul is removed from its source, the greater the intoxication. In a way this intoxication helps the purpose of the soul's journey towards its accomplishment, but the purpose of the soul is accomplished by its longing. What does it long for? Soberness. And how is that soberness attained? By discarding the veils which have covered the soul, and have thus divided it from its real source and goal. What uncovers the soul from these veils of illusion? The change which is called death. This change may be forced upon the soul against its desire, and it is then called death; it is a most disagreeable experience, like snatching away the bottle of wine from a drunken man, which is for the time most painful to him. Or else the change is brought about at will, and the soul, throwing away the cover that surrounds it, attains the same experience of soberness while still on earth, even if it is but a glimpse; the same experience which the soul, drunken by

illusion, arrives at after millions and millions of years, and yet
not exactly the same.

The experience of the former is *Fanà*, annihilation, but the
realization of the latter is *Baqà*, resurrection. The soul, drawn by
the magnetic power of the divine Spirit, merges into it with a joy
inexpressible in words, as a loving heart lays itself down in the
arms of its beloved. The intensity of this joy is so great that
nothing the soul has experienced in its life has ever made it so
unconscious of the self; yet this unconsciousness of the self becomes in reality the true self-consciousness.

It is then that the soul realizes fully, 'I exist'. But the soul which
arrives at this stage of realization consciously, has the greatest
experience. The difference is like that between the person journeying towards the goal, enjoying at every step each experience he
meets with and rejoicing at every moment of this journey in
approaching nearer to the goal, and another person who is not
aware of the journey at all.

THE MYSTICAL MEANING OF THE
RESURRECTION

WHAT IS the exact meaning of the resurrection which is spoken of in the Bible? The resurrection is that moment after death when the soul becomes conscious of all its experiences. As the soul is connected with everything in the universe, the individual resurrection is a universal resurrection.

After Christ had risen from the dead he said, 'He that believeth shall be saved'. The dead are those who have not realized their immortality; he rises who realizes his immortality; and Christ's saying means that he who has the knowledge of God, of immortality, shall never die, and that those who have belief in God—which is the same as knowledge of God—are never dead.

What death is can only be understood by man; birds and beasts feel the inactivity resulting from death, the absence of life, but they do not realize what death really is. I have seen a bird, when its mate was shot and fell dead, settle beside it, feel it with its beak, and when it felt that it was still and lifeless, drop its head and give up its life before the hunter could approach. I have also seen a dog die instantly when it saw that its companion dog with which it had spent its life was dead. But still, animals feel only the inactivity, the absence of the friend. They do not fully realize the true nature of death.

In the East Sufis often build their houses or cottages near cemeteries and also in the jungles, so that by seeing the dead they may remember that now is the time to conquer death, in order to realize their immortality after death. And time and again man, in the form of a holy being, awakens humanity to the knowledge of its immortality.

If the resurrection merely meant that Christ after his death rose again, it would be a story which could either be believed or disbelieved. If it were only believed as such, how long would that belief last? Its lesson is much greater than that; it means the resurrection from this mortal life to immortality. Those who have risen to that immortal one Being, where there is no distinction between husband and wife, brother and sister, father, mother, and child, they are the sons of the resurrection.

The story tells that when Mary Magdalene and the other Mary came to the tomb where Christ had been laid, they found that the stone that was before the tomb had been rolled away; and, looking in they saw his wrappings lying about and the head-cloth in a place by itself; but the body of Christ was not there. The stone is the same stone that is spoken of in the Hindu myths. The Lord Krishna is called *Girwara*: he who holds the stone, who lifts it up. Under this stone every individual soul in the world is oppressed; it is the stone of the external self. When this is lifted up, then man rises to immortality. And above what does he rise? He rises above the body and above the mind; the wrappings and the head-cloth lying separately symbolize the body and the mind.

Great poets, great musicians, great writers, often rise above the body. They do not know where they are sitting or standing, they are lost in their imagination, unconscious of their physical existence; but they do not rise above the mind. When the consciousness can rise above the mind, above the thoughts, then it is free, then it is active in its own element, and then the higher consciousness can give of itself to the mind.

The rising to that consciousness in which there is no distinction is the highest degree of resurrection; but there are other degrees, just as in a lift one cannot arrive at the seventh floor without passing the second, third, fourth, and all the other floors.

There is that resurrection in which the exact counterpart of the physical body walks, sits down, and can do all that the physical body can do. This is called by Sufis *Alam-e Mithal*. There are mystics who have mastered this so completely that they are quite independent of their physical body. There is no death when this is mastered.

If a poet is writing his poetry, his wife, his servant, a hundred people may pass before his eyes, but he will not see them; he will not know that anyone has been near. If a little love of poetry can do this, how much more will the love of the inner life, the absorption in the inner life, draw the consciousness within!

It is told in the gospel that after his resurrection Christ was seen several times by his disciples. It is the experience of every person who has practised concentration and who has meditated, that he sees that which he has held in his consciousness, not only inwardly but outwardly before him. This is the first experience that every mystic has. The disciples were lost, absorbed in the thought of Christ; how should they not see him?

Christ said, 'Handle me, and see; for a spirit hath not flesh and bones, as ye see me have.' The word spirit is used in many different senses. It is used for a ghost or for the soul, but really it means the essence, which is the opposite pole to substance; in manifestation spirit is the opposite of matter in every way.

All that the eye has seen resurrects in the eye. If someone mentions a certain person to us, even though we had forgotten that person altogether he rises up in our eye, and we see him in a certain house, in a certain place where we have seen him before. It is not in this physical eye, but in that eye which is beyond. The materialists may say it is all in the brain, but how could the brain contain so many thousands and millions of things and beings? No doubt without training a person does not see the spirit, but it can be said that in a dream one sees oneself, one experiences oneself in different surroundings in the company of different people. And when someone says, 'That is a dream', I would answer, 'When do you call it a dream? You call it a dream when you are awake and when you see the contrast with your surroundings; then you say, "It was a dream; if not it would have remained with me, but everything was different there"; but if while you are dreaming someone came to you and said, "It is a dream", you would never believe it.'

The resurrection is the rising to that real life, that true friend upon whom alone, from among all other things and beings, we can lean, who alone is always unchanged, who has always been with us and always will be.

THE SYMBOL OF THE CROSS

MANY THINK that this symbol has existed only from the time of Jesus Christ, and no doubt it became better known after the time of the Master; but in fact this symbol is an ancient one used at different times and in all ages by the mystics. It has many mystical meanings.

The cross shows a vertical and a horizontal line. Everything that exists has come from these two lines and extends vertically and horizontally, as may be seen in the leaf which develops in length and in breadth. In its first meaning, therefore, the cross is the symbol of manifestation; it belongs also to the journey towards the spiritual ideal, and no better picture could be given of this journey than a cross.

Then, whenever someone begins to speak or act for the truth, he finds his way barred; there is a cross standing in his way. Speak the truth before the nation, in the face of the world, and the cross, the bar will come from the nation or the world to oppose one. Thus another side of this mystery is the destiny, the life of a teacher: the cross signifies what he has to meet with when delivering the message of truth in the world.

There is still another great mystery of the cross which is very little understood. Everywhere outside us there is space—space being that which can accommodate, which can contain. But within us also there is space, a space which extends in another direction.

Besides these symbolical meanings the cross is a natural sign that man has always made either from his artistic faculty or from his reasoning faculty. It is the nature of light to spread its rays, especially when the light is in its perfection. By looking at the sun —at the setting sun in particular—one finds lines forming on the sky and on the earth: first there is one straight line, and if one watches carefully out of that first vertical line a horizontal line develops. By keen observation of light one realizes that it is the nature of light to form a perpendicular and a horizontal line; and if it is the nature of the external light to form a cross it is also the nature of the inner light. The external light is the reflection of the inner light, and it is the nature of the inner light that is expressed in the outer light; by this one can see that the inner light is not only manifested in the outer light, but that the outer light is the picture of the inner light.

We can also see by observing nature's forms—the form of a tree, of a plant, of a flower, the forms of the animals and birds, and in the end the most developed and finished form of the human being—that they all present a cross. One cross may be seen by observing the formation of man's head. Another cross is suggested by the whole human form. It is always a horizontal line and a perpendicular line that suggest the symbol of the cross, and there is no form that has not a horizontal and a perpendicul·.r line; it is these two different aspects or directions which form the cross. In this way one can understand that in the mystery of form the cross is hidden.

Now coming to one of the first mysteries mentioned above, namely that man's journey towards spiritual progress can be pictured as a cross: in the first place man's ego, man's self, is his enemy and stands as a hindrance to his progress. Feelings such as pride, conceit, selfishness, jealousy, envy, and contempt are all feelings which hurt others, and which destroy one's own life and make it full of that misery which springs from that selfish personal feeling: the ego of man. The more egoistic, the more conceited he is, the more miserable a life he has in the world and the more he makes the lives of others miserable. This ego, or *Nafs*, is a natural development in man's life or heart: the more he knows of the world, the more egoistic he becomes; the more he understands and experiences the world, the more avaricious he is.

It is not that man brings his faults along with him when he is born. He arrives with innocence, with the smiles of the infant, the friend of everyone who comes near him, ready to cast his loving glance on everybody, regardless of whether they are rich or poor, friend or foe, attracted by beauty in all forms; and it is that quality in the infant which attracts every soul. This shows that the same soul which comes with such purity of heart, purity of expression, beauty in every movement, develops in his nature as he grows up in the world all that is hurtful and harmful to himself and to others. It is in the world that, as he grows up, he creates his Nafs. Yet at the same time there is in the depths of the heart that goodness which is the divine goodness, that righteousness which man has inherited from the Father in heaven.

A longing for joy and rest and peace is in him, and this shows that in man there are two aspects: there is one nature which is in the depths of his heart; and there is another nature which has developed after his coming on earth. And then there arises a conflict, a struggle between these two natures, when the nature which belongs to the depths begins to feel that it yearns for something. It must have goodness from other people, it must have peace in life, and when it cannot find these the inner conflict arises.

Man creates his own disharmony in his soul and then treats others in the same way; therefore he is neither satisfied with his own life, nor is he satisfied with others because he feels that he has a complaint against them, although it is caused mostly by himself. What he gives he takes back, yet he never realizes that. He always thinks that everybody should give him what he yearns for in the depths of his being: love, goodness, righteousness, harmony, and peace; but when it comes to giving he does not give because he lives in the other life he has created. This makes it plain that in every man a being is created, and that being is the Nafs; in point of fact it is the same as the conception of Satan found in all the scriptures and traditions.

People have often divided the world between two spirits: a small part of humanity for God, and a greater part of humanity for Satan, making the dominion of that Satan-spirit even more extensive than the dominion of God. But if one understands the meaning of the word Satan, one sees that it is this spirit of error which has been collected and gathered in man after his coming on earth, this Nafs, which acts as Satan, leading him continually astray and closing the eyes of his heart to the light of truth. As soon as a revolution comes in the life of a man, as soon as he begins to see more deeply into life, as soon as he begins to acquire goodness, not only by receiving it but by giving it, as soon as he begins to enjoy not only the sympathy of others, but the giving of sympathy to others, then comes a time when he begins to see this Satan-spirit as apart from his real original being, standing before him constantly in conflict with his natural force, freedom, and inclination; and then he sees that sometimes he can do what he desires, but at other times this spirit gets hold of him and does not allow him to do what he wishes. Sometimes he finds himself weak in this struggle, and sometimes he finds himself strong. The result is that when he finds himself strong in this battle he is thankful and satisfied; but when he finds himself weak in it he repents and is ashamed, and wishes to change himself.

This is the time when another epoch begins in the man's life, and from this time on there is a constant conflict between himself and that spirit which is his ego. It is a conflict, it is a kind of hindrance to his natural attitude, his natural inclination to do good and right; and he constantly meets with that spirit because it was created in his own heart and has become part of his being. It is a very solid and substantial being, as real as he feels himself to be and often more real, and something within him in the depths of his being is covered up by it. And this constant conflict between his real, original self and this self which hinders his spiritual progress, is pictured in the form of a cross.

This cross he carries during his progress. It is the ugly passions, the love of comforts, and the satisfaction in anger and bitterness that he has to fight first; and when he has conquered these the next trouble he has to meet is that still more subtle enemy of himself in his mind: the sensitiveness to what others say, to the opinion of others about himself. He is anxious to know everybody's opinion about him or what anybody says against him, or if his dignity or position is hurt in any way. Here again the same enemy, the Nafs, takes another stand, and the crucifixion is when that Nafs is fought with—until there comes an understanding that there exists no self before the vision of God.

It is this which is the real crucifixion; but with it there comes still another which always follows and which every soul has to experience, for the perfection and liberation of every soul depend on it. This is the crucifixion of that part of a man's being which he has created in himself and which is not his real self, although on the way it always appears that he has crucified his own self.

The mystery of perfection lies in annihilation, not annihilation of the real self, but of the false self, of the false conception which man has always cherished in his heart and has allowed to torture him during his life. Do we not see this among our friends and acquaintances? Those who attract us, and those whom we love and admire deeply, have always only one quality which can really attract us: personality. It is not only that their selflessness attracts us, but what repels us in the life of others is nothing but the grossness of the Nafs, or one might call it the denseness and hardness of that self-created spirit or ego.

The teaching of Christ when he said, 'Blessed are the poor in spirit', is little understood. He does not mean poor in divine spirit, but poor in this self-created spirit; and those who are poor in this self-created spirit are rich in the divine spirit. Therefore one can call the Nafs the spirit of grossness; but a better word is ego.

There have always been two tendencies: one of sincerity, and the other of insincerity and falsehood. They constantly work together. The false and the true have always existed side by side in life and nature. Where there is real gold there is false; where there is a real diamond there is an imitation diamond; where there are sincere people there are insincere ones; and in every aspect of life—in a life of spirituality, in the acquisition of learning, in art or science—we can see both sincerity and insincerity. And the only way to recognize real spiritual development is by understanding the extent of selflessness; because however much a person pretends to spirituality and wishes to be godly or pious or good, nothing can hide his true nature. For there is the constant tendency of that ego to leap out; it will leap out from his control, and if he is insincere he cannot hide it. Just as the imitation diamond, however bright, is dull compared with the real one, and when tested and examined will prove to be an imitation, so real spiritual progress must be proved in the personality of a soul. It is the personality that proves whether a man has touched that larger realm where self does not exist.

The next and still greater mystery of the cross can be observed in the life of the messengers, the prophets, the holy beings. In the first place no one has entrance into the kingdom of God who has not been so crucified. There is a poem by the great Persian poet Iraqi, who tells us how he went to the gate of the Beloved and knocked at the door; and a voice answered, 'There is no place for anyone else in this abode. Go back to where you came from', and he went back. Then, after a long time, and after having gone through the process of bearing the cross and being crucified, he came again, this time full of that spirit of selflessness, and he knocked at the door and the word came, 'Who art thou?' and he said, 'Thyself alone, for no one else exists save thee.' And God said, 'Enter into this abode for now it belongs to thee.'

It is this selflessness, to the extent that even the thought of self is no longer there, that it is dead, which is the recognition of God. One finds this spirit to a small extent in the ordinary lover and beloved, when a person loves another from the bottom of his heart. The one who says, 'I love you but only so much; I love you but I give you sixpence and keep sixpence for myself; I love you but I keep a certain distance, I never come closer; we are separate beings', his love is mixed with self. As long as that exists, love has not done its full work. Love accomplishes its work when it spreads its wings and veils man's self from his own eyes. That is the moment when love is fulfilled. And so it is in the life of the holy ones who have not only loved God by professing it or showing it, but to the extent that they have forgotten themselves. It is that state of realization of being which can be called a cross.

But then such souls have a cross everywhere; every move they make is a cross, a crucifixion. In the first place living in the world, a world full of falsehood, full of treachery and deceit and selfishness, every move they make, all their actions, everything they say and think prove that their eyes and hearts are open to something which is different from what the world is looking at. It is a constant conflict. It is living in the world, living among people of the world, and yet looking at a place which is different. Even if they tried to speak they could not. Words cannot express the truth; language is too inadequate to give a real conception of the ultimate truth. As it is said in the Vedanta, the world is Maya. Maya means something unreal; to these souls the world becomes most unreal as soon as they begin to see the real, and when they compare the world with this reality it seems even more unreal. No ordinary being can imagine to what an extent this world manifests itself to their eyes.

People in the world who are good yet without having arrived at spiritual perfection, who are sensitive, tender, and kind, see how the world treats them; how they are misunderstood, how the best is taken by the selfish, how the one who is generous has to give more and more, how the one who serves has to serve more and more, how the one who loves has to love more and more; and still the world is not satisfied. How jarring life is to these! And think of those who have arrived at such a stage of realization that there is a vast gulf between the real and the unreal, whose language when they arrive at that realization is not understood any more, so that they are forced to speak in a language which is not their own, and to say something different from what they are realizing. It is more than a cross. Not only Jesus Christ had a cross to bear; every teacher who has a portion of the message to give has his cross.

But then one may ask why the masters of humanity who have come throughout the ages and have had such a cross to bear did not go to the forests, to the caves, to the mountains; why did they stay in the world? Rumi has given a beautiful picture of this. He tells why the melody of the reed flute makes such an appeal to our hearts. It is, he says, because first it is cut away from its original stem, and then holes have been make in its heart so that the heart has been broken, and it begins to cry. And so it is with the spirit of the messenger, with the spirit of the teacher: by bearing and by carrying his cross, his self becomes like a reed, hollow. This makes it possible for the player to play his melody; when it has become nothing, the player uses it to play his melody. If there were still something there the player could not use it.

God speaks to everyone, not only to the messengers and teachers. He speaks to the ears of every heart, but it is not every heart that hears Him. His voice is louder than the thunder and His light is clearer than the sun—if one could only hear it, if one could only see. In order to hear and to see man should remove this wall, this barrier, which he has made of his self. Then he becomes the flute upon which the divine player may play the music of Orpheus which can charm even the hearts of stone; then he rises from the cross into the life everlasting.

ORPHEUS

THERE IS always a deep meaning attached to the legends of the ancient Greeks, as to those of the Indians, Persians, and Egyptians. And it is also most interesting to see how the art of the Greeks, however beautiful it is, had a far deeper meaning than would appear on the surface; by studying it we find the key to this ancient culture.

An example of this is the symbolic meaning of the story of Orpheus. We learn from the first part of this story that there is no object that a person has once desired from the bottom of his heart which will be lost for ever. Even if the object of love that a person has once desired were in the deepest depths of the earth, where only reason could behold it and not the eye, even then it could be attained if one pursued it with sufficient purpose. The next thing we learn is that in order to attain an object, the love-element is not sufficient; besides love we need wisdom, that wisdom which awakens in harmony and harmonizes with the cosmic forces, helping one to attain one's object.

The wise of all ages and of all countries admit the truth that the one who possesses the knowledge of sound knows the science of the whole of life, and thus the invoking of the gods by Orpheus means his coming into touch with all the harmonious forces which, united together, brought him the object which he wished to attain. But the most fascinating part of the story is the ending, both artistically and on account of its meaning. Orpheus was proceeding with Eurydice following him, and he had promised that he would not look back. The moment he looked back Eurydice would be taken from him. The meaning of this is that the secret of all attainment is faith. If the faith of a person endures for ninety-nine miles, and only one mile remains before the gaining of the object, even then if doubt comes attainment can no longer be expected. From this we can learn a lesson, a lesson which can be used in everything we do in life, in every walk of life: that in order to attain anything we need faith. Even the slightest lack of faith in the form of doubt, will spoil all we have done.

'Verily faith is light, and doubt darkness.'

THE MYSTERY OF SLEEP

WE SEE in our daily life that the child's greatest friend is the one who helps it to go to sleep. However many toys we may give it, however many dolls and sweets, when the child is helped to sleep, it is then that it is most grateful. When the mother with her blessed hand rocks it to sleep, this is of the greatest benefit for the child; it is then that it is happiest.

If those who are sick and in pain can sleep they are happy. Then all their pain is gone. If they can only sleep they feel they can endure all else. They will ask the doctor to give them anything to make them sleep. If a person were offered a king's palace and every enjoyment, every luxury, the best surroundings, the best dishes, on condition that he should not sleep, he would say, 'I do not want it; I prefer my sleep!'

The difference between the happy and the unhappy is that the unhappy cannot sleep. The sorrow, care, anxiety, and worry have taken their sleep away. Why do people take alcoholic drinks and drugs of all sorts? Only for this. When a man has drunk alcohol, because of the intensity of the stimulant a slight sleep comes over him. His feet and hands are asleep, his tongue is asleep; he cannot speak distinctly; he cannot walk straight and falls down. The joy of this sleep is so great that when he has drunk once he wants to drink again. A thousand times he resolves that he will not drink any more, but he does it all the same. Rumi says in one of his poems, 'O sleep, every night thou freest the prisoner from his bonds!'

The prisoner when he is asleep does not know that he is in prison; he is free. The wretched is not wretched; he is contented. The suffering have no more pain and misery. This shows us that the soul is not in pain or in misery. If it were it would also be so when the body is asleep. The soul does not feel the misery of the body and the mind; it is when a person awakes that the soul thinks that it is in pain and wretched. All this shows us the great bliss of sleep. And this great bliss is given to us without cost, like

all that is best in life. We do not pay for sleep. We pay thousands
of pounds for jewels, for gems that are of no use to us, while we
can buy bread for pennies.

Man does not know how great the value of sleep is, because the
benefit it gives cannot be seen and touched. If he is very busy, if he
has some business that brings him money, he would rather occupy
himself with that even at the cost of his sleep, because he sees
that he has gained so many pounds, so many shillings; but he
does not see what he gains by sleep.

When we are asleep we generally experience two conditions:
the dream and the deep sleep. The dream is the uncontrolled
activity of the mind. When we are awake, when our mind works
without control, it shows us pictures which come from its store
of impressions and we call this imagination. When we control
the activity of the mind we call it thought. The imaginings that
come during sleep we call dreams. We do not call them real,
because our waking state shows us something different; but while
we are not in the waking state the dream is real.

During a deep sleep a person is usually not conscious of anything, and when he wakes up he feels refreshed and renewed.
What are we doing when we are fast asleep? The soul is then
released from the hold of the body and the mind. It is free; it
goes to its own element, to the highest spheres, and it enjoys
being there and is happy. It experiences all the happiness, all the
bliss and peace that are there.

Besides the dream and the deep sleep there are visions. These
are seen when the soul in sleep is active in the higher spheres.
What it sees there the mind interprets in allegorical pictures. The
soul sees plainly the actual thing, and whatever the mind
receives from its impressions is more or less what the soul sees.
Therefore the thing is seen as a picture, an allegory, a parable,
which the sage can interpret, because he knows the language of
those spheres. If he sees himself going down or walking up a
mountain, if he sees himself in rags or very richly dressed, on an
aircraft or in the desert, he knows what it all means. The ignorant
one does not know; he merely thinks it is a dream and nothing
important.

A person sees in a vision either what concerns himself, or what concerns others in whom he is interested; if he is interested in his nation or in the whole of humanity, he will see what he has to do in regard to the nation or the whole of humanity.

In a dream a voice may be heard, or a message given in letters. This is the higher vision. The saints and sages see in the vision exactly what will happen or what the present condition is, because their mind is controlled by their will. Even in sleep their mind does not for one moment think that it can act independently of their will. And so whatever their soul sees is shown exactly as it is seen. They see visions even while awake, because their consciousness is not bound to this earthly plane. It is awake and acts freely upon the higher planes.

Besides the dream, the vision, and the deep sleep, the mystics experience two other conditions, the self-induced dream and the self-induced deep sleep. To accomplish this is the aim of mysticism. It is so easy that I can explain it in these few words, and yet it is so difficult that I bow my head before him who has achieved it. It is accomplished by concentration and meditation.

To hold one thought in our mind, keeping our mind free from all other thoughts, from all pictures, is very difficult. A thousand thoughts, a thousand pictures come and go. By mastering this the mystic masters all; then he is awake upon this plane as well as upon the higher plane, and to him the one becomes sleep and the other waking. People may say that those mystics who can do this are great occultists, very psychic people; but that is not their aim. Their aim is the true consciousness, the real life which lies beyond: God. When this is open to them then all wisdom is open to the soul, and all the books, all the learning in the world, become intelligible to them.

CONSCIOUSNESS

WHETHER the consciousness sees without eyes, or whether it needs the eyes to see, is a question which comes to the mind of all metaphysicians. If the consciousness can see alone, without the help of the eyes, then why were these eyes created? There are people who can see things that are happening at a distance of many hundreds of miles, and things that may happen many years later. In Hyderabad there was a dervish who had the habit of smoking very strong hashish. When he let the smoke out of his mouth he used to look into it and answer any questions that were put to him. If someone asked him, 'Where is my uncle at present?' he would say, 'Your uncle? In Calcutta, near the bazaar, the second house on the left. Your uncle is sitting in his room, his servant is at his side and his child is standing in front of him.' Whatever question he was asked, he answered. His consciousness had not the external self before it and therefore it was able to see through the eyes of another, through the eyes of the uncle or any other. He did not see it without eyes.

When I was in Russia there was an African there, a very ordinary man, not a man of any education. At night when he was asleep, he knew what anyone who came to that house had said or done. This was because his soul was in and about that house and it saw through the eyes of whoever came there.

The faculty of seeing exists in the consciousness from the beginning. Therefore among the names of God are Basir, the Seer, and Sami, the Hearer. *Basárat*, the faculty of seeing, becomes more exact the nearer it approaches manifestation. In the same way the universal consciousness sees through the eyes of every being on earth. It is looking at one and the same time through the eyes of all the millions of beings upon the earth. The thief may steal something, hide it, carry it off and think that no one sees him; but he cannot escape the sight of that consciousness which is within himself, looking through his eyes. It is not that God looks down from a distance and sees all the creatures on earth; he sees through the very eyes of the beings themselves. One might ask if God is not limited by this, made helpless and dependent; but if it seems so to us, it is because we have reduced God to a part of His being. We take a part and call it ours, our self, while in reality it is all God, the one Being. A Hindustani poet has said, 'What shall I call my self? Whatever I see it is all Thou; body, mind, soul, all are Thou. Thou art, I am not.'

The mystics not only see what may be happening at a distance in their sleep, but at all times. Some time ago there was in Delhi a mystic or murshid whose name was Shah Alám. One day he was having a hair-cut. He was looking in a little looking-glass, such as are used in India, while the barber was cutting his hair. Suddenly he dashed the mirror on the ground so that it broke into pieces. His mureeds who were with him were astonished; the barber also was amazed, wondering what had caused him to throw down the mirror with such violence. Afterwards he told them what had happened. At that time one of his mureeds was travelling by sea from Arabia to India; and a storm had struck the ship he was sailing in and he was in great danger. He called upon his murshid for help, and the murshid saw his peril in the mirror and saved him.

To some extent an illuminated soul can be conscious of all the past events in the evolution of man. But does this eye which is so accommodating, collect within itself all that it sees? And does the mind, through which man receives his memory, the most wonderful source of record there is, always remember everything it sees and experiences through life? No, only certain things which have made a deeper impression upon it. If we could remember everything, all the good and bad words people have spoken, all the literature we have read and all the foolish and crazy things we have heard, where would we be in the end? Human beings have a mind; they have a body; and their health depends entirely upon what they take in and then put out. If it were not so, man would not be able to live, so he takes the essence and the rest is discarded. Also, that which one takes from the angelic world and from the jinn world is only the essence; the essence of experience. The one who remembers all the good and bad things of the past is not to be envied, for he must have had many experiences of remorse and these would only create bitterness in him. It is the greatest relief to forget, it is like bathing in the Ganges. The present has so many beautiful things to offer us; if we only open our eyes to look at them we do not need to look for beauty in the past. Beauty is always here.

CONSCIENCE

CONSCIENCE is a product of the mind, and the best that the mind produces. It is the cream of the mind. But the conscience of a person living in one country may be quite different from the conscience of someone living elsewhere, for it is built of another element. For instance in ancient times there used to exist communities of robbers, who considered themselves entitled to rob the caravans passing through their territory. Their morals and principles were such that if one of their victims said, 'All I possess I will give you, if you will only let me go', they would say, 'No, I wish to see the blood of your hand'. They did not let him go without hurting him; the idea was, as they said, 'We do not accept anything from you; we are no beggars, we are robbers. We risk our lives in our profession; we are brave, and therefore we are entitled to do what we do.' It was the same with some of the sea-pirates. They believed their profession to be a virtuous one; and from that thought they became kings. The same people, when small, were robbers; but when they became great, they were kings.

Conscience, therefore, is what we have made it. At the same time it is the finest thing we can make; it is like the honey made by the bees. Beautiful experiences in life, tender thoughts and feelings gather in ourselves and create a conception of right and wrong. If we go against it, it brings discomfort. Happiness, comfort in life, peace, they all depend upon the condition of our conscience.

The whole of life in this world is built on conventions and accepted ideas, and conscience is erected on this edifice. In order to develop, conventions need the exclusiveness of the environment. They are the cause of the diversity of humanity, and no civilization, however advanced, can quite avoid them. The progress of civilization creates necessities of this kind. People do not like to admit this, but they will live according to conventions all the same. The artist is not conventional because he lives in his own world, and the greater artist he is, the more he will do so; but the ordinary man cannot live in the midst of the world and ignore conventionality.

The best way to understand civilization is the spiritual way. Once a person understands spiritual morality, he does not need to learn man-made morality; it will come by itself. As soon as a man begins to regard the pleasure or displeasure of God in the feeling of every person he meets, he cannot but become most refined, whatever his situation in life. He may live in a cottage, but his manner will surpass the manner of palaces. Furthermore, once a man has begun to judge his own actions, fairness will develop in his nature, and everything he does will be just and fair; he does not need much study of outer conventionalities. And then there is the Sufi conception of God as the Beloved. When this conception—that, in a greater or lesser degree, the divine spirit exists in everyone—is practised in everyday life and is considered in dealing with everybody, one will come to regard them all with the same devotion and respect, with the same thought and consideration, which one would give to the Beloved, to God.

In these ways the spiritual life teaches man what is best in conventionality; and when a civilization comes to be built on a spiritual basis, which is bound to happen one day, the conventionality of the world will become genuine and worth having.

Conscience is made from the cream of facts, but not from truth. For truth stands above all things; it has nothing to do with conscience. But the understanding of truth is just like a spring which rises and expands into an ocean, and then one arrives at such a degree of understanding that one realizes that all is true, and that all is truth. Of absolute truth there is nothing more to be said, and all else is Maya; when one looks at it from that point of view, nothing is wrong and nothing is right. If we accept right we must accept wrong. Einstein's theory of relativity is what the Hindus have called Maya, illusion; illusion caused by relativity. Everything exists only by our acceptance of it; we accept a certain thing to be right, good, beautiful, and once accepted that becomes part of our nature, our individual self; if we do not accept it as such, then it does not. A mistake, unless we accept it as such, is not a mistake; but once accepted it is a mistake. One might say that we do not always know that it is a mistake; but do we not know it from the painful consequences? That also is acceptance.

There are dervishes who work against accepted fact; for instance that fire causes burns. They jump into the fire and come out unharmed. They say that hell-fire is not for them. When they can prove that fire cannot harm them here, certainly there will be no fire for them in the hereafter.

The best way of testing life is to use one's conscience as a testing instrument with everything, to see whether there is harmony or disharmony. But in oneself there is also a constant action and reaction of conscience. The reason is that a human being has different phases of existence. In one phase he is less wise; if he dives deeper into himself he will become wiser. What he does in one sphere he would reject in another sphere. Man has so much to reject and to fight in himself, that he has that action and reaction even without contact with others.

Sometimes a person in a certain mood is a devil, and in another a saint. There are moods and times when a person is quite unreasonable; there are fits of goodness and fits of badness—such is human nature. Therefore one cannot say that an evil person has no good in him, nor a good person no evil. But what influences one's conscience most is one's own conception of what is right and wrong; and the next greatest influence is the conception of others. That is why a person is not free.

It is with conscience as with everything else. If it has become accustomed to govern one's thought, speech, or action, it becomes stronger; if it is not accustomed to do this, then it becomes weaker and remains only as a torture, not as a controller.

Conscience is a faculty of the heart as a whole, and the heart consists of reason, thought, memory, and heart itself. The heart, in its depth, is linked to the divine Mind, so in the depth of the heart there is a greater justice than on the surface; and therefore there comes a kind of intuition, inspiration, knowledge, as the inner light falls upon our individual conception of things. Then both come together. In the conscience God Himself sits on the throne of justice.

A person who is condemned by his conscience is more miserable than the one who is condemned by the court. The one whose conscience is clear, even if he is exiled from his country or sent to prison, still remains a lion, albeit a lion in a cage; for even in a cage there can be inner happiness. But when one's conscience despises one, then that is a bitter punishment in itself, more bitter than any court can mete out. Sa'di says it so beautifully; he sees the throne of God in the conscience, and says, 'Let me confess my faults to Thee alone, that I may not have to go before anyone in the world to humiliate myself'.

As soon as we accept humiliation, we are humiliated whether we think so or not. It does not depend upon the one who humiliates us; it depends upon ourselves. Even if the whole world does not accept it, it is of no avail if our mind is humiliated; and if our mind does not accept it, it would not matter if the whole world did. When a thousand people come and say that we are wicked, we will not believe it as long as our heart tells us that we are not. But when our own heart says, 'I am wicked', a thousand persons may say, 'You are good', but our heart will continue to tell us that we are wicked. If we ourselves give up, then nobody can sustain us.

The best thing certainly is to avoid humiliation, but if a person cannot avoid it he is as a patient who needs to be treated by a physician. Then he needs someone who is powerful enough to help him, a master-mind, so that he can be attended to and get over that condition. When a person is a patient he cannot help himself very well; he can do much, but there will always be the need of a doctor. However, when the feeling of humiliation has entered the mind, one should accept it as a lesson, as a necessary poison. But poison is poison. What is put into the mind will grow there. It should be removed; if it remains it will grow. All impressions such as humiliation, fear, and doubt, will grow in the subconscious mind bearing fruit, and there will come a time when one is conscious of them.

THE GIFT OF ELOQUENCE

WHEN WE consider the mineral, vegetable, and animal kingdoms together with mankind, we see that not only man, but also
every other being has the gift of expression. The rock expresses
least and we feel least for it. We strike it and break it and quarry
it and make use of it in every way, and we do not sympathize with
it at all, for it does not speak to us. It tells us very little. We
sympathize much more with the plant; we love it, tend it, and
give it water, and because it has more expression we care more for
it. But among the stones there are some that speak to us more than
others; we prize the diamond, the ruby, and the emerald most.
We pay thousands of pounds for them; we wear them.

An animal has a much greater gift of expression than a plant
or a rock, and we feel that animals are much nearer to us. The
dog by wagging his tail, by jumping about, by his every movement says, 'I love you,' and we care much more for him. We
do not want the plant on the chair next to us, but if the dog
sits on the chair it is all right. The cat has no words either, but all
the same it speaks to us with its voice. In all parts of the world
people have praised the nightingale because of its voice, its
expression. There are many birds in the forests of which we never
think because they have no voice. But the song-birds we all
know, and we like to keep a parrot because it can speak.

It is said in the Qur'an that Allah has made man the Khalif,
the chief of creation, because of this one gift: speech. Man alone
has the gift of eloquence. But while some men are like a rock,
and some like a plant or an animal, others possess the human
quality. The man who is like a rock has no expression; he has no
magnetism. He has only what is in his appearance, just like the
stones, even the emerald or the ruby; when that is gone, nothing is
left. The man who is like a plant has no intelligence, only some
feelings, some personality. There may be some beauty in him,
or he may be like a thorn, or poisonous. The man who is like an
animal has feelings and passions, but he cannot give expression to

them. That man only is a human being who has the gift of expression, and who can speak out about what he feels.

The gift of eloquence is symbolized by the Hindus as *Vāk*, the goddess of speech. Why not a god? Because the one who speaks is responsive to the Creator, the God within. The Hindus have also distinguished three sorts of men, *Rakshasa*, the monster, *Manusha*, the man, and *Devata*, the godlike man. The monster is he who is without speech and without feeling. The human man has feeling but no expression. The godlike man is he who has eloquence; it is his eloquence alone that makes him what he is.

Eloquence existed from the beginning, for the Word was in the beginning, before the creation of man. But neither the rock nor the plant nor the animal could express that Word; it was only man who could do so, and when he expressed it he became the pen of the divine Being. That is why the creation is perfected in him and why he is the highest of all beings. But to speak, and by this speech to hurt or wound the heart, the feelings, of another is the misuse of eloquence. There is a Russian saying, 'A sweet tongue is a sword that conquers the world.' The sword has two aspects, it conquers and it kills; and the tongue also can win and slay. The same idea is expressed in the gospels, 'Blessed are the meek, for they shall inherit the earth.'

The world is like a dome in which whatever is spoken comes back to us. If we say, 'How beautiful!' these words come back to us. If we say, 'You stupid!' the echo comes back: you stupid. A man may think that he is such an important person that he can say what he pleases, but some day the echo of his bad words will come back to him.

Sometimes a person does not wish to speak to his friend in a way that would hurt him, but without wishing to speak harshly he may do so, as his mind may be full of the bad impressions that he has stored there. Therefore we should store up only good impressions and not hold on to the others, in order that only good may come from us.

There are two ways of speaking about a subject. Before speaking one may ponder upon it, and then speak with all the reasonings that have come to one's mind. This is parrot-speech. One repeats what one has learned just as the parrot says certain words because it has been taught to do so. The other way of speech is to depend upon the store, the knowledge, that is always ready within oneself. In order to lay bare that knowledge an arrow is needed, and that arrow is the deep feeling that pierces everything. The knowledge is always there, but without eloquence we are shut off from that knowledge.

If we see a lop-sided person walking crookedly in the street, it is very easy to laugh at him, but a little feeling will produce pity, and a deep feeling will bring with it the expression of pity and compassion.

THE POWER OF SILENCE

IN THE Vedanta breath is called *Prana*, life. Breath is the chain which links body, heart, and soul together. It is so important that when it is gone from the body, this body which is so much loved and cared for that the slightest cold or cough is treated by doctors with medicines, is then of no more use. It cannot be kept alive.

Speaking is a breach in the breath. That is to say, when one speaks one has to take many more breaths than one would take otherwise. The breath is like the hoop a child plays with: according to the force of the blow of the stick, so many times the hoop turns; and when the force is spent the hoop falls down. It is also like the ticking of a watch. The watch goes for the time for which it is wound; it may be for twenty-four hours, or for one week, but longer than that period it cannot go, however far it is wound. Or compare it with a child's top; it turns so many times according to the strength with which it is spun, and when the force is spent the top falls over.

In accordance with the first breath, so long will our life last: so many breaths. By speaking we take away much of our life; a day's silence means a week longer of life and more, and a day's speech means a week less of life. Silence is the remedy for much, although of course a person living in the world cannot practise it continually. But he should keep a watch on his words; he should remember that for every word he speaks he will be awarded heaven or hell.

In India from ancient times there have been mystics who are called *Muni*. They never speak, although they do all kinds of other things. These mystics have often lived very much longer than we live at the present time: three hundred, five hundred years and more.

By not speaking the breath is not interrupted; it remains regular and even. The mystics have always given great importance to the breath, and have made its study the principal object in their training. Those who have mastered the breath have mastery over their lives; those who have not mastered it are liable to all kinds of diseases. There are some who have mastered it unconsciously, such as boxers and wrestlers, and also some people who have led a righteous life.

In the present age we have become so fond of speech than when a person is alone in the house he likes to go out, if only to find somebody to talk to. Often when people are alone they speak to the objects round them. Many people speak to themselves when they have no one else to talk to. If it were explained to them, perhaps they would understand how much energy they lose with each word spoken. Silence is relaxation of mind and body; it is restful and healing. The power of silence is very great, not only for the gaining and preservation of energy and vitality, but also morally there are many benefits to be obtained by silence.

Most of the follies we commit are follies of speech. In one week, for every single folly of action we commit a thousand follies of speech. Often we offend or hurt someone only by talking too much; if we had refrained from speech we would not have hurt him.

Then there is exaggeration. All idealists, those who like to admire something, have the tendency to exaggerate. If a person has gone out and read on a poster that a Zeppelin is coming* he wants to frighten his friends, and at once he says that twenty Zeppelins are coming. And when his friends are alarmed he feels a certain satisfaction. When idealists take a fancy to a person they tell him that he is the sun and the moon in the heavens. There is no need to say all this.

By speaking a person also develops a tendency to contradiction. Whatever is said, he wants to take the opposite standpoint. He becomes like a boxer or a wrestler: when there is no one to box or to wrestle with he is disappointed, so intense is his inclination for speech.

Once I was at a reception at a friend's house, and there was someone there who disputed with every guest, so that they were all tired out. I tried to avoid him but someone introduced us, and when he heard that I was a teacher of philosophy, he thought,

* During World War I in London.

'This is the person I want'. And the first thing he said was, 'I do not believe in God.' I said, 'Do you not? But do you believe in this manifestation and in the beauty of this world of variety, and that there is a power behind it which produces all this?' He said, 'I believe in all that, but why should I worship a personality, why should I call him God? I believe in it but I don't call it God.' I said to him, 'You believe that every effect has a cause, and that for all these causes, there must be an original cause. You call it cause, I call it God; it is the same. There is some officer whom you salute, some superior before whom you bow, for instance your father or mother, some fair one whom you love and adore, for whom you have a feeling of respect, some power before which you feel helpless. How great then must that Person be who has produced and controls all this and how much more worthy of worship!' He answered, 'But I do not call that a divinity, I call it a universal power, an affinity working mechanically, harmonizing all.' When I tried to keep him to one point, he ran to another; and when I followed him there, he ran to another, until at last I ceased, thinking of the words of Shankaracharya, 'All impossible things can be made possible save the bringing of the fool's mind to the point of truth.'

The tendency to contradiction can grow so much, that when some people hear even their own ideas spoken about before them, they will take up the contrary point of view in order to prepare a position for discussion. There is a Persian saying, 'O Silence, thou art an inestimable bliss, thou coverest the follies of the foolish and givest inspiration to the wise!'

How many foolish things we say only through the habit of speech! How many useless words we speak! If we are introduced to someone we must speak; if not we are thought impolite. Then come such conversations as, 'It is such a fine day; it is cold', or whatever the weather is, and so on; such speech without reason in time turns into a disease, so that a person cannot get on without emptying the head of others by speaking about useless things. He can no longer live one moment without it owing to his self-interest; he becomes so fond of speech that sometimes he will tell the whole story of his life to a stranger, preventing him from speaking, although that man may be very bored and would like to say, 'What do I care about all that?' And people also give out secrets that afterwards they regret having told.

Under the same spell a person shows impatience in his words, a pride, a prejudice, for which he is sorry afterwards. It is the lack of control over speech which causes all this. The word is sometimes more prized than the whole world's treasure, and again it is the word which puts a person to the sword.

There are different ways of receiving inspiration, but the best is silence. All the mystics have kept silence. During my travels through India all the great people that I met kept silences at least for some hours, and some for twenty hours a day.

In Hyderabad there was a mystic called Shah Khamush. He was called so because of his silence. In his youth he was a very clever and energetic young man, and one day he went to his murshid and as usual he had some question to ask as is natural in a pupil. The murshid was sitting in ecstasy, and as he did not wish to speak he said to him, 'Be quiet.' The boy was much struck. He had never before heard such words from his murshid, who was always so kind and patient and willing to answer his questions. But it was a lesson which was enough for his whole life, for he was an intelligent person. He went home and did not speak to his family, not even to his parents. Then his murshid, seeing him like that, did not speak to him any more. For many years Shah Khamush never spoke, and his psychic power became so great that it was enough to look at him to be inspired. Wherever he looked he inspired. Wherever he cast his glance he healed. This happened not long since, perhaps twenty-five years ago.

There is an intoxication in activity, and nowadays activity has increased so much that from morning till evening there is never any repose, owing to our daily occupations which keeps us continually on the move. And at night we are so tired that we want only to sleep, and next morning the activity begins anew. By this kind of life much is destroyed; man is so eager for his enjoyments that he does not think of the life that is there to be enjoyed. Every person should have at least an hour a day in which to be quiet, to be still.

After the silence of speech comes the silence of thought. Sometimes a person is sitting still without speaking, but all the time his thoughts are jumping up and down. The mind may not want the thoughts, but they come all the same. The mind is let out to them like a ballroom, and they dance around in it. One thought should be made so interesting, so important, that all other thoughts are driven out by it.

When the thoughts have been silenced, then comes the silence of feeling. We may not speak against some person, there may be no thought against him in our mind, but if there is a slight feeling against him in our heart, he will feel it. He will feel there is bitterness for him in that heart. Such is also the case with love and affection.

The abstract means that existence beyond this world where all forms of existence commingle, where they all meet, and this abstract has its sound. When that sound too is silenced and a person goes beyond it, then he reaches the highest state, *Najat*, the Eternal; but surely a great effort is needed to attain to this state.

HOLINESS

ONE OFTEN wonders what the word 'holy' means. Sometimes people understand it as meaning spiritual, pious, pure, religious; but none of these words can fully explain its meaning. Holy is the next degree beyond pious. God-realization is pious, self-realization is holy. The first step to self-realization is God-realization; it is not through self-realization that man realizes God.

Holiness is the spark of divinity in man, and no soul should be regarded as being deprived of this spark of divinity. This spark is light itself, and though it also exists in the lower creation, among animals and birds, in trees and plants and in any form of life, it is in man that it has the opportunity to blaze into a flame. At first this light is buried in the heart of man, but as soon as this spark of divinity begins to shine from his heart he shows the sign of holiness. This is because holiness is not a human heritage; it is inherited by every soul from God. But it manifests only when the heart is open, and when out of that divine spark there rises a tongue of flame which illuminates the path of man in life's journey towards the spiritual goal. It is lack of understanding of this subject which has made man accept a certain teacher in whom he or his friends or ancestors recognized divinity, and at the same time reject another with all his apparent holiness. Holiness does not belong to a particular race, community, or family. It manifests naturally in the life of some; in the life of others it has to be dug for. The fire is there, but it is buried; it needs to be brought to the surface. Sometimes blowing is needed to help the flame to leap up.

Holiness has different meanings according to its connection. Religious holiness is morality, philosophical holiness is truth, spiritual holiness is ecstasy, magical holiness is power, heroic holiness is bravery, ascetic holiness is indifference, poetical holiness is beauty, and lyric holiness is love.

Many stories are told about holy people who live in caves in the Himalayas. One reads of them in books. No doubt souls who

reach a higher realization naturally feel inclined to get away from
the world and its strife, and to seek a corner where nobody can
reach them, though many extremely meditative people can be
found in the midst of the crowd. I have seen illuminated ones in
all kinds of guises: as beggars, as rich men, as paupers, as kings, as
religious men, or as irreligious men. Spiritual vibrations were
emanating continually from them all, and the universal brotherhood which naturally inspires the soul that is conscious of its
self, showed in their everyday life.

For nine years of my life in India I travelled from south to
north and from west to east on a pilgrimage to the holy souls, and
never did the thought enter my mind that the holy ones belonged
to any particular religion or denomination. The Hindu bows
before his deity, the Muslim cries out to his Lord, the Parsi
worships the fire, but the devotee seeks the sacred dwellings of the
holy men. It is through the lips of the holy man that the God of
the devotee speaks, while the God of the orthodox is hidden in
theories, the God of the idolaters is concealed in the shrine, and
the God of the intellectual seeker is lost in obscurity. The love of
spiritual realization which was born in my heart has kept me in
the pursuit of these sacred beings all through life. He who seeks,
finds; and so I found the souls I sought after. And I met them
not only in the heart of the forest or in the mountain caves,
but even in the midst of the crowd.

There is the question whether a man's holiness can be recognized by his actions. The answer is that it can certainly be seen in
his actions, but who can judge the action when it is already difficult
for the wise to judge the action of the worst sinner? Who would
be ready to judge a holy man except a fool? No doubt holiness
can be recognized in goodness, and yet no one can fix a standard
of goodness, for what is good for one is bad for another; sometimes that which is poison for one is a remedy for another. The
goodness of every person is peculiar to himself. If he wanted to
the worst person in the world could accuse the best person of lack
of goodness, for no man's goodness has ever proved, nor will it
ever prove, to be to the satisfaction of everybody. But holiness
in itself is goodness; even if it is not in accordance with people's
standards of goodness. Holiness is a continually rising fountain of

light, a phenomenon in itself; it is illumination and it is illuminating. Light has no other proof than itself. Holiness needs no claim, no pleading, no publicity. It is its own claim, it pleads for itself, light itself is its publicity.

Many in this world seem to be confused between false and true. But there comes a moment when one can distinguish without any difficulty between false and true. Because what is false cannot stand for any length of time all the tests that come from all sides. It is the real gold that stands all tests, and so it is with true holiness. Holiness is enduring, knowing, forgiving, understanding, and yet it stands beyond all things, above all things. It is unbreakable, unshakable. It is beauty, it is power, and it is divinity when it reaches its perfection.

THE EGO

THE SUFI term *Nafsaniat* expresses the blindness of the personal ego, which first began to eclipse the soul when man tasted the forbidden fruit, as is described in the story of Adam and Eve. In the beginning man started his life on earth by obtaining his sustenance at the expense of the vegetable kingdom. He never for one moment paused to consider whether the plants, flowers, and fruits have life within them, and demand from him the love which he himself demands from every being around him.

His blindness increased when he robbed the calf of the food which nature had provided for it, enjoying the milk himself. As his blindness became more intense the ego grew still more tyrannical, and he began to sacrifice the lives of birds and beasts to satisfy his fancy and appetite. In this way he sustained his physical self, which was thus built up with such unjustly gathered properties, and this caused a thick veil of darkness to cover his eyes, making him selfish and sensual, so that he considered the satisfaction of his passions and appetites, the achievement of comfort and grandeur, as the sole purpose of life. Thus he descended from man to animal, and from the level of an animal to that of a devil. When he reached this stage there remained for him neither God nor virtue. The command of Christ to love one's enemy could not be obeyed, for he was not even able to love his neighbour, his fellow-man, when the question of self-interest arose.

It is this aspect of involution which has brought about floods, volcanic eruptions, and such disasters as the loss of the *Titanic*, and the recent upheaval of society.

Man has considered civilization to be that which the ancient Hindus termed Kali Yug, or the Iron Age. What they called Krita Yug, the Golden Age, man today calls barbarism, which shows how the heart of man has hardened. At the present time a man's word is no longer his bond; a signed contract is needed. A superficial politeness has taken the place of love, and artificiality has taken the place of truth. Machinery has usurped the place of personal bravery. Religion and morality have been superseded by trade unions, and material investigation has taken the place of life's realization.

Man can no longer distinguish the difference between a fleeting joy and an everlasting peace. The objective world is so concrete before his eyes that he cannot see beyond it. He wants to realize the material results of his efforts, even at the cost of his life, and the call of heaven itself fails to attract him to the Infinite.

There is a saying, 'The load of collected sin will sooner or later crush the bearer.' Every criminal is haunted by the hideous spectre of his crime. We need not be surprised that there is not a single nation or race which was not involved, directly or indirectly, to a greater or lesser degree, in the recent world-wide upheaval. No corner of the globe has entirely escaped this terrible visitation; it has taken its toll from every race and religion. So we know that the catastrophe of modern history was intended for humanity in general; it was a cleansing with the purpose of inaugurating an ideal period of peace which can only be possible when instead of the will of man the purpose of God is fulfilled.

THE BIRTH OF THE NEW ERA

THAT THE new era will not be worse is plain enough, for when the worst has happened there cannot be anything beyond that. The worst condition ends the cycle, and the new cycle must necessarily begin better. If we look back with keen sight and with a true sense of justice, it is clear that as individuals, as communities, as nations, and as races, the world has been going from bad to worse in the way of selfishness. There is not one religion in this world whose followers are not in revolt against their leaders on the path. Religion has gradually lost its truth and has survived in name only. So we can no longer be unaware of our sins in the past.

When we look at racial distinctions, we see that the hatred of one race for another has always increased with civilization. Colour prejudice, class distinction, differences between East and West, and the dominion of one sex over the other are not yet out of sight; they are rather on the increase.

In whichever direction we look—at the prosperity of commerce, the great progress in education, art, and science—we can see everywhere the demoralization of the world bringing to an end the ideal of friendship and personal relationship. In the progress of education, the knowledge of the soul's purpose, the only thing worth while in life, is overlooked. Education qualifies a man to become selfish to the best of his ability, and to get the better of another. Art has lost its freedom of grace and beauty, since its reward depends on the approval of the heartless and blind. Science has degenerated for the very reason that the scientist has limited his view to the objective world and denied the existence of the life which is beyond perception. In the absence of a higher ideal the constant striving after material inventions has led man to such devices as have set the world on fire. Those who are under the spell of destruction are unaware of all this; they cannot know it until the clouds of gloom have dispersed, their hearts are clear, and their minds have recovered from this intoxication which prevents them from thinking and understanding.

The races in the coming era will mix more and more every day, developing finally into a world-wide race. The nations will develop a democratic spirit, and will overthrow every element which embitters them against one another. There will be alliances of nations until there is a world alliance of nations, so that no nation may be oppressed by another, but all will work in harmony and freedom for common peace.

Science will probe the secrets of the life unseen, and art will follow nature closely. The people of all classes will be seen everywhere. The caste system will vanish and communities will lose their exclusiveness, all mingling together, and their followers will be tolerant towards one another. The followers of one religion will be able to pray by offering the prayers of another, until the essential truth will become the religion of the whole world and diversity of religions will be no more.

Education will culminate in the study of human life, and learning will develop on that basis. Trade will become more universal, and will be arranged on the basis of a common profit. Labour will stand side by side with capital on an equal footing.

Titles will have little importance. Signs of honour will become conspicuous. Bigotry in faiths and beliefs will become obsolete. Ritual and ceremony will be a play. Women will become freer every day in all aspects of life, and married women will be called by their own names. The sons and daughters will be called by the name of their town, city, or nation, instead of by the family name. No work will be considered menial. No position in life will be humiliating. Everybody will mind his own business, and all will converse with one another without demanding introductions. The husband and wife will be like companions, independent and detached. The children will follow their own bent. Servant and master will be so only during working hours, and the feeling of superiority and inferiority among people will vanish. Medicine will take away the need for surgery, and healing will take the place of medicine. New ways of life will manifest themselves, hotel life predominating over home life. Grudges against relatives, complaints about servants, finding fault with neighbours will all cease to occur, and the world will continue to improve in all aspects of life until the day of *Gayamat*, when all vain talk will cease, and when everywhere will be heard the cry, 'Peace, peace, peace!'

THE DEEPER SIDE OF LIFE

IN THESE modern times people consider an intellectual life, or a life of manual labour, a normal life. A practical man is considered a man of common sense, and common sense reaches no further than its limited boundaries. A practical man is the one who knows best how to guard his material interests in the continual struggle of life. Some call common sense positivism: believing only in all that proves to be real to our senses and in all that can be perceived, felt, and experienced by our mind. For this reason, in spite of great and unceasing progress in the material world, we have closed the door to another world of progress which can only be entered by opening the door to the deeper side of life. By his form and features, by his physical construction, man looks at one side and covers the other side with his own self. Man sees what is before him, but not what is behind him. As he is made so by nature he cannot look into the deeper side, being absorbed in the life on the surface.

Today there seems to be greater need of the inner life than there has ever been before. It is the head quality which is developed these days, whereas the heart quality needs to be developed in order to bring balance to life. Life, so balanced, can then be prepared for the inner culture or the spiritual life. Many consider sentiment to be quite unimportant, something which should be kept apart from the central theme of life which today is intellectuality. No one who has given a thought to the deeper side of life will deny for one moment the power and inspiration that arise when once the heart is kindled. A person with heart quality need not be simple, he need not discard intellect; only, the heart quality produces a perfume in the intellect like the fragrance in a flower. Morals learnt from logic are dry morals—a fruit without juice, a flower without fragrance. The heart quality produces naturally virtues which no one can teach; a loving person, a person with sympathy in his heart, teaches morals through himself. It is the balance of thought and feeling that makes the soil ready for the sowing of the seed of the inner life.

There are three steps which one must take in order to come to the spiritual life. The first step is the knowledge of the nature and character of man. A seeker takes his first step in the path of truth when he is able to understand his fellow-men fully and find the solution to every problem connected with them.

The next step is to have insight into the nature of things and beings, to understand cause and effect and to be able to find the cause of the cause and the effect of the effect; to be able to see the reason of the reason and the logic of the logic. When a person is able to see the good side of the bad and the bad side of the good, and when he is able to see the wrong side of the right and the right side of the wrong, then he has taken the next step on the spiritual path.

The third step is to rise above the pains and pleasures of life, to be in the world and not of the world, to live and not to live at the same time. Such a one becomes a living-dead person, a dead person living for ever. Immortality is not to be sought in the hereafter; if it is ever gained, it is gained in one's lifetime. In this third stage of development one is able to attain happiness, power, knowledge, life, and peace within oneself, independently of all things outside.

The spiritual knowledge which has always been sought by awakened souls will always be sought by them. In past ages the seekers looked for a guide on this path, a guide who initiated them into the mysteries of the deeper side of life, and once the secret was revealed it no longer remained a mystery to them. The man who is not yet awakened to the inner side of life has not experienced life fully; he has only seen one side of life, maybe the more interesting side, but the less real. The one who has experienced both sides of life, the outer and the inner life, has certainly fulfilled the purpose of his life on earth.

LIFE'S MECHANISM

BY LIFE'S mechanism I mean one's environment. There are many who realize that life's mechanism has a great deal to do with one's success or failure, but nevertheless not everyone thinks deeply enough about it to know to what extent it affects one's life. The mystic always teaches that one should treat oneself as a patient and cure oneself of one's weaknesses, but from a practical point of view conditions have also to be taken into consideration. And this point of view is supported by the words of Christ. One should not be surprised if man cannot accomplish soon enough that which he wishes to accomplish in life when it is even difficult for the Creator to do so. It is to teach this philosophy and secret that Christ has said, 'Thy will be done on earth as it is in heaven'. What did Christ mean by this? He meant, 'Thy will is easily done in heaven, and I wish that people would help to let it be done as easily on earth.'

If one had to swim across the sea it would take great courage, great perseverance, and great faith to make that journey, and still one would not know when one would arrive at one's destination; but when one boards a ship the journey is made easy. Then one does not need to exhaust one's faith and perseverance to the same extent, because there is a mechanism at one's disposal to attain the object. Mechanism, therefore, is most necessary for the attainment of every object. If one wishes for comfort in the home one needs a mechanism; if one has a business or an industry, a certain amount of organization improves the conditions. In a state the government answers the purpose of keeping order and peace, and when it is cold one needs warm clothes, while in the summer a different environment is necessary.

Now this idea is easy to understand, but to make the right mechanism is most difficult. For in the first place there are so many who have not got their object clear in their mind. They will go on day after day, not knowing what they really want, thinking differently every day, and this deprives them of the mechanism which can only be produced after knowing one's definite object in life. Very often by too much enthusiasm, by too much tampering with the mechanism, one spoils one's scheme, defeats one's object. At other times when the mechanism does not answer the purpose, one falls short of the purpose which one had in mind.

One can never say that one knows enough about this subject; for in treating oneself one needs only one's own knowledge, but in arranging mechanisms one has to deal with many different natures, and one must possess much more knowledge of human nature and of life. People have often come to me and said. 'I have been able to manage myself as I was instructed, and I have been able to keep up my concentrations and meditations which were given to me, yet my goal is far from being reached.' But what is lacking is not always practice or self-training; it may be that the necessary mechanism is lacking. For instance, if a person says, 'I have been able to discipline myself and now I can meditate fairly well. Now I will go and sit at a seaport and meditate on the thought that I am in a town across the ocean', will he arrive there? Or a person with self-discipline will meditate on the thought, 'All the wealth that is in the bank will come to my house'; will it come? Even if he continues to meditate upon the bank for a thousand years he will not succeed in getting its wealth!

In this objective world one needs an objective mechanism to produce certain results, and if people who are on the spiritual path do not see this side of it, they will only prove that, in spite of their goodness and spirituality, they lack balance, and then the practical man has good reason to laugh at the mystical-minded person. Therefore the work of the Sufi Movement is not only to guide souls towards a higher ideal, but also to keep their eyes open on the way, in order that they may see where they are going. Sufis should give an example to those who have no belief in spiritual ideas by striking a balance throughout their lives. A person may take good care of himself and may concentrate upon good health, and yet his surroundings may be the cause of an illness. That cannot be helped; it is not lack of spirituality in that person; it is lack of materiality. Does this not show that we ought to balance the two? It does not give a person great exaltation to become so spiritual that he floats in the air by levitation, if he is no better than a balloon. It is the one who can stand firmly on earth who has accomplished something. We cannot say of every man that he stands on his own feet. Nothing in the world is worse than to be dependent, and if spirituality makes a man more dependent, in other words at the mercy of other people in the practical things of life, then spirituality is not to be wished for. Spirituality is mastery, both materially and spiritually: to be able to manage oneself and to be able to keep the mechanism right.

THE SMILING FOREHEAD

BY FOREHEAD I mean a person's expression, which depends solely upon his attitude to life. Life is the same for the saint and for Satan; and if their lives are different it is only because of their outlook on life. The same life is turned by the one into heaven and by the other into hell.

There are two attitudes: to one all is wrong; to the other all is right. Our life in the world from morning to evening is full of experiences, good and bad, which can be distinguished according to their degree; and the more we study the mystery of good and bad, the more we see that there really is no such thing as good and bad. It is because of our attitude and the conditions that things seem good or bad to us.

It is easy for an ordinary person to say what is good or bad, just or unjust; it is very difficult for a wise man. Everyone, according to his outlook on life, turns things from bad to good and from good to bad, because everyone has his own grade of evolution and he reasons according to that. Sometimes one thing is subtler than others, and then it is difficult for him to judge. There was a time when Wagner's music was not understood, and another time when he was considered the greatest of musicians. Sometimes things are good in themselves, but our own evolution makes them seem not so good to us. What one considered good a few years ago, may not seem good at a later evolution. A child appreciates a doll most, later he will prefer the work of great sculptors.

This proves that at every step and degree of evolution man's idea of good and bad changes, and thus when one thinks about it one will understand that there is no such thing as right and wrong. If there is right, then all is right. No doubt there is a phase when man is a slave of what he has himself made right or wrong; but there is another phase in which he is master. This mastery comes from his realization of the fact that right and wrong are made by man's own attitude to life; and then right and wrong, good and bad, will be his slaves, because he knows that it is in his power to turn the one into the other.

This opens the door to another mystery of life which shows that as there is duality in each thing, so there is duality in every action. In everything that is just something unjust is hidden; and in everything that is bad something good; and then one begins to see how the world reacts to all one's actions: one person sees only the good and another only the bad. In Sufi terms this particular attitude is called *Hairat*, bewilderment; and while to the average man theatres, moving pictures, and bazaars are interesting, so to the Sufi the whole of life is interesting, a constant vision of bewilderment. He cannot explain this to the world, because there are no words to explain it.

Can one compare any joy to that of taking things quietly, patiently, and easily? All other joys come from outer sources, but this happiness is one's own property. When a person arrives at this feeling, it expresses itself not in words but in the 'smiling forehead.'

There is another side to this subject, which is that man is pleased to see the one he loves and admires and respects; and if he frowns at someone, it is because it is someone he does not admire or respect. Love is the divine essence in man and is due to God alone; and love for man is a lesson, a first step forward to the love of God. In human love one begins to see the way to divine love, as the lesson of domestic life is learnt by the little girl playing with her dolls. One learns this lesson by loving one person, a friend, a beloved father, mother, brother, sister, or teacher. But love is wrongly used when it is not constantly developing and spreading. The water of a pond may turn bad, but the water of a river remains pure because it is progressing, and thus by sincerely loving one person, one should rear the plant of love and make it grow and spread at the same time.

Love has done its work when a man becomes all love—his atmosphere, his expression, every movement he makes. And how can such a man love one and refuse another? His very countenance and presence become a blessing. In the East, when people speak of saints or sages it is not because of their miracles, it is because of their presence and their countenance which radiate vibrations of love; and this love expresses itself in tolerance, in forgiveness, in respect, in overlooking the faults of others. Their sympathy covers the defects of others as if they were their own; they forget their own interest in the interest of others. They do not mind what circumstances they are in, be they high or humble; their foreheads are smiling. In their eyes everyone is the expression of the Beloved, whose name they repeat. They see the divine in all forms and beings.

Just as the religious person has a religious attitude in a temple, so the Sufi has that attitude before every being, for to him every being is the temple of the divine. Therefore he is always before his Lord. Whether a servant, a master, a friend, or a foe is before him, he is in the presence of God. For the one whose God is in the high heavens, there is a vast gulf between him and God; but the one who has God always before him is always in God's presence, and there is no end to his happiness.

The idea of the Sufi is that however religious a person may be, without love he is nothing. It is the same with one who has studied thousands of books; without love, he has learnt nothing. And love does not reside in a claim to love; when love is born one hears its voice louder than the voice of man. Love needs no words; they are too inadequate to express it. In what small fashion love can express itself, is in what the Persians call the 'Smiling Forehead'.

THE SPELL OF LIFE

ONE SOMETIMES wonders why God made man so weak that he is often liable to be bad, and one may even think that this is very unjust of God. But it is not so, and this point is very well explained in a story from the Arabian Nights.

There was a king who had a servant who was a great drunkard. Once, wishing to amuse himself, the king told the other servants to give the man a lot to drink and to put him into his own bed when he was completely overcome. When the day broke, there were musicians playing, as was the custom, and ten or twelve girls were singing in the king's room to waken him.

When the servant awoke he thought, 'What has happened to me? Last night I was a servant; now I am in the king's bed and everything is kingly! Am I a servant or am I a king?' When he looked at the girls, they all bowed. Every one called him 'Your Majesty'.

He got up and went out. Then he came to the Durbar. There he was seated on a throne and all the vizirs came, bowed before him, and presented their addresses. He thought, 'I must be a king. If I had only been a king in the bedroom, it would have been nothing, but here too everyone bows and says "Your Majesty!"'

The whole day he enjoyed his kingship. But in the evening his wife came. The night before, when he did not come home, she had thought that perhaps he was lying drunk somewhere. She looked for him everywhere, and when she could not find him she went to the palace. No one stopped her, because the king had given his orders. When her husband saw her he looked at her as if she were death; he thought, 'I cannot be a king, because if I were, my wife would not be here. I shall have to go with her!' She said, 'What are you doing here? You did not come home; I have had no food, and you are enjoying yourself here. Come with me.' He said, 'I do not know you; go away.' But she said, 'You are my husband, come with me.' And she dragged him away, while he kept on saying, 'I am a king, I am a king.'

It is the situation we are in which makes us believe we are this or that. Whatever the soul experiences, that it believes itself to be. If the soul sees the external self as a baby it believes: I am a baby. If it sees the external self as old it believes: I am old. If it sees the external self in a palace it believes: I am rich. If it sees that self in a hut it believes: I am poor. But in reality it is only: I am.

This is the spell of life, by which man is spellbound. Hafiz says, 'Before our birth, Thou gavest us a draught of wine.' And Jami says, 'O Saki, wine-giver, forgive me, it is my youth. Sometimes I embrace, the wine-bottle and kiss it. Sometimes I throw it away.' So are we all. A child's doll is sometimes embraced and kissed, and at another time it is thrown on the floor and broken, and something else is taken up instead. At one time we say that a person is our friend, and at another we say he is our enemy. At one time we say that we like this nation, that race; at another it is our enemy. According to our childishness we change.

Man in his dream of life is always running after the passing clouds. And when does he awaken? When the wife comes. And what is the wife? The wife is the destructiveness of nature; and when she comes as death he sees that all that he has and all that he calls his own will be left behind: his name, his fame, his possessions. Everything is for those who live, and for him there is only the grave. He can take nothing with him. Then he realizes that none of these things can give him everlasting peace and satisfaction, and he looks for something which can give him these.

It is only a question of his ego, his consciousness. There is a saying in Hindustani, 'The humility of the wise is not lost. The seed goes into the dust to become a plant.' When the wise man has humiliated himself in the dust, this dust will make him flourish. This is not the same as mastery, although it prepares him for the higher grades.

The Qur'an says, 'Mutu kubla anta Mutu.' Die before death. The Sufi dies before his death, and experiences in life what the condition will be after death. In other words, he invites his wife to visit him, and welcomes her through his kingship, so that he may not have to be dragged away by her but may even enjoy life with her, with his wife on earth; in other words: he becomes living dead.

When a person has understood intellectually that all this manifestation has come from one Being, he is inclined to say, 'What should we worship, what should we adore, if we ourselves are all? Or whom should we fear?' But he forgets his own person; if he is composed of so many different organs and different atoms and planes and yet can be a person at the same time, why should not the whole Being be a person? We know intellectually that all are one. But when someone insults us, we cannot bear it, we no longer think that he is the same as we are. When someone has done us harm, we blame him; we do not stop to think that he is the same as ourselves, so why should we blame him?

SELFLESSNESS

SELFLESSNESS, called *Enkesar* by the Sufis, not only beauti-
fies one's personality, giving grace to one's word and manner,
but it also gives dignity and power together with a spirit of
independence, which is the real sign of a sage. It is selflessness
which often produces humbleness in one's spirit, taking away the
intoxication which clouds the soul. Independence and indifference,
which are as two wings which enable the soul to fly, spring from
the spirit of selflessness. The moment the spirit of selflessness has
begun to sparkle in the heart of man, he shows in his word and
action a nobility which no earthly power or wealth can give.

There are many ideas which intoxicate man, many feelings
which act upon the soul like wine, but there is no stronger wine
than the wine of selflessness. It is a might and it is a pride that no
worldly rank can give. To become something is a limitation,
whatever it may be; even if a person were to be called the king of
the world, he would still not be the emperor of the universe.
The master of the earth is still the slave of heaven. The selfless
man is he who is no one and yet is all.

The Sufi, therefore, takes the path of being nothing instead of
being something. It is this feeling of nothingness which turns the
human heart into an empty cup into which the wine of immortality is poured. It is this state of bliss which every truth-seeking soul
yearns to attain. It is easy to be learned and it is not very difficult
to be wise; it is within one's reach to become good; but there is an
attainment which is greater and higher than all these things, and
this is to be nothing. It may seem frightening to many, the idea of
becoming nothing, for human nature is such that it is eager to hold
on to something, and the self holds on to its own personality, its
own individuality. Once one has risen above this, one has climbed
Mount Everest; one has arrived at the spot where the earth ends
and heaven begins.

The whole aim of the Sufi is, by the thought of God, to cover
his imperfect self even from his own eyes; and that moment when

God is before him and not his own self, is the moment of perfect bliss to him. My murshid, Abu Hashim Madani, once said that there is only one virtue and one sin for a soul on this path: virtue when he is conscious of God, and sin when he is not. No explanation can fully describe the truth of this except the experience of the contemplative, to whom when he is conscious of God it is as if a window facing heaven were open, and to whom when he is conscious of the self the experience is the opposite. For all the tragedy of life is caused by being conscious of the self. All pain and depression are caused by this, and anything that can take away the thought of the self helps to a certain extent to relieve man from pain; but God-consciousness gives perfect relief.

THE CONSERVATIVE SPIRIT

THERE ARE two different points of view open to one about everything in the world: liberal and conservative, and each of these points of view gives a person a sense of satisfaction, because in both there is a certain amount of virtue. When someone looks at his family from the conservative point of view he becomes conscious of family pride and acts in every way so as to keep up the honour and dignity of his ancestors. He follows the chivalry of his forefathers and by looking at it from this point of view he defends and protects those who belong to his family, whether worthy or unworthy. In this way he helps to keep going a flame which has perhaps been alight for many years, by holding it in his hand all through life as a torch to guide his way. And when one looks at one's nation from a conservative point of view it gives one a feeling of patriotism, which is the substitute for religion in the modern world. It is no doubt a virtue, in the sense that one begins to consider one's whole nation as one family. It is not only for one's own children that one cares, but also for the children of the whole nation. Man gives his life when occasion arises to defend his nation, or the dignity, the honour, and the freedom of his people.

The conservative spirit is the individualizing spirit, which is the central theme of the whole of creation. It is the spirit which has functioned as the sun; but for this spirit there would be only the all-pervading light, and it is its power working in nature which keeps many branches together on one stem and a number of leaves together on one branch. Again, it is this spirit working in man's body which keeps man's hands and feet together, thus keeping him an individual entity. But there is always a danger that this spirit, if increased, may produce congestion. When there is too much family pride man lives only in his pride, forgetting his duty towards mankind and not recognizing anything which unites him with others beyond the limited circle of his family. When this congestion is produced in a nation it results in all kinds of disasters, such as wars and revolutions with violence and destruction. The nightmare that humanity has recently experienced has been the outcome of world-congestion produced by the extreme of this same spirit.

This shows that it is not true that virtue is one thing and sin another. The same thing which was once virtue may become sin. Virtue or sin is not any action; it is the condition, it is the attitude which prompts one to a certain action, and it is the outcome of an action which makes it a sin or a virtue. Life is movement, death is the stopping of the movement; congestion stops it, circulation moves it. The conservative spirit is useful in so far as it is moving, in other words, as it is broadening itself. If a person who is proud of his family, after doing his duty to his own people takes the next step which is to help his fellow-citizens, and the third step which is to defend his nation, he is progressing. Both his family pride and his patriotism are no doubt virtues, for they lead him from one thing to another which is better.

Congestion comes when a person is absorbed in his own interest. If he is so taken up with his family and its pride and interest that nobody else in the world exists to him except his own people, then his patriotism becomes a veil over his eyes, making him blind so that he is neither able to serve others nor even his own. In selfishness there is an illusion of profit, but in the end the profit attained by selfishness proves to be worthless. Life is the principal thing to consider, and true life is the inner life, the realization of God, the consciousness of one's spirit. When the human heart becomes conscious of God it is like a bubble which turns into the sea; it spreads and it extends the waves of its love to both friend and foe; and spreading further and further it attains perfection.

CHARACTER-BUILDING

CHARACTER is, so to speak, a picture with lines and colours which we make within ourselves. It is wonderful to see how the tendency of character-building springs up already in childhood, just as one sees in a bird the instinct of building a nest. A child begins by noticing all kinds of things in grown-up people, and then it adopts whatever it likes most and whatever attracts it. By this we understand that when a person is absorbed in himself he has no time for character-building, for he has no time to think of others. For instance, if even the greatest actors do not forget themselves on the stage, they cannot act. The musician, if he cannot forget himself while playing, cannot play well. As with everything else, the whole task of building oneself depends entirely on forgetting oneself; and this is the key to the whole of life. I have met people distinguished in art, science, philosophy, religion, in all fields, and found that they had all reached greatness by means of this quality, the quality of forgetting themselves; and again I have seen people with great qualities but who could not bring out the best in their lives because they did not possess this one quality.

I remember a vina-player, a very wonderful musician, who used to play and study many hours a day, but whenever he had to play before an audience he became self-conscious. The first thought that came to him was himself; and when that happened all the impressions of the people there would fall upon him. Generally he would then take his vina, cover it up, and run away. But on the other hand I have heard Sarah Bernhardt simply recite the Marseillaise, that was all; but when she appeared on the stage and recited this poem, she would win every heart in the audience, for at that time—it was during the war—she was France. What enabled her to be France was her concentration, her way of forgetting herself.

Character-building is much greater and more important than the building of a house, a city, a nation, or an empire. One might ask why it is so important, as it is only the building of our insignificant self, but many have built an edifice, or even a nation, and they are gone and there is no memory of them left. The Taj Mahal is one of the most wonderful buildings in the world. Those who see it—artists, architects—have a great admiration for it, but that is all; no one cares who made it; no one's heart is moved on account of the builder.

To this day the Hindus repeat, early in the morning, 'Ram, Ram'; the Buddhists call on the Lord Buddha and the Christians on Christ. Why? Only because of the personality of these holy ones, of the magnetism that was theirs. The words of Christ spoken so many hundreds of years ago are remembered today simply because of his personality. It is not spirituality alone: there have been many madzubs who were very spiritual. They were united with God, but they have gone and no one remembers them. It is not piety: there are many pious people sitting in the mosques and the churches telling their rosaries. Their piety is for themselves; they cannot move the world. So if it is not spirituality and not piety, what is it then? It is the development of humanity in us.

This development concerns our intelligence, our heart, and our mind. It concerns the intelligence because if we have love, but no intelligence to know the pleasure of the beloved, then we can be a great lover, but our love will be of no avail. It concerns the heart, because if we have intelligence but no feeling, no sympathy, we may speak very politely, we may be very polished in manner, but if there is bitterness within, if we do not feel what we say, it would be better if we had not said anything. It concerns the mind, because if we have intelligence and feeling but no thoughtfulness, no sense of what is appropriate, we are ignorant. One may be well acquainted with European manners and decorum, but if one is sent to the court of an Eastern king, one will be at a loss. Or a person may know all the etiquette of an Indian court, but if he comes to Europe he knows nothing about Western ways.

It is a great privilege to be human, so that we can develop our humanity and be human in mind, in reality as well as in form. The privilege consists in being man, who is the ideal of God.

It is not the rock, which does not know whether a king or a

beggar, a holy man, or a wicked person stands upon it. It is not the angels, who have no heart to feel with and for another; they feel the praise of God, they praise God. It is man who has been given a heart.

A Hindustani poet says, 'To become Nabi, a saint or prophet, Ghauth, Qutb, is very difficult. What shall I tell you of the struggles of their life, since it is even difficult for man to become human?' Indeed, to attain to spiritual grades is very difficult. We should first try to become human. To become an angel is not very difficult; to be material is very easy; but to live in the world, in all the difficulties and struggles of the world, and to be human at the same time, is very difficult. If we become that then we become the miniature of God on earth.

RESPECT AND CONSIDERATION

THERE IS a virtue which the Sufi calls *Muruat*, a virtue which is too delicate to express in words. It means refraining from certain actions out of respect for someone else, whether in consideration for his age, position, knowledge, goodness, or piety. Those who practise this virtue do not do so only towards someone important or pious, for when this quality develops it manifests in one's dealings with everyone.

Muruat is the opposite of bluntness. It is not necessarily respect; it is something more delicate than that; it is both consideration and respect together. In its full development this virtue may even become so intense that a person out of consideration and respect tries to bear with the lack of the same virtue in another; but when one arrives at that stage the human manner ends, and the saintly manner begins. Man is not born into this world only to eat, drink, and make merry; he is born in order to perfect the human character. The way he realizes this is by great thoughtfulness and consideration; otherwise, with all power, position, wealth, learning, and all the good things of the world, he remains poor if he lacks this richness of the soul which is good manner.

All the beauty which surrounds us is something which is outside of us; the only beauty which is dependable is to be found and developed in our own character. A person may show lack of Muruat, if not in words, in his glance. One does not need to speak in order to be rude. In one's look, in one's intonation, in one's manner of standing or walking, in the way one closes the door on leaving the room, one can show one's feelings. Even if one does not speak, one can make the door speak. It is not an easy matter to control oneself when one's mind is out of hand.

Delicate ideas such as these are most difficult to learn and practise in life. And today many wonder if they are not weaknesses;

but something that can only be practised by mastering oneself can never be a weakness. There is no loss even if thought or consideration is given to someone who does not deserve it; for if such an action did not bring any profit, it was still practice; and it is practice which makes a man perfect.

GRACIOUSNESS

AS SOON as the soul touches the inner kingdom, which is the divine kingdom, its true nobility becomes manifest in the form of graciousness or *Khulk* as the Sufis call it. Kings and those belonging to aristocratic families were trained to be gracious, yet it is a quality born in the heart of man. This means that every soul shows the aristocratic manner from the moment it touches the inner kingdom. Thus true aristocracy is the nobility of the soul: when the soul begins to express in every feeling, thought, word, and action that graciousness which belongs to God Himself. Graciousness is quite different from a patronizing attitude, which is a wrong manner. A gracious person, before expressing that noble attribute, tries to hide himself even from his own eyes.

The reason why the great ones, the truly noble people, are gracious, is that they are more sensitive to all the hurt and harm that comes to them from those who are unripe and try therefore out of kindness to keep themselves from doing the same to someone else, however lowly his position.

There is a great truth in what Christ has said in the sermon on the mount, 'Blessed are the meek: for they shall inherit the earth.' This will always prove true whatever be the age and whatever the evolution of the world. Whether it be a time of aristocracy, or whether it be a time of democracy, the value of that nobility of nature which is expressed in graciousness will always command its price. It is easy to use this word, but it is most difficult to practise it through life, for there is no end to the thought one has to give to every action in life in order to achieve it. It needs judgment and a sense of fairness, of weighing and measuring all one does; besides it needs a fine sense of art and beauty, for in perfecting the personality one attains to the highest degree of art. Verily, the making of the personality is the highest form of art there is. The Sufi considers the cultivation of human attributes, in which lies the fulfilment of the purpose of his life, as his religion.

A young man one day showed some impatience with his aged

QSM

father, who could not hear very clearly any more and asked him two or three times to repeat what he had said. Seeing the irritated expression on his face, the father said, 'My son, do you remember that there was a day when you were a little child and you asked me what a certain bird was and I told you: a sparrow? You asked me perhaps fifty times, and I had the patience to repeat it to you again and again without being hurt or troubled about it; I was only pleased to tell you all I knew. Now when I can no longer hear so well, you can at least have patience with me and explain something twice if I did not hear you the first time.' What is needed most in order to learn that noble manner of life is patience, sometimes in the form of endurance, sometimes in the form of consideration, and sometimes in the form of forgiveness.

In dealing with people who lack education one should keep in mind that real civilization means progress. Those who are not educated should be educated to understand life better. There are only two possibilities: to go forward or to go backward. Either one will begin to think like those who are not educated, or one must help the one who is uneducated to advance; one must take the one who is uneducated gently by the hand and lead him towards more beautiful ideas.

Once in India I was staying near a Hindu temple, and there were two porters who took care of that temple. They were Afghans, proud and rough, and rigid in their behaviour; yet in their expression there was honesty and goodness. Often I passed that way and every time they ignored my entering and leaving, lest they should have the trouble of observing the conventional politeness. One day one of them came to me with a message from his master. I got up from my seat and received him most cordially; and since that day, every time I passed I was very well received, with smiles and a very cordial welcome, and they ignored me no more. This happened because education was given to him without hurting his feelings, and as that gave him pleasure he thought he would return the politeness.

To force a virtue upon anyone is pride; to let him see the beauty of good manners is an education. We should consider it our sacred task to approach the people who need improving with such gentleness and with such a manner that culture and beauty are developed in them, which will then be shared by us both.

OVERLOOKING

THERE IS a tendency which gradually manifests in a person who is advancing spiritually, and that tendency is overlooking, or *Darguza* as the Sufis call it. At times this tendency might appear to be negligence, but negligence is not overlooking; negligence is not looking. In other words overlooking may be called rising above things. One has to rise in order to overlook; the one who stands beneath life could not overlook anything even if he wanted to. Overlooking is a manner of graciousness, it means to look and at the same time not to look, to see and not take notice of being seen, not to be hurt or harmed or disturbed by something, not even minding it. It is an attribute of nobleness of nature, it is the sign of souls who are tuned to a higher key.

One may ask, is it practical? Perhaps not always, but in the end it is practical all the same; the one who overlooks will also realize the practicality of it. Perhaps he will only realize this at last, after he has met all its numerous disadvantages; nevertheless, all is well that ends well.

Very often overlooking costs less than taking notice of something that could well be overlooked. In life there are things which matter and there are things which do not matter; and as one advances through life one finds there are many things that do not matter, that one could just as well overlook. The one who takes notice of everything that comes his way, will waste time on a journey which takes all his life to accomplish. While climbing the mountain of life, the purpose of which is to reach the top, if a person troubles about everything that comes along he will never be able to reach the top; he will always be troubling about everything at its foot. After having realized that life on this earth lasts only a few days, a person will not trouble any more about little things; he will only trouble about things which really matter. By striving for little things a person loses the opportunity of accomplishing great things in life. One who troubles about small things is small; the soul who thinks of great things is great.

Overlooking is the first lesson of forgiveness. This tendency comes out of love and sympathy; for when one hates one takes notice of every little fault, but when one loves another one naturally overlooks the faults, and very often one tries to turn the faults of the beloved into merits. Life has endless things which suggest beauty, and numberless things which suggest ugliness; there is no end to the merits and no end to the faults, and one's outlook on life is according to one's evolution.

The higher one has risen, the wider one's horizon becomes. The tendency to sympathize, which is an analytical tendency, weighing and measuring and taking good notice of everything, brings a person the desire to overlook. Judge not, said Christ, lest ye be judged. The more one thinks of this lesson, the deeper it goes into one's heart, and what one learns from it is to try and overlook all that does not fit in with one's own ideas as to how things ought to be in life, until one comes to a stage of realization where the whole of life seems one sublime vision of the immanence of God.

CONCILIATION

ANY EFFORTS made in developing the personality or in character-building must be made not for the sake of proving oneself superior to others, but in order to become more agreeable to those around one and to those with whom we come in contact. Conciliation, or *Ettefaq* as it is called by the Sufis, is not only the moral of the Sufi, but it is the sign of the Sufi. This virtue is not learned and practised easily, for it needs not only goodwill but wisdom. The great talent of the diplomat is to bring about the desired results by agreement. Disagreement is easy; among the lower creation one sees it so often; what is difficult is agreement, for it requires a wider outlook, which is the true sign of spirituality. Narrowness of outlook makes the horizon of man's vision small; the person with a narrow outlook cannot easily agree with another. There is always a meeting-ground for two people, however much they differ in thought; but the meeting-ground may be far off, and a man is not always willing to take the trouble to go so far, in order to come to an agreement. Very often his patience does not allow him to go far enough to meet another. What generally happens is that everyone wants the other to meet him where he himself is standing, and there is no desire on his part to move from there.

This does not mean that a person in order to become a real Sufi must give up his ideas so that he may meet in agreement with another; and there is no benefit in always being lenient with every thought that comes from somebody else, nor is there any benefit in always erasing one's own idea from one's heart. That is not conciliation. The one who is able to listen to another is the one who will make another listen to him. It is the one who agrees easily with another who will have the power of making another agree readily with him. Therefore in doing so one really gains in spite of the apparent loss which might sometimes occur. When man is able to see both from his own point of view and from the point of view of another, he has a complete vision and a clear insight; he so to speak sees with both eyes.

No doubt friction produces light, but light is the agreement of the atoms. It is a stimulus to thought if two people have their own ideas and argue about them, and in that way it does not matter so much; but when a person argues for the sake of argument, the argument becomes his object and he gets no satisfaction out of conciliation. Words provide the means of disagreement, reasons become the fuel for the fire; but wisdom resides where the intelligence is pliable; then one understands all things, both the wrong of the right and the right of the wrong. The man who arrives at perfect knowledge has risen above right and wrong. He knows them and yet he does not know, he can say much and yet what can he say? Then it becomes easy for him to conciliate each and all.

There is a story that two Sufis met after many years, having travelled their separate ways. They were glad to meet each other after many years of separation because they were both mureeds of the same murshid. One said to the other, 'Tell me, please, what has been your experience. After all this time of study and practice of Sufism I have learned one thing: how to conciliate others; and I can do it very well now. Will you please tell me what you have learned?' The other one said, 'After all this time of study and practice of Sufism I have learned how to master life; all that exists in this world is for me, and I am the master. All that happens, happens by my will.' Then came the murshid, whose mureeds they had been, and they both told him about their experiences during their travels. The murshid said, 'Both of you are right. In the case of the first it was self-denial in the right sense of the word which enabled him to conciliate others; in the case of the other there was nothing left of his will; if there was any will, it was the Will of God.'

OPTIMISM AND PESSIMISM

OPTIMISM represents the spontaneous flow of love; optimism also represents trust in love. This shows that it is love trusting love which is optimism. Pessimism comes from a disappointment, from a bad impression which continues to be a hindrance on the path. Optimism gives a hopeful attitude to life, while with pessimism one sees darkness on one's path. No doubt sometimes pessimism shows conscientiousness and cleverness, and it may also show experience. But conscientiousness alone will never be enough to overcome the difficulties one meets in one's life; it is trust that solves its problems. The wise have understood that cleverness does not reach far; it goes a certain distance and then no further, for cleverness is knowledge which belongs to the earth. And as to experience, what is man's experience? One is only proud of one's experience until one has seen how vast the world is. In every line of work and thought there is no moment when experience is not needed, but the further man goes in experience the more he sees how little he knows.

The psychological effect of optimism is such that it helps to bring success, for it is by the spirit of optimism that God has created the world. Optimism comes from God, and pessimism is born from the heart of man. By what little experience of life he has, man learns, 'This will not succeed, that will not do, this will not come right'. For the one who is optimistic it does not matter if it does not come right in the end; he will take his chance. For what is life? Life is an opportunity, and to the optimistic person this opportunity is a promise, while for the pessimistic person this opportunity is lost. It is not that the Creator makes man lose it, but it is man himself who fails to seize the opportunity.

Many people prolong an illness by giving way to pessimistic thoughts. One will often find that for those who have suffered for many years from a certain illness, that illness becomes so real that its absence seems unnatural. They believe illness to be their nature, and its absence is something they do not know; and in that way they keep the illness in themselves. Then there are pessimistic people who think that misery is their lot in life, that they were born to be wretched, that they cannot be anything else but unhappy, that heaven and earth are against them; but they themselves are their misery, and pessimism belongs to them. Man's life depends upon the object of his concentration, so if he concentrates upon his misery, he must be miserable. A person who has a certain habit of which he does not approve, often thinks he is helpless before it as it is his nature; but nothing is man's nature except what he makes for himself. As the whole of nature is made by God, so the nature of each individual is made by himself; and as the Almighty has the power to change His nature, so the individual is capable of changing his nature. Among all the creatures of this world, man has the most right to be optimistic, for man represents God on earth, God as Judge, as Creator, and as Master of all His creation. Man is master of his life, of his own affairs—if he only knew it.

A man with optimism will help another who is drowning in the sea of fear and disappointment; while on the contrary, if someone who is ill or downhearted comes to a pessimistic person, that pessimist will pull him down and make him sink to the depths together with himself. On the side of the one is life, on the side of the other is death. The one climbs to the top of the mountain, the other descends to the depths of the earth. Is there any greater helper in sorrow or misfortune, when every situation in life seems dark, than the spirit of optimism which knows that all will be well? It is no exaggeration to say that the very spirit of God comes to man's rescue in the form of the optimistic spirit.

It does not matter how hard a situation in life may be, however great the difficulties, they can all be surmounted; but a person's own pessimistic spirit weighs him down when he is already at a low ebb. Death is preferable to being weighed down in misery by a pessimistic spirit, and the greatest reward there can be in the world is the spirit of optimism, while the greatest punishment that can be given to man for his worst sin is pessimism. Verily, the one who is hopeful in life will succeed.

HAPPINESS

DOES happiness depend upon circumstances or upon our outlook on life? It is a question that is often asked, and is most difficult to answer. Many with some philosophical knowledge will say that this material world is an illusion and its conditions a dream, but yet there are very few who can make themselves believe it. To know a thing in theory is different from practising it. It is very difficult to rise above the effect that conditions produce. No doubt there is only one thing that helps us to rise above conditions, and that is a change of outlook on life; and this change is made possible by a change of attitude.

Happiness is a flourishing condition of the soul. A child which has started by being ill-mannered, hurtful, and destructive, will attract the same power, and the same things will happen to it. Whatever the child gives out will rebound. How many people are acquainted with this fact? They never think that they can be hurt by their own words, their own action, thought, or feeling; they go on, and then in time it all comes back to them, sweeping them off the ground of happiness.

In Sanskrit life in the world is called *Sansara*. It is pictured as living in a mist. One thinks and says and does and feels, yet all the time one does not fully know why. If a person knows one reason for it, there is another reason hidden behind it which he does not yet know. Very often conditions in life give the effect of captivity; sometimes it seems as if one has to walk between a river and a precipice; and to rise above conditions one needs wings, which not everyone has got. Two wings are attached to the soul: one is independence, the other indifference. It needs a great deal of sacrifice before one can feel independent in life, and indifference is against one's nature of love and sympathy; it is as if one has to cut one's heart in two before one can practise indifference throughout life. No doubt when once the soul is able to spread its wings one sees the conditions of life as being far removed; then one stands above all conditions that make man captive.

There is no difficulty which cannot be surmounted sooner or later, but even if one has achieved something one desires in life there always remains something else that seems to be incomplete; and so if a person goes from one thing to another, achieving all he desires, the objects of his desire will multiply and there will never be an end to it. The more he has to do in life the more difficulties he must meet with, and if he keeps away from the life of the world then his being here is purposeless. The more important the task, the more difficult is its accomplishment.

And so the evening follows the day, and this goes on till eternity. For a Sufi, therefore, it is not only patience to bear all things that is necessary to relieve him momentarily from difficulty and pain, but also seeing all things from a certain point of view. Very often it is the outlook which changes a person's whole life. It can turn hell into heaven; it can turn sorrows into joy. When a person looks from a certain point of view, every little pinprick feels like the point of a sword piercing his heart, but when he looks at the same thing from a different point of view the heart becomes sting-proof; nothing can touch it; all the things which are thrown at him like stones drop down without having touched him.

What is the meaning of walking upon the water? Life can be symbolized as water: there is one who drowns in the water, there is another who swims in it, but there is still another who walks upon it. The one who is so sensitive that after one little pinprick he is unhappy all day and night, is the man of the first category. The one who takes and gives back, making a game of life, is the swimmer. He does not mind if he receives one knock, for he derives satisfaction from being able to give two knocks in return. But the one whom nothing can touch is in the world and yet above the world. He is the one who walks on the water; life is under his feet, both its joy and sorrow. Verily, independence and indifference are the two wings which enable the soul to fly.

VACCINATION AND INOCULATION

THE THEORY behind vaccination and inoculation is the same as the one taught as Hatha Yoga by Shiva, or Mahadeva as he is often called. It is said of Mahadeva that he used to drink poison, and by doing so he got over its effect. Mahadeva was the most venturesome among the ascetics. He is pictured carrying a serpent round his neck. If one can be such friends with a serpent as to keep it round one's neck, one can no doubt sit comfortably in the presence of someone one does not like. The hatred and prejudice and nervousness which are felt in the presence of someone one does not like would then not arise. The soul which has forgotten its battle with everything that made it fear and tremble and run away, has conquered life and has become the master of life; it attains the kingdom of heaven. No doubt the methods which Mahadeva adopted were extreme measures; no one could recommend them to his pupils and be thought sane in this modern world!

It is the same with vaccination. When new, such methods have met with a great deal of prejudice and opposition, yet there is much to be said for the principle behind them. It brings us to a higher realization of life, and makes us understand that even that which is called death, if it were put in a cup and given us to drink, could bring us life. By absorbing the destructive element in one's body, the body becomes destruction-proof, so that that particular destruction is no longer a destruction but becomes part of one's nature. This is the method of destruction from the spiritual point of view.

Death is death as long as man is not acquainted with it. When man absorbs it then he is master of death. That was the message of Jesus Christ, who spoke of eternal life from beginning to end; and the mystery of that message is that when once a person has absorbed death he has obtained eternal life.

People say, 'I do not like to touch vinegar, it harms my health; I cannot bear to eat cream, I cannot digest it; I cannot stand

sugar in my tea, I do not like it'. For them these things are poison.
By saying such things a person makes certain substances foreign,
exclusive, to his nature; and he thereby subjects himself to them.
There comes a time when they rule him, when he is in their power.
The way of Shiva was always to work against his own weaknesses.
Though he counted them as weaknesses and not as belonging to
his nature, he acted as if everything belonged to his nature and
absorbed all that was foreign to it in order that no situation would
arise where he would become subjected to it. Snake-charmers, by
making snakes bite them a little at a time, become inured to the
poison, and it was the same with Shiva: out of death he had made
a necklace. One can go to extremes in this way, but it is a law
which should be studied and which it is good to know. It teaches
us all that is to be found in us, all the destruction which is the
source of fear and pain and disappointment.

MARRIAGE

MARRIAGE is the most sacred of all sacred things. It is certainly not in the first place a contract, a business; when we look at marriage from a higher point of view, it appears that marriage is the fulfilment of life.

From a physical point of view, this life which is full of struggle and strife can be met with greater strength and greater courage and greater capability when two harmonious forces are united together. There is a saying of a Persian poet, 'When two hearts unite, they become powerful enough to remove mountains.' Life is a continual struggle. And in order to become capable of meeting this struggle, it is necessary to be strong and powerful. When two hearts are united they are more capable, more powerful, and greatly blessed.

Looking at marriage from a mental point of view, no matter how wise, how strong, how courageous, how powerful a person is, he still lacks something. Every individual, after all, has defects. No matter how many merits he has, he needs something better: at the time of doubt, conviction; at the time of anxiety, support from another source; at the time of confusion, a little light; at the time of sorrow, a word of consolation, of happiness. No matter what a person has—wealth, power, rank, position—this will not balance his life. If there is anything that will balance his life, it is another soul to provide that which is missing at the moment when he needs it in his life. Therefore from a physical point of view marriage is a power, and from a mental point of view it brings balance.

Lastly there is the spiritual point of view. Among the ancient people the wise gave an answer to the ever-recurring question as to why the world was created; and this answer was that God felt lonely. And no matter how many rays of the light of wisdom we may throw upon life, we shall always receive this one answer as the reason for creation: that if anything exists it is only one Being, and that is God. Therefore the whole of manifestation which is created by Him, is in Himself. If God created it, it was only because He felt lonely. It is the same idea that can be seen symbolically in the belief of the ancient people, that Eve was created out of the rib of Adam. It only means that this world was created out of God Himself; that it is God's own manifestation. He wanted to see, in order to remove the monotony of being alone; and if it was the need of God to create something and put it before Himself to remove the monotony of being alone, it is natural that every human being has this inclination too. But this inclination leads to what? To greater perfection; because an individual man is limited, no matter how powerful, how great, how wise and learned he may be, and in order to become greater he must become another person.

Marriage is the first step towards becoming another person. The one who formerly thought that he would attain pleasure, comfort, happiness in life, and enjoy it for himself, from the moment he is married thinks first of his wife and of how he can give her comfort; for without her he can no-longer enjoy life.

When this outlook comes to a person, his consciousness changes. It rises and expands and becomes the source of all revelation and bliss. Why is it so? Because by this expansion the spirit of God becomes awakened in man. It removes what stands between his limited and his unlimited self, and gradually raises him to a stage where he fully realizes the One who is his source and goal, who is the essence of his being. As Rumi says, 'Whether you have loved man or whether you have loved God, if you have loved enough you will be brought in the end into the presence of the supreme Love itself'.

From a spiritual point of view, therefore, marriage is a step forward on the path to perfection, that path by which the ultimate purpose of life is attained.

LOVE

IN REALITY wisdom is love and love is wisdom, although in one person wisdom may be predominant and in another love. The cold-hearted man is never wise, nor is the really warm-hearted person foolish; yet both these qualities, love and wisdom, are distinct and separate, and it is possible that a person may be loving but lacking in wisdom. It may also happen that a person who is wise is lacking in love to some extent; but no one can be wise if love is absent from his heart, and no one will be truly loving if wisdom had not illuminated his heart, for love comes from wisdom and wisdom comes from love.

It is very difficult to say what love is, and how one should love. Is it embracing people and running after them and saying pleasant things to them? Not everyone finds it easy to show his love. One person perhaps has a love hidden in his heart, and another person's love comes out in his words. The love of one person changes the whole atmosphere, and that of another is like a spark hidden in a stone. To judge who has love and who has not is very difficult. There is love for instance which seems as if it comes from a cracker, calling out,' I am love', but it burns out and is gone. There is also love like a spark in a pebble; it may never manifest. and if you hold the pebble it feels cold, but at the same time it is there, it is dependable and it lasts; therefore one can never judge.

In the East there is a well-known story about a young man called Hakim and a princess who was renowned for her beauty. There were many who loved her and wanted to marry her, but she had made a condition: that the one who brought her a certain pearl which she longed to possess would be accepted. There was one lover of this princess who loved her perhaps more than anybody else, but he could not find a way of getting that pearl. Now Hakim's task in life was to roam about from country to country doing what he could for those who needed his services. He met this lover who was very unhappy; and Hakim consoled him and said,

'Continue in your pursuit of love even if it be difficult, and remember that I shall go on until I have brought rest to your heart by finding for you the pearl you are looking for'. Hakim went in pursuit of the pearl, and the story goes on to tell what difficulties he had in obtaining it. At last he got it and brought it to the palace, and then the princess was so impressed by Hakim that she declared that she wanted him as her husband. But Hakim told her of the promise he had made to his friend, who was her real lover. He himself was the lover of those in need.

The explanation of this story is that the princess represents God, and the pearl the knowledge of God. And the lover in the story is a lover of God who, however, does not want to take the trouble which is necessary to obtain the pearl. But there was someone else ready to delve deeper, even if it were not for himself but for others, in order to get the knowledge and give it to them. Thus there are two types of workers. The first type is the one who works for himself, but at a higher stage is the one whose task is doing work for others; he brings into the life of others that blessing which is their need.

Why is it, one may ask, that as love grows difficulties arise from all sides? This happens because before one fell in love one was unconsciously linked with the source alone; but when once love has awakened on the physical plane, one becomes attached to someone on earth. It is like Adam and Eve being exiled from the garden of Eden. This naturally causes every influence to work against one; even the throne of God is shaken by love's outburst, for by a sincere link on earth, which is very powerful, every other influence is automatically pulled and pushed, thereby causing a commotion in the world of the heart. The soul of man is happiness; yet man is never really happy since he is occupied with the world of woes. It is only love that can being about that happiness which is spoken of in legends, that happiness which is beyond all the pleasures of this mortal world. And those who see or feel, consciously or unconsciously, the happiness experienced by the lover and the beloved, naturally either knowingly or unknowingly react against it.

The love of God is everywhere in nature; yet we see destruction and misery and inequalities all around us. It is a difference of focus.

If we focus our mind upon all that is good and beautiful we shall see God's love in spite of all the ugliness that exists in nature and especially in human nature. In doing so we will spread a cover over it; and by collecting everything beautiful in us we will be able to give to whatever lacks beauty from the supply in our own heart. But if we focus our attention upon ugliness it will grow in us, and there will come a time when we shall not be able to see any good anywhere; everywhere we look we will only see cruelty, unkindness, wickedness, and ugliness.

One may ask if in focusing one's mind on beauty alone, one is not in danger of shutting one's eyes to the ugliness and suffering one might otherwise alleviate. The answer is that in order to help the poor one needs to be rich, and in order to take away evil from a person one needs to have so much more good. That goodness has to be earned as money is earned; and that earning means collecting goodness wherever we find it. What happens is that man becomes agitated by the abundance of goodness that he sees; being himself poor he cannot add to it, and then he is drawn towards evil. Although he may unconsciously develop in his own nature a craving for the goodness he sees, that does not help him in his agitation; his looking at evil only adds another wicked person to the whole.

The one whose eyes are focused on beauty in time will join the good; he is getting the same impressions but the result is different. Besides, by criticizing, by judging, by looking at wickedness with contempt, one does not help the one who needs it. The person who is ready to overlook, forgive, and patiently tolerate all those disadvantages that he may have to meet with, is the one who can help.

One should love for the sake of love, not for a return. When one serves, one should serve for the sake of serving, not for acknowledgment or appreciation in any shape or form. In the beginning such a person may perhaps seem a loser, but in the end he will be the gainer, for he has lived in the world while yet holding himself above the world; the world cannot touch him. Yet if one asks whether one can separate jealousy from love, it is like asking whether one can separate the shadow from the body. Where there is human love there is jealousy.

Furthermore, the tendency to doubt, the tendency to distress, the tendency to fear, suspicion, and confusion, where does it all come from? It all comes from the thought of getting something in return, anxiety as to whether anyone will give one back what one has given him. That is the thought behind it. And as to doubt, what is doubt? Doubt which gathers round the soul is like a cloud passing before the sun, keeping its light from shining out. But the unselfish one has good reason for his trust; he looks through the clouds and says, 'What do I care if I am not rewarded, I don't mind. I know what to do: give service; that is all the satisfaction I want. I do not look for anything in return. This is where my duty ends.' He is blessed because he has conquered; he has won his battle.

It is through lack of knowledge of divine justice that man doubts. He always wonders whether he will get his right portion or whether another will get it, or whether someone will get the better of him. If one would only look up and see the perfect Judge, God Himself, whose justice is so great that in the end every portion is made equal and even! Inequality is only a question of the beginning, not of the end. If man saw the justice of God he would become brave, he would trust, and he would not trouble about a return; for if man will not return something, God is responsible for returning a thousandfold what one has given.

Sometimes a person cannot give the love which friends require, and he even forgets his friends when absorbed in work and his occupation. One may wonder whether this is lack of charity. But the question is, what work and occupation? There are kinds of work and occupation of a high character which ask one's whole attention, and such work requires sacrifice. And that is no lack of charity, because every one likes to love, but if one can manage to love and be loved at the same time, it is better.

A person who is able to help others should not hide himself but do his best to come out into the world. 'Raise up your light high', it is said; all that is in you should be brought out; and if the conditions hinder you, break through the conditions! That is the strength of life.

If there is any power that will attract, it is the power of one's love. The only question is, is there anything one loves more than the ordinary things of life? And if there is one should strive for that.

Love can take many forms, even that of indifference. I remember I went once, for a relative, to the house of a physician, an Indian physician who had a very ancient method of writing his prescriptions. Each took him nearly ten minutes. I was shown into a small room where fifteen to twenty people were already waiting, and I sat down among them. He continued to write prescriptions for all who came; and when he had finished with those who were before me, he began to write prescriptions for those who had come after me. I had thought that the physician, as a friend of the family, would have seen me first, but he went on until he had seen everyone, and I was the last.

Finally he said to me, 'Now tell me what you want.' I told him, and he wrote out the prescription without any haste; and when I was leaving he said, 'I hope you understand that I did not want to see you while all the other patients were still there. I wanted to see you at leisure'. He was doing me a favour, and though he tried my patience it was still a majestic sort of favour. It gave me a good example of love in the form of indifference.

If somebody truly loves one person, he will end by loving everybody. The one who says, 'I love this person, but hate that other one', does not yet know what love is. For love is not limited; it is divine and therefore unlimited. By opening the love element in oneself, one opens the divine element in oneself; and when the fountain of love begins to rise in the heart, then divine realization will rise like a fountain. The great saints, who had love for even the smallest beings, came to divine realization without great study or meditation. Their love taught them.

Love is divine from its beginning in all aspects. Rumi says, 'If you love a person or if you love God, by journeying on the path of love in the end you will arrive in the presence of the Sovereign of love.' Love is a conqueror who in the end will always conquer. It is not only the one we love whom love will conquer; love's conquering is the conquering of the kingdom of God. The power of love is penetrating; nothing can resist it in the end. And by giving love and kindness we never lose anything; love is an element that is never lessened, it is a treasure that is divine.

When we stop to consider whether a person is worthy or unworthy, then we confine our love within a channel; but when we allow that feeling to flow it will develop into a continually flowing condition; then it will work out its own destiny without any intention on our part.

THE HEART

FROM A mystical point of view personality is formed around the heart. For a materialist the heart is the piece of flesh hidden in the breast, but for the mystic the heart is the centre of the person round which the personality is formed. Consciously or unconsciously man loves the word 'heart', and if we were to ask a poet to leave out that word and write his poems without using it, he would never satisfy himself or others. Few people think of this; yet the poets who have most appealed to humanity, have used the word 'heart' most. For what is man? Man is his heart. A dead heart means a dead man, a living heart a living man.

People look for wonder-workings and surprises, for phenomena of all kinds. Yet the greatest phenomenon, the greatest surprise, and the greatest wonder is to be found in one's heart. If there is anything that can tune man to the highest pitch, that can tune the strings of his soul to the right note, it is only by the tuning of the heart. The one who has not reached his heart has not reached God. People may be relations, friends, partners, collaborators, and yet be quite separate; nearness in space does not make people real friends. There is only one way of coming near to one's friends, and that is by way of the heart. If there is anything which is the most wonderful in heaven and earth, it is the heart. If a miracle is to be found anywhere, it is in the heart. For when God has tuned the heart, what is there which is not to be found in it?

The Nizam of Hyderabad once wrote, 'If one only knew how large the heart is! It accommodates heaven and earth, all the sea and all the land.' The greatness or smallness of men does not depend on outer things. Whatever rank or position a man has, if his heart is not great he cannot be great; and if his heart is great he remains great under all circumstances. It is the heart that makes one great or small.

Hearts can be of different kinds; there is the golden heart, the silver heart, the copper heart, the iron heart. The golden heart

shows its colour and its beauty; it is precious and at the same time
it is soft. The silver heart shows inferior qualities compared with
the golden heart; yet coins are made of silver; it is useful. Of the
copper heart pennies are made, and pennies too are useful in everyday life; they are even more used than gold and silver coins.
Copper is strong and hard, and it needs many hammerings to
shape it and make something out of it. And then there is the
iron heart, which must be put into the fire before anything can
be done with it. When the iron becomes hot in the glowing fire,
then we can make something out of it; but the blacksmith must be
always ready; as soon as the fire begins to glow, he must start at
once. If he lets it go, it will turn cold in a moment.

And besides these aspects there is the heart of rock and the heart
of wax. The heart of rock must be broken; it must be cut;
nothing reaches it. Cold, heat, fire, sun, or water has little effect
upon the heart of rock. But when the heart is of wax, it melts as
soon as the sun falls upon it, and when heated one can mould it
any way one likes. Then there is the heart of paper that flies like
a kite in the wind; to the north, to the south, to the east, to the
west. One can control it as long as the string is strong enough
to hold it; but when there is no wind it drops down.

Are these examples sufficient? No, there are innumerable hearts,
each differing in quality, and once we begin to distinguish the
qualities of the heart, we begin to see miracles, living phenomena,
every moment of our life. Is there anything that can be compared
with the heart? It dies and lives again; it is torn and mended
again; it is broken and made whole; it can rise and it can fall, and
after falling it can rise again, and after rising it can fall again
instantly. There is one heart that can creep, another that can walk,
another that can run, another that can fly, and yet we cannot limit
the action of the heart. We cannot imagine how the heart can be
illuminated and darkened in a moment! It is a maze we enter and
when we are inside we can never get out. The heart can be confusion and it can be paradise, it can be heaven itself; and if we ask
where we can see the soul manifest to view, it is in the heart.
Where is paradise, where is heaven, where is love, and where is
God? We can answer each of these questions by saying: in the
heart of man.

Imagine, how wonderful and at the same time how obscure! If we call the heart the spark of fire, then we can see its different aspects as sympathy in the form of heat, as longing in the form of fire, as affection in the form of glowing, as devotion in the form of flame, as passion in the form of smoke that blinds one's eyes. That which gives courage to stand firm in the battlefield, to struggle through life, to endure all that comes, that which strengthens one to have patience, what is it? It is the heart. If the heart fails, one falls; if the heart rises, one rises.

When the heart is directed towards one ideal, one object, one point, it develops; when the heart is going from one point to another, it is weakened, for then the fire element of the heart dies. The little spark is brought to a blaze when one blows upon it; and yet the fire is put out by blowing. Why? Because man's blowing is directing the air to one single spot, but the wind blowing all around extinguishes the fire.

When man says, 'I love everybody', one can be sure he loves nobody; but when he says, 'I love my mother, my father, my son, my daughter, my friend, or my beloved', then he has taken the first step on the path of love. But no one in the world can claim to love and at the same time know love. The moment one knows what love is one loses the claim. Before one can say, 'I love', one must be able to show it by jumping into the fire and losing oneself in it.

The Hindu poet says, 'The first initiation in the order of lovers is to become nothing'. And another poet says, 'O Love, you have taught me first the lesson which many learn at the end!' When someone says, 'If you will be good to me I will be kind to you, I will respect you', it is a business proposition. And when a person says, 'I wish someone loved me', he is very mistaken, for he will never be loved; he may wait for eternity. Love never asks to be loved. Love is more independent than anything, and it is love that makes one independent.

There is love that is like an infant. It must be taken in one's arms; it cannot stand; if it is not taken up it cries. It is not mature; it is not developed; it is not yet love. And then there is love that is like a child that has not yet learned to walk. It has to hold on to the table or the chair to steady it; that love too is undeveloped. But then there is love that stands on its own feet and walks alone; that is independent love, and one can depend upon it.

Love shows its quality by constancy. Where there is no constancy there is no love. People have wrongly understood the meaning of love; the real meaning is life itself. The feeling that one is alive, that feeling itself is love.

Then what is love? Love is God and God is love. As long as one is involved in selfish thoughts and actions one does not understand love. Love is sacrifice, love is service. Love shows itself in regard for the pleasure and displeasure of the beloved. And that love can be seen in all aspects of life, once it is understood. Love for those who depend upon one, for those with whom one comes in contact in every aspect of life, love for one's country, for one's race, for humanity; it can extend even to love for every little creature, for the smallest insect that lives. Thus the drop of water becomes the ocean, thus can limited man expand through love. The more sympathy expands, the further it reaches heavenward, until man becomes as great as the Absolute.

Sufis, instead of teaching the lesson of indifference, have taught the lesson of love and sympathy, and have called it the cultivation of the heart. In Sufi terminology this is called *Suluk*, which means the divine manner, the loving manner. When a refined manner is directed by the heart quality, it becomes a loving manner, the manner of God, and all such attributes as gentleness, tolerance, kindness, forgiveness, mercy, and compassion spring from it. The great teachers and prophets did not become what they were by their miracles, their wonder-workings; what was most apparent in them was the loving manner.

Read the lives of the prophets. Look at the way Jesus Christ had with all those who came to him. When the sinners who were condemned and expelled from society were brought to the Master he raised them up with his compassion. He was on the side of the accused ones. The fishermen who were with the Master never understood him, and even the most educated could not. Yet the Master lived with them and won their hearts in the end. This was by his loving manner. Think of the Prophet Mohammad whose most beloved daughter was killed by an Arab before his eyes; and when the Arab said, 'I did not do it on purpose. Will you forgive me?' the Prophet forgave him instantly. When he became a conqueror and judge, and his enemies, who had ill-treated him and turned him out of the country, were brought before him in rows and asked him, 'What will you do to us?' the Prophet said, 'You are my brothers; God will forgive you.' Think also of the compassion of Buddha towards even the smallest insect.

For attainment on the spiritual path study is secondary and magical powers are unimportant. The first and most important principle is the cultivation of the heart quality, and there is only one way to cultivate this heart quality: to become more and more selfless at each step that we take. For what prevents the loving manner is the thought of self; the more we think of our self, the less we think of others, until at the end of the journey our self meets us like a giant, a giant who will prove to be the stronger. But if with the first step we take on the spiritual path we struggle with this giant, we can only conquer him by the power of love.

Love is the stream which when it has risen up falls again like a fountain, each drop forming a virtue. Virtues taught in books have not the same power, but virtues springing naturally from the spring of love in the depth of the heart are love itself. There is a Hindu saying, 'No matter how much wealth you have, if you do not have the treasure of virtue, it is of no use.' True riches are the ever-increasing fountain of love, from which all virtue comes.

THE HEART QUALITY

THERE ARE people who look at life with their brain, or their head as they call it, and there are others who look at life with their heart. And between these two points of view there is a vast difference; so much difference that something that one sees on the earth the other sees in heaven, something that one sees as small the other sees as great, something that one sees as limited the other sees as unlimited. These two types of people become opposite poles. No one will admit that he looks at things with his head; everyone will say that he looks at life with his heart. But if one only knew what it is to look at life from the heart! The most evolved person in the world will only go as far as to say, 'I have not yet learned to look at life from the heart; I would like to know how to do it, I would like to learn it.'

One might say that emotional and devotional people are flying in the clouds, and that the others who act with reason and logic are standing on the earth. This is true; but in the first place angels ride on clouds, and if the soul has an angelic quality the clouds are its sphere, not the earth. One may ask where then is the place for practicality in life; but what is practicality, as one calls it, and all that one is so careful about? And how long does it last, what is it worth? No doubt it is true that man is born on earth to bear the weight of his physical body and its needs, a roof over his head, and a piece of bread to sustain him. But if man believes that this is all there is to think about, he is making a great mistake, devoting all his life to what he calls practicality, practical life, and never thinking of the heavenly treasure that is hidden in the heart of man.

The heart of man is like water. Either it is frozen and then it is snow or ice; or it is water and then it is liquid. When it is frozen it has turned into a crystal; when it is liquid it is in a condition to flow, and it is natural for water to be running. Then there are two principal kinds of water, salt water and sweet water. The sea, which is quite contented with itself, indifferent to all, has salt water because it is independent of all else. It gives health, happiness, and pleasure to those who are near it, because it asks nothing from anyone. It rises and falls within itself, it is independent, it is immense; and in that way it shows perfection. But with that independent perfection its water is not sweet. The ascetic who has closed his heart with the perfection of God and with the realization of truth, is like the sea: independent, indifferent to all things. His presence heals people, his contact gives them joy and peace, and yet his personality is uninteresting to others, as is the salt water of the sea.

When the sea is calm it is a pleasure to travel on it, and when the sea is rough there is no worse illness than sea-sickness. And it is through its tranquillity and calmness and peace that the powerful mind, the mind of a soul which has touched perfection, opens itself to everyone, as the sea lays itself before those who journey on it with open heart. Ships and boats pass over it; those who journey enjoy travelling on the sea. But when the sea is disturbed by wind and storm it is also perfect in its annoyance, it can shake the boats and steamers; and in the same way the mind of the sage can have an effect upon all things in nature: it can cause volcanic eruptions, it can cause disasters, revolutions, all manner of things, when once its tranquillity is disturbed. Aware of this quality of the heart and knowing the great powers possessed by a man who has touched divine perfection, people in the East give careful regard to the pleasure or displeasure of the sage. They believe that to annoy a sage is like annoying the whole of nature, to disturb his tranquillity means to shake the whole universe. Compared with this a storm on the sea is a very small thing; the heart that has touched perfection, if once upset, can upset the whole universe.

The water of the river is sweet. It is sweet because it is attracted to the sea, it is longing to reach the sea. The river represents the loving quality, a quality that is seeking for the object it loves. A heart that loves God and His perfection may be likened to the river that seeks the sea; that is why the personality of the seeker is more pleasant than the personality of the one who is contented with what he knows.

There is little danger in travelling on the river, there is great joy in swimming in the river, and along its banks there is fine scenery to look at. And so it is with the personality which is like the river; that continual flowing of the feeling of sympathy means that the sympathy is living. As the river helps the trees and plants and the earth along it, so it is with the kind, sympathetic person whose feeling is liquid; everywhere he goes he takes with him that influence which nourishes, which helps souls to flourish and to progress.

And then one sometimes finds a little stream; it is not a river, it is only a small running stream; but it is even more beautiful to look at. It expresses modesty, fineness of character, beauty; for its water is pure. The little stream expresses the nature of an innocent heart, the heart that cannot be prevented from being sympathetic and loving by any experiences of the world which make water turn bitter. Bitter experiences have not touched it, and it remains pure and clear. It inspires poets, it uplifts the composer, it quenches the thirst of the thirsty, it is an ideal subject for the painter to paint. With its modesty it has purity, and with its purity it has life.

There is also the water of the small pool. It is sometimes muddy, sometimes dirty because of its narrowness, its smallness. In the same way the narrow heart always has mud in it. Because it is narrow and because it is not deep enough, all the elements of the earth enter it and take away its purity.

Again, there is the water of the large pool, where water-lilies grow, where fish swim, where the sun is reflected and where the moonlight produces a beautiful vision, where one would like to sit and look at it, because it expresses to everyone that can see it the liquid nature of the heart, the heart that is not frozen, the heart that is like water. It is still, it is calm. Sitting by its side can make one's heart tranquil and because of its stillness one can see one's reflection in it.

Spring water is most healing and most inspiring, because it comes from above and runs downhill. That is the character of the inspired mind. The heart that like a spring pours out water in the form of inspiration, in poetry or music, or some other form, has beauty, has a healing quality. It can take away all the worries and anxieties and difficulties and troubles of those who come to it, like the water of the spring; it not only inspires but it heals.

There is also the fountain which rises and falls in so many drops. This is man-made, in the same way that personality also is man-made. When man has made a personality of himself, then the feeling that rises from the heart through that personality is like a fountain. Each drop falling from it takes the form of a virtue.

Then the water that rises from the sea towards the sky in the form of vapour represents the aspiration of the heart. The heart that aspires upward, that wishes to reach upward, that heart shows the quality of vapour. It is the heart of the devotee, of the one who is always conscious of seeking the higher ideal, touching the higher principles. That heart of inspiration forms itself as clouds, and pours down just like the rain, bringing celestial beauty in the form of art or poetry or music, or of anything that is good and beautiful.

There are hearts which have been exposed to fire for a long, long time, and there comes a sulphury water from them, purifying and healing; for it has gone through fire, it has gone through suffering, and therefore it heals those who suffer.

There are hearts with many different qualities, like water with different chemical substances: those who have suffered, those to whom life has taught patience, those who have contemplated. They all represent one or other kind of the water that heals, and so do their personalities. People who have had deep experiences of any kind, of suffering, of agony, of love, of hate, of solitude, of association, of success, of failure, all have a particular quality, a quality which has a special use for others. And when a person realizes this, he will come to the conclusion that whatever has been his life's destiny, his heart has prepared a chemical substance through sorrow and pain, through joy or through pleasure, a chemical substance that is intended for a certain purpose, for the use of humanity, and that he can only give it out if he can keep his heart awakened and open. Once it is closed, once it is frozen, man is no longer living. It does not matter what he has gone through, for even the worst poison can be of some use. There is no person, however wicked, who is of no use, if only he realizes that the first condition for being useful to humanity is to keep his heart open.

As to spiritual attainment, it is something that we can never absorb through the head; it can only be received through the heart. Let two persons, one with his heart and the other with his head, listen to the teachings of a teacher. The latter will be thinking, 'Is it so or is it not so?' or, 'How is it, if it is so? How can it be;

and if it is, why is it?' And there is never an end to the 'why'. But another person will listen with his heart; and while both logic and reason are at his disposal they are not troubling him. His heart is open, he listens to it; and the quality of the heart is such that whatever falls upon an open heart becomes instantly revealed. When one says, 'I cannot understand you', it is just like saying, 'I have my heart closed to you'; there is no other reason for not understanding another person. But when one can say that one has understood it all, it means one's heart was open; that is the reason why one has understood it.

Thus understanding does not depend upon the head; it depends upon the heart. By the help of the head one can make it more clear, it becomes intelligible and one can express it better. But to begin with it must come from the heart, not from the head. Besides a person who only uses his head says, 'It must be so because I think it is so', whereas the person who has the heart quality says, 'It is so because I believe it to be so'. That is the difference. In one person there is a doubt, in the other there is conviction.

There is in Arabic a word which is very difficult to translate: *Iman*. It is not exactly faith or belief; the nearest word one can find for it is 'conviction', a conviction that cannot be changed by anything, a conviction that does not come from outside. One always seeks for conviction, but nothing convinces and nobody convinces; conviction is something that comes from one's own heart, and it stands above faith and belief; for belief is the beginning of that same thing of which faith is the development and conviction the culmination.

Spiritual attainment is nothing but conviction. A man may think, 'Perhaps it is so'. He may think about the best doctrines or about the highest ideas that there are, but he will still think, 'It is so, perhaps'. There is always 'perhaps' attached to it. But then there is another person who cannot use the word 'perhaps' because he does not think about it. He cannot say, 'It may be so', when he knows that it is so. When a person arrives at the stage when the knowledge of reality becomes a conviction, then there is nothing in the world that will change it. And if there is anything to attain to, it is that conviction which one can never find in the outside world; it must rise from the depths of one's own heart.

THE TUNING OF THE HEART (1)

NO ONE in this world may be called loveless; at the same time, everyone is not necessarily full of love. Either the fire is burnt out and the heart has turned to ashes, or the heart has a spark of love in its depths just as the stone has a spark of fire which hardly ever shows itself. One may ask if it is not a weakness to be sympathetic, as it is the sympathetic person who gives in, and the one without sympathy holds on to himself; but sometimes the one who gives in is more powerful than the one who thinks that he should not give in. Very often a person does not give in owing to fear, doubt, or lack of confidence in himself, and often it is the brave and courageous who give in. It is not always a weakness, although in some cases it may be so.

Sentiment is often underestimated when it is compared with reason. This is a mistake, for where there is real sentiment it is much stronger, much more powerful than reasoning. The one who goes from one reason to another, and then again to another reason, is often found to be very weak. Besides the man of reason has no magnetism, he has only reason. He can argue, discuss, talk too much, but he does not attract. The man of sentiment has strong magnetism, he can attract without words because he has something living in him. In the man of sentiment is to be found the divine element, the heart quality.

Someone came to the great poet of Persia, Jami, and asked him if he would take him as a pupil and teach him spiritual truth. And Jami asked, 'Have you ever loved in your life?' He said, 'No, never'. Jami said, 'Go and love first. Let your heart by tuned, let it be melted first. Then come to me. Then I will show you the spiritual path'.

Sympathy is the main quality to be cultivated in order to develop the spiritual faculty; but if one would ask me what I mean by sympathy, it is something I cannot explain. All such words are different names, different aspects of one and the same thing. What is called sympathy, kindness, mercy, goodness, pity, compassion, gentleness, humility, appreciation, gratefulness, service, is in reality love. And what is love? Love is God.

Someone will say, 'Yes, once I was very friendly and loving.' And if you ask him, 'Why not today?' He will answer, 'I was digging and I found mud.' But in every place you dig there is water. One need only dig deep enough, until one has found water. If one does not dig till one finds water one only gets mud. Those who are disappointed in human nature and those who allow their heart to become cold because of this have lost a great deal. Somebody once said to me, 'I have lost my friend, and since then I have lost sympathy for human nature.' And I said, 'Your first loss was not so great, but I pity you for your second loss. It was then that you should have kept your sympathy.'

There are five different aspirations the wise may have in their search for spirituality: seeking for knowledge, seeking for life, seeking for happiness, seeking for peace, and seeking for an ideal. And all these five can only be sought in one's own heart, and then only when the heart is tuned to a certain pitch.

One may say, 'I seek for knowledge', but there are two kinds of knowledge. The one kind of knowledge is that of names and forms, in other words, the knowledge of facts. But there is a difference between a fact and truth. In our everyday language we often confuse these two words, and we say truth for fact and fact for truth. In order to attain to higher knowledge we should not try to gain it in the same way as we try to gain outer knowledge of names and forms. The outer knowledge we gain by learning; the inner knowledge we gain by unlearning. The inner knowledge we can only gain when the heart is tuned to its proper pitch. Criminals and those who are repulsive, and all those who are working towards their own defeat, one will mostly find to be devoid of heart quality. It is because of the lack of heart quality that all the inclinations come that drag a person downward. However highly a man may be qualified or however intelligent, whatever his profession, it does not matter; if the heart quality is lacking a person will go down. The ultimate result is that this person goes downward and not upward. It cannot be otherwise.

The inner knowledge is beyond words, and to try to put it into words is like trying to put the sea into a bottle. It is impossible to put it into words. It is something which we can only realize of ourselves, and then only when we have tuned our heart to the proper pitch. How can anybody explain what a high note means? One cannot explain it; we must sing ourselves and find out what a high note is; when we produce it ourselves we know what it means. Thus inner knowledge should be acquired by the tuning of the heart, in order that the heart itself knows what it is. Many have tried to describe the inner knowledge by saying they are one with God, or a part of God, or that they are God. But all these are insolent terms. Why try to put something into words which cannot be expressed? Apart from inner knowledge, can even a deep sentiment such as gratefulness, sympathy, admiration, respect, be put into words? Words would only limit these sentiments.

The power that the heart quality has is immense. The hen, when it is taking care of its young ones, will not hesitate to fight an elephant in defence of its chicks. The heart full of love for its young gives the hen such power that it does not even see the size of the elephant. Its confidence in its own power is greater than the strength of the elephant.

Those who have accomplished great things, those who have held their life cheap for a high ideal, have not thought about it with their brain; it is their heart which has felt it. It is the heart quality that gives courage and bravery, not the brain. Therefore, if one wants to seek for the divine power of the Almighty God, it should be sought for in one's own heart.

We also confuse pleasure and happiness. Sometimes we say pleasure for happiness, or happiness for pleasure. In reality very few in this world know what happiness means. Pleasure is the shadow of happiness, for pleasure depends upon things outside ourselves; happiness comes from within ourselves. Happiness belongs to the heart quality; pleasure to the outer world. The distance between pleasure and happiness is as vast as that between earth and heaven. As long as the heart is not tuned to its proper pitch one will not be happy. That inner smile which shows itself in a man's expression, in his atmosphere, that belongs to happiness. If position were taken away and wealth were lost in the outer life, that inner happiness would not be taken away. And the smiling of the heart depends upon the tuning of the heart, the heart must be tuned to that pitch where it is living.

The fourth aspiration is peace. Peace is the longing of our soul, but not necessarily for rest or comfort; it is far greater than that. Peace is something that relieves every atom of our body and mind from stress. It is a kind of relief, a kind of upliftment. It cannot be compared with any earthly experience; it is like being raised to the higher spheres, for it is there that a person really experiences peace. And where does it come from? It comes from the same tuning of the heart.

The fifth aspiration is the ideal. Again it is the heart quality which is necessary for the ideal; if one has no heart then the brain cannot make an ideal. It is the heart which tries to reach it. Christ has said, 'Seek ye first the kingdom of God, and all these things shall be added unto you.' By getting in tune with the God-ideal one will become so attuned that one will find a way open to the heart of every person one meets and a connection with every condition and with every object, thereby realizing at-one-ment with the Absolute.

Thus the five different aspects of spiritual attainment are all attained by the tuning of the heart. What is this tuning of the heart in reality? When a string of the violin is loose it does not give the sound it is meant to give, and therefore it does not fulfil the purpose for which it was put on the violin. It can only be used for that purpose when one has tuned it to the right pitch. And the same condition is needed with the heart. The heart must have a certain awakening, a certain amount of life in it, that can only be brought about by sympathy. When that sympathy is not there, then the heart is like a loose string on the violin.

Many will object, 'But does not our heart depend also upon our everyday environment, on the circumstances of life? If the environment is not agreeable, how can we make it right?' Indeed, the first stage of our development depends upon environment and circumstances; but there is nothing in this world which we cannot try to improve. There are many things that we can help and improve, if we would only try. Sometimes it is difficult, but often we think it is difficult while it is not really so. The greatest difficulty is loss of patience. When patience is exhausted things cannot be made better, and then they remain in the same condition; but when one really wants to make one's environment better and sacrifice all one can in order to do so, then one can. Too often one expects from others more than they are able to give, and that makes one helpless and dependent. Once a person has become so independent that without the help of others he can keep his feelings untouched, he becomes like the sun which burns without oil; and in that it differs from lamps which burn with oil, for when the oil is finished then their light goes out.

The relationship between the heart and the conditions of the outside world is such that it is the condition of the heart which influences one's life's affairs. When the heart is out of tune everything goes wrong; it makes the whole atmosphere out of tune. Once a lady said to me, 'I have had bad luck this week. I lose or break many things; everything tears and gets destroyed.' I said, 'There is something wrong with yourself. You yourself are out of tune; especially this week something has upset your rhythm.' And on thinking this over, she found out that it was so.

The more keenly one studies life, the more one will find that the heart has an influence on both failure and success, on rise and fall, on favourable and unfavourable conditions in life. No sooner has the heart been tuned than conditions in life become better and ill luck is averted; wrong reasoning, people becoming tired and disappointed with one another, things going wrong, losses, all these things disappear as soon as the heart is tuned. It is difficult enough to keep a delicate instrument like the violin tuned, and the heart is incomparably more delicate; it is the instrument on which the soul, the spirit, plays. It is on the model of the heart that the harp we know has been made, and the ancient artists have put a harp or a lute in the hands of the angels. Symbolically the angels mean heart, the heart quality.

The reason why the heart influences our life, is that the heart is like the seed out of which the plant has grown which we call our self. Thought, speech, and action, like fruits and flowers, are the effect of the heart; what the heart produces is the same as that which was already in it. For instance a person cannot conceal his feelings all the time. He may play at being a friend, he may play at being brave; whatever he plays at he is able to maintain for a certain time and no longer, for what is in the heart must come out some time or other in the form of actions or words, from the lips, in the expression, or as atmosphere. The heart never fails to express itself in some form or other. And what does it express? What it possesses, what it is. A person may be our bitter enemy and for a long time try to hide it, but in some form or other it will come out. A person may be our friend and like to show indifference in some form or other, but his love will leap out. If a person has something against us or if he has an admiration for us, it cannot remain hidden. He will close his lips, not showing anything in his actions and never saying it, but even through his eyes it will come out, through the expression it will show, through the atmosphere it will manifest. The heart will speak louder than words.

Our heart is also closely related to the people we meet; to such an extent that in industry, business, profession, science, politics, and domestic life, in every aspect of life, the people we meet are affected and influenced by the condition of our heart. If the heart is out of tune, let a man be in his office, the factory, his home, among friends, in the club, in society, whatever he says or does not say, or whatever he does, his very presence will upset the atmosphere. Therefore the secret of magnetism, the mystery of attraction in a person, is solved by the study of the heart. Very often we are uncomfortable in the presence of someone; or the presence of someone attracts us without that person having said one word. We may feel as if we had always known a person, as if we had always been friends though we had never seen him before. If we are in tune, we tune others also; but if a person's heart is not in tune, then everyone in his presence also gets out of tune. That is the mystery of attraction and repulsion.

Very often we will see that people attract one day and perhaps the week after or a month or a year later, there is repulsion. The reason why that person attracted for the moment, was that his heart was in tune; but then after some time his heart got out of tune again. It is because of this that a person who was once attracted may feel repulsion another time; and because he does not know the reason he will always blame the other. Human nature is such that man sees himself last; especially if it comes to blame he never thinks of himself, he first blames the other.

If we go still deeper into this subject, then we shall find that not only with human beings, but even with nature, with the atmosphere, with the weather, with the climate, there also is the tuning of the heart. Even flowers feel it. Many people can keep flowers in their hand for a long time, while with others, no sooner have they touched a flower than it fades. The fading of the flower means that it becomes out of tune. There are stories of sages in the East, who after having left a place of rest and peace where they were staying, perhaps under the shade of a tree or in a village, came back after ten years and found the place in a bad state; but the moment they returned it became fertile again and the place flourished. What does it mean? That they were in tune.

When we begin to think more about human nature and study it more, we shall find that there is no creature as selfish as man can be. With all his intelligence and goodness and kindness, the most unjust and inconsiderate creature is man; inconsiderate about the feelings of his fellow-men, towards a relative who depends on him, or someone who waits upon him, who cares for him, or towards someone who relies upon his word. Man has always *his* motive, *his* convenience, *his* joy, *his* object before him; all else he sets aside. But he is the victim of his own inconsiderateness, though he does not know that it is really the cause of all failure, ill luck, difficulties, problems, or anything else he has to face.

There are so many debts to pay in life; not only money, but there are obligations to those around us, obligations to those who justly or unjustly, foolishly or wisely expect something from us: thought, consideration, love, service, our obligations towards friends and acquaintances, obligations towards strangers. Today the life we live keeps our minds so much at work that every day we become less and less considerate, less and less thoughtful. Thus the unknown influences which come upon us and bring about changes in our life are such that we blame this or that person or the stars and planets and other things; but in reality it all belongs to the realm of the heart. As soon as we realize this, we consider our relationship to others. Our duty, our interest, our virtue in the world is to be thoughtful, to be considerate about every word we say, every thought we think, every feeling we have, considering what influence it will have upon someone else and whether it will bring him pleasure. If there is any religion or spirituality it is in this.

There is a still higher stage of our development, and that is the attitude of going forth and sympathizing with all we meet. This comes by understanding; the more understanding we have of human nature the more sympathetic we become. Even for those who do not deserve it we should have sympathy. In this way sympathy, which is symbolically like water, spreads in time; it will expand like the water of the ocean. It becomes an everlasting spring that rises and falls. In order to teach this the wise of India turned the river Ganges and the river Jumna into places of pilgrimage and called them sacred. These rivers rise in the same place on the top of the Himalayas, and from there they divide and descend, becoming larger streams; and the place where they join, near Allahabad, is a place of pilgrimage. Those who go there are purified from all sin.

Its symbology is this, that the water which rises from the top of the Himalayas is like a spring of love coming from the heart. That which rises from the heart is the first place of pilgrimage. Then it goes on like the holy rivers Ganges and Jumna, and the place where these rivers meet is called Sangam, which means 'sympathy'; and where the river reaches the sea it is called the 'Unity with God'. It is a beautiful picture of life which one can observe in that symbolic form. If interpreted rightly we could have the sacred pilgrimage to the Ganges here and everywhere; the sacred river is the sympathy coming out of our own heart, and the reaching towards God is the perfection, the spiritual attainment.

THE TUNING OF THE HEART (2)

SPIRITUALITY is not necessarily intellectuality, nor orthodoxy, nor asceticism. Orthodoxy, ascetism, or intellectual pursuit
after truth, are all the various ways people have taken in order to
reach the spiritual goal; but the way is not the goal. If there can be
a definition of spirituality, it is the tuning of the heart.

In this material age of ours heart quality is totally forgotten, and
great importance is given to reason and logic. When we argue with
a person, he wants us to argue with reason; we must be logical.
Sentiment and idealism have no place. It is because of this that
humanity is getting further and further away from spiritual
attainment. That which is the chief and the best quality is ignored;
and by ignoring that quality it becomes dead. If a poet happens to
live in a village where no one understands poetry, if an artist
lives in a town where no one cares for his pictures, if an inventive
genius has no opportunity of bringing his inventions out, their
faculties and talents become blunted and finally they die; and the
same happens to the heart quality: if it is not taken notice of, if it
has no opportunity to develop, if it is ignored, then this quality
becomes blunted and in the end it dies. As it is expressed in a song,
'The light of a whole life dies when love is done.' What remains?
There is no sign of life; what remains is intellectuality expressing
itself by the power of egoism. It is difficult to live in the world
because selfishness is ever on the increase.

There is a certain fineness that belongs to human nature, a
certain nobleness, a certain independence. There is a certain
ideal, a certain delicacy, a certain manner. And all these become
blunted when the heart quality is left undeveloped.

I have been travelling for many years, seeing people engaged
in the pursuit of truth; and to my very great disappointment I
have found many who, although interested in higher things, are
yet arguing and discussing, 'Do you believe what I believe?' or,
'My belief is better than your belief', always intellectually. But
we do not need to use so much intellect in seeking God, in

attaining spirituality, for this does not come through intellect; it comes by the tuning of the heart.

People will say that this may be so, but that all the same there are many emotional and affectionate people. But emotional people are not always loving people. Maybe outwardly, but very often the more emotional people are, the less loving; for one day their love is on the rise, next day it drops. They are just moved by emotions like clouds. One day the sky is clear, next day it is covered over. One cannot depend upon emotions. That is not love; it is the feeling nature that should be developed, the sympathetic nature.

Besides there exists, especially in the Western world, a false conception of the strength of personality. Many have understood this wrongly, and under the guise of strength they want to harden their hearts. Many think that for a man to be touched or moved by anything is not natural or normal. On the contrary, if a man is not touched or moved it is not natural; he is then still in the mineral kingdom and not yet in the human kingdom. To be human and not to be touched or moved by something touching, appealing, only means that the eyes of the heart are closed and its ears blocked; that the heart is not living. It is the wrong understanding of a high principle. The principle is that man must be feeling yet at the same time so strong that however much feeling he has he should have enough strength to hide it. It does not mean he must not have feeling; a man without feeling is without life.

However much one studies psychology, theoretically or practically, one will not attain to spirituality. Spirituality does not belong to intellectuality. It has nothing to do with it. In connection with spirituality, intellectuality is only useful in so far as an intellectual person can better express spiritual inspiration.

One might ask if it is not natural to attain spirituality. Does it not come without any effort on our part? And if it is not natural, then what is the use of attaining spirituality? The answer is that spirituality is not only for human beings but also for the lower creation, for every being; not spirituality in the sense we usually understand it, but in the sense of being tuned to one's natural pitch. Even birds have their moments of exaltation. At the setting or the rising of the sun, the breaking of dawn, in moonlight, there come times when birds and animals feel exalted. They sing and dance and sit on the branches of the trees in exaltation. Every day they feel this exquisite joy. And if we go still further and if we have eyes to see life in those forms in which others do not see it, in the rock or the tree, we find that there are times when even the trees are in a complete state of ecstasy. Those who live naturally, who open the doors of their heart, whose soul is in contact with nature, find nature singing, dancing, communicating. It is not only a legend, a story of the past, that saints used to speak with the trees. It is an actual fact and is the same today as in the past. Souls are always of the same nature. They are the same, only we have become unbelievers, we have no confidence in life. We have become material, we have closed our eyes to what is before us. Souls can become saints and sages today just as in the past. Are the stars not the same as ever?. They communicate also today with the one who is able to understand them. But we have turned our back on nature; we live in an artificial world; we have not only become material, we have become matter itself.

Sufis in all ages, mystics of India, Persia, and Egypt have considered the awakening of the heart quality to be the principal thing in life. For all the virtues that the priest can teach and pre-scribe, all the virtues that one is told to practise in life, come naturally when the heart opens. One need not learn virtue; virtue becomes one's own. Virtues that are taught, how long do they last? If there is any virtue it must come by itself; spirituality is natural. And if animals and birds can feel spiritual exaltation, why not we? But we do not live a natural life. We have tried in our civilization to be as far removed from nature and natural life as possible, breathing an artificial atmosphere contrary to climatic influences, eating food which we have manufactured, turning it into some-thing quite different from what nature had made it.

The most important question is how to make the best of our life, how to make the best of this opportunity which is passing by us. Every moment lost is incomparably more valuable than the loss of money. As man comes to realize this, he will more and more come to the conclusion that while he thought that he was progressing, he has really been moving around in the same maze.

If only he had found the door, that door which is called by the wise spiritual attainment! However well educated one may be, however much one has collected or accomplished, however much power and position one has gained, none of this will be lasting; there is only one thing which is everlasting and that is spiritual attainment. Without this there will always be dissatisfaction, an uncomfortable feeling. No knowledge, power, position, or wealth can give that satisfaction which spiritual attainment can give.

There is nothing more easy and nothing more difficult in the world: difficult because we have made it difficult; easy because in reality it is the easiest thing possible. All other things one has to buy and pay for. We have even to pay for our water. But for spiritual attainment we do not need to pay any tax. It is ours, it is our self; it is the discovering of our self. And yet what one values is what one gets with difficulty. Man loves complexity so much; he makes something big and complicated and says, 'This is valuable.' If it is simple he thinks that it has no value. That is why the ancient people, knowing human nature, told a person when he said he wanted spiritual attainment, 'Very well; for ten years go around the temple, walk around it a hundred times every evening. And go to the Ganges. Then you will get inspiration.' That is what should be done with people who will not be satisfied with a simple explanation of the truth, who want complexity.

One often hears people say, 'I once had deep feeling but that feeling is all gone, it is lost. Now I have no more feeling.' That really means that something in them has died. They do not know it, but something of great importance has died as a result of their being affectionate, loving, kind. Perhaps they have met with the bad qualities of human nature and have become disappointed; and so the feeling heart has taken the bowl of poison and died. There are others who out of self-righteousness or keen perception of human defects, out of their critical tendency, begin to hate before they can love someone, letting hate come first and giving love no chance.

What is necessary is to develop a sympathetic nature and to sustain its gradual growth. Just as it is difficult for the student of voice-culture to practise with his voice and yet not to let it be spoiled, so it is with a sympathetic person. While developing, he runs the risk of spoiling the faculty of sympathy; in other words, the more loving a person, the more chance he has of being disappointed. The greater the love, the greater the fragility of the heart and the more susceptible it becomes to everything, until it can break at any moment. The one who walks in the path of sympathy should take great care that his way is not blocked; everything will be trying to block his way, and it is his own perseverance that will keep it open.

By lack of development of the sympathetic nature a block is produced in the mind and in the body. In the physical body there are some nervous centres, centres which are awakened by sympathetic development. And by lack of sympathetic development they remain closed. It is for this reason that a butcher is less intuitive. Everything that keeps man from sympathy robs him of intuition, for in these finer centres sympathy develops life, and the absence of that sympathy takes away that life.

So it is in the mind. When the heart is not sympathetic there is something missing in the mentality of man, and it is sympathy which opens it. The Sufis know the medicine for this disease, and it is the practice of the art which is called *Zikr* or *Mantram*. By practising that particular art in the right way one activates these fine centres by vibrations. By the repetition of certain mystic words the centres begin to vibrate. Very often after only a short time of doing these practices a person feels quite different, especially when a mental thought is held during that time; thus concentration is developed at the same time. It helps the love-nature or sympathetic nature to be deepened or centralized, and as it begins to flow out an atmosphere is created, a spiritual atmosphere; this all comes from the development of feeling.

During my pilgrimage to the holy men of India I saw some whose presence was more illuminating than the reading of books for a whole lifetime, or arguing a thousand times about any problems. They do not need to speak; they become living lights, fountains of love. And as there is infection in disease so there is also infection in spiritual attainment. One feels uplifted and full of joy, ecstasy, happiness, enlightenment.

No doubt one person may be more impressed than another;

upon one the influence is much greater that upon another. It all depends upon the individual. I remember a lady once telling me, 'Since you came my husband has been very nice to me.' But eight days after I had left the town where I was staying, she wrote to me that her husband was just as he had been before. It makes a great difference what person it is, for it is just like the effect of fire. On stone, on iron, on wax, on paper, on cloth, on cotton, on every object the effect of fire is different, and so on every person the effect of spiritual personality is different.

Once I met a learned man, a doctor of philosophy with a great many degrees. We spoke about the deeper side of life. And he became very interested in what I said and told me that he thought very highly of me; so I thought that if I were to tell him about my teacher how much more interesting it would be for him. I told him, 'There is a wonderful man in this city; he has no comparison in the whole world.' 'Are there such people?' he asked, 'I would very much like to see him. Where does he live?' And I told him, in such and such a part of the city. He said, 'I live there also, where is his house? I know all the people there. What is his name?' So I told him. He said, 'For twenty years I have known this man, and now you are telling me about him!' I thought to myself, 'In a hundred years you would not have been able to know him.' He was not ready to know him. If people are not evolved enough they cannot appreciate, they cannot understand others. They cannot even understand the greatest souls. They may sit with them, talk with them; they may be in contact with them all their life, but they do not see; while another, if he is ready to understand, needs only one moment. This philosopher had known my teacher for twenty years and yet he did not know him; I saw him once and became his pupil for ever. This man was learned, he was very intellectual, but he saw him with his brain; I saw my teacher with my heart.

The one principle to be remembered in the path of sympathy is that we should all do our best with regard to the pleasure of those whom we love and whom we meet. But we should not expect the same from those whom we love and whom we meet. For we must realize that the world is as it is, and we cannot change it; we can only change ourselves. The one who wants others to do what he wishes will always be disappointed. That is the complaining soul, the one who all day long and every day of the month is complaining. He is never without a complaint; if not about a human being, then it is the climate; if not about the climate, then about the conditions; if not about someone else, then about himself.

He should remember that self-pity is the worst poverty. The person who takes life in this way, who considers his poor self to be forgotten, forsaken, ill-treated by everybody, by the planets, even by God, for that person there is no hope; he is an exile from the garden of Eden. But the one who says, 'I know what human nature is, I cannot expect any better, I must only try and appreciate what little good comes from it and be thankful for it, and try and give the best I can to the others', has the only attitude which will enable him to develop his sympathetic nature. The one who keeps justice in the foreground will always be blinded by it; he will always talk about justice, but he will never really know it. For the one who keeps justice in the background, the light of justice falls on his way and he only uses justice for himself. When he has not done right towards others he takes himself to task, but if others do not do right towards him he says that this also is justice. For the just person all is just; for the unjust everything is unjust. The one who talks too much of justice is far from justice; that is why he is talking about it.

Is there then no reward at all in sympathy if it leads only to disappointment? Life's reward is life itself. A person may suffer from disease or be most unhappy and sad; but if he were asked, 'Do you want to be turned into a rock?' He would say, 'No, rather let me live and suffer.' Therefore life's reward is life; and the reward of love is love itself. Loving is living, and the heart that closes itself to everyone closes itself to its own self.

The difference between human love and divine love is like that between drill and war. One has to drill in order to prepare for war. One has to know the phenomenon of love on this plane in order to prepare to love God who alone deserves love. The one who says, 'I hate human beings, but I love God', does not know what love means; he has not drilled, he is of no use in war. Whether a loving person loves a human being or whether he loves God, he shows no trace of hatred. And the one who has hatred in him loves neither man nor God, for hatred is the sign that the doors of his heart are closed.

Is it not a great pity that we see today among the most civilized nations one nation working against the other, a lack of trust and the fear of war between them? It is dreadful to think that humanity, though it appears to be progressing, is actually going backward to a greater extent than has ever been seen in the history of the world. Are we evolving or going backward? What is missing is not intellectuality, for every day people are inventing more and more ingenious things. Then what is missing? It is the heart quality. It seems as though it is being buried more deeply every day. Therefore today the real man is being destroyed, and the false part of his being is continuing. Better conditions can only be brought about by the individual who realizes that it is the development of the heart which can accomplish this, and nothing else.

Very often people coming to hear me say afterwards, 'Yes, all you say is very interesting, very beautiful, and I wish too that the world could be changed. But how many think like you? How can you do it? How can it be done?' They come with these pessimistic remarks. And I tell them, 'One person comes into a country with a little cold or influenza and it spreads. If such a bad thing can spread, could not then the elevated thought of love and kindness and goodwill towards all men also spread? Thus we should see to it that there are finer germs of goodwill going from one to the other, of love and kindness, of the feeling of brotherhood, of the desire for spiritual evolution; they will have greater results than the other ones. If we all took this optimistic view, if we all worked in our small way, we could accomplish a great deal.'

There are many good, loving, and kind people whose heart goes out to every person they meet. But are they spiritual? It is an important question to understand. The answer is that they are very close to spiritual attainment, but they are unconsciously spiritual. They are not spiritual consciously. Very often we meet a mother or father or child in whom we see a deeply loving tendency; love is pouring out from them, they have become fountains of love. Yet they do not know one word of religion or of mysticism. But this does not matter. After all what are these names? Nothing but nets for fishes to be caught in, which may then remain in those nets for years. Sometimes these are big names with little meaning to them, but much is made of them by those who want to commercialize the finer things. Very often it is a catering on the part of so-called spiritual workers to satisfy human curiosity and to create a sensation even in the spiritual world. Nevertheless truth is simple. The more simple one is and the more one seeks for simplicity, the nearer one comes to truth.

The devotional quality needs a little direction; that direction allows it to expand itself. The loving quality is just like water. The tendency of water is to expand, to spread, and so the loving quality spreads; but if a person is not well directed or if he does not know himself, then instead of deepening it becomes limited. The love quality must be deepened first before it spreads out. If not, what generally happens to those who set out to love all human beings is that in the end they hate all human beings, because they did not first deepen themselves enough and so lacked more and more the strength of attraction.

The Sufis have therefore considered spiritual culture to be the culture of the heart. It consists of the tuning of the heart. Tuning means the changing of pitch of the vibration. The tuning of the heart means the changing of the vibrations, in order that one may reach a certain pitch which is the natural pitch; then one feels the joy and ecstasy of life, which enables one to give pleasure to others even by one's presence because one is tuned. When an instrument is properly tuned one does not need to play music on it; just by striking it one will feel great magnetism coming from it. If a well-tuned instrument can have that magnetism, how much greater should be the magnetism of the heart which is tuned! Rumi says, 'Whether you have loved a human being or whether you have loved God, if you have loved enough you will be brought in the end into the presence of the supreme Love itself.'

THE SOUL, ITS ORIGIN AND
UNFOLDMENT

WHEN WE look at life and at the process of its development,
either from a mystical or from a scientific point of view, we shall
find that it is one life developing itself through different phases.
In other words: there is one vital substance—call it energy,
intelligence, force, or light, call it God or spirit—which is forcing
its way through the most dense aspects of nature, and which
leads to its finest aspects. For instance by studying the mineral
kingdom we shall find there is a life in it which is forcing its way
out. We see that from the mineral kingdom come substances
such as gold and silver and precious stones. This means that there
is a process by which matter becomes finer and finer until it
begins to show that the Spirit is of such radiance, intelligence,
and beauty, that it even manifests through precious stones.

This is the scientific point of view; but when one adopts a
mystical point of view then, if one is among rocks, if one stands
still in the mountains, if one goes alone into the solitude, one
begins to feel an upliftment, a sense of peace, a kind of at-one-ment
with the rocks, hills, and mountains. What does this mean?
It means that the same spirit which is in us, is also in the mountain
and rocks, it is buried in the rocks as it is in a less degree in ourselves, but it is the same spirit. That is why we are attracted to
mountains, although mountains are not as living as we are. It
is we that are attracted, not they. Besides what can we give to the
mountains? Restlessness, discord, our lack of harmony, our limitations. What can the mountains give us? Harmony, peace,
calmness, a sense of patience, endurance. They inspire us with
the idea that they have been waiting for perhaps thousands of
years for an upliftment which comes through the development
of nature from rock to plant, from plant to animal, from animal
to man. This gradual unfoldment of the spirit is buried in all these
different aspects of nature; and at each step, from rock to plant,

from plant to animal, and from animal to man, the spirit is able to express itself more freely, is able to move more freely.

In this way the spirit finds itself in the end; this shows that there is one purpose working through the whole of creation. The rocks are working out the same destiny as man, the plants are growing towards the same goal as man. What is that goal? Unfoldment. The spirit is buried in them and wants to make its way out. At each step of evolution there is a new unfoldment, a greater opening. From the animal, Darwin says, man has come. It might have seemed at the time that this was a new scientific discovery, but it was not so. A Persian poet, who lived seven hundred years before Darwin, says in poetic terms and in a religious form that God slept in the rock, dreamed in the plant, awoke in the animal, and realized Himself in man. And fifteen hundred years ago the Prophet Mohammad said the same in the Qur'an: that first was the rock, and afterwards the animals, and from them man was created.

The mystic sees a development of material life from rock to plant, from plant to animal, and from animal to the human physical body. This is one aspect, but only one. There is something else also, and that is the divine Spirit, the Light, the Intelligence, the All-consciousness. The one makes the earth, the other heaven. It is this Sun, this divine Spirit, which shines and projects its rays, each ray becoming a soul. Thus it is not true to say that man has developed from a monkey, and it is degrading the finest specimen of nature that God has created if it is called an improvement of matter. It is a materialistic, limited conception. The soul comes direct from the divine Spirit. It is intelligence itself, it is the consciousness; but not the consciousness we know, for we never experience the pure existence of our consciousness. What we know of our consciousness is what we are conscious of, and therefore we only know what consciousness is in name.

There is no difference between pure intelligence and consciousness. We call pure intelligence consciousness when that intelligence is conscious of something, yet what we are conscious of is something that is before us. We are not that. We are the being who is conscious, not that which we are conscious of. The mistake is that we identify ourselves with what we see, because we do not see ourselves. Therefore man naturally calls his body himself, because he does not know himself. As he cannot find himself, what he identifies himself with is his body. In reality man is not his body, man is his soul. The body is something man possesses; it is his tool, his instrument with which he experiences life, but the body is not himself. Since he identifies himself with his body, he naturally says, 'I live', 'I die', 'I am happy', 'I am unhappy', 'I have fallen', or 'I have risen'. Every condition of his limited and changeable body makes him think, 'I am this'. In this way he loses the consciousness of the ever-changing aspect of his own being.

The soul is the ray which in order to experience life brings with it an instrument, vehicles, and those vehicles are the body and the mind. Therefore instead of 'spirit', we could just as well say the soul with its two vehicles, body and mind. Through the body it experiences outer conditions, through the mind it experiences inner conditions of life. The soul experiences two spheres, the physical and the mental sphere; the mental sphere through the mind, and the physical sphere through the body and the five senses.

When we come to the evolution of the world according to the point of view of the mystic, we shall see that it is not that man has come from the plant and animal and rock, but that man has taken his body, his physical instrument, from the rock, from the animal, from the plant, whereas he himself has come direct from the spirit and he is directly joined to the spirit. He is, and always will be above that physical instrument which he has borrowed from the earth. In other words, man is not the product of the earth, but the inhabitant of the heavens. It is only his body which he has borrowed from the earth. Because he has forgotten his origin, the origin of his soul, he has taken the earth for his origin, but this is only the origin of his body and not of his soul.

There is the question of what is the soul's natural unfoldment towards spiritual attainment. Spirituality apart, at every stage in one's life—infancy, the time from infancy to childhood, from childhood to youth, from youth to middle age—at every further step there is a new consciousness. Childhood is quite a new consciousness compared with infancy. Youth is quite a different consciousness compared with childhood. In that way every soul, no matter what stage of life it is in and whether it knows it or not, has gone through many different unfoldments, each of which has given it a new consciousness. And there are experiences such as failure in business, or misfortune, or an illness, or some blow in life—it may be an affair of the heart or of money or a social matter: there are many blows which fall upon a person—and then a shell breaks and a new consciousness is produced. Very few will see it as an unfoldment, very few will interpret it as such, but it is so. Have we not all known among our acquaintances someone very uninteresting or with a disagreeable nature to whom we were never attracted, and then perhaps after a blow, a deep sorrow, or some other experience, he awakens to a new consciousness and suddenly attracts us because he has gone through some kind of process?

Spiritual unfoldment is the ultimate goal of all mankind, and it comes at the moment when a person begins to be more thoughtful. When he begins to remember or to realize this yearning of the soul, consciously or unconsciously, a feeling comes, 'Is this all I have to do in life, to earn money, to have high rank or position? If this is all it is all a game. I have become tired of this game, I must think of something else. There is something else I have to attain to.' This is the beginning; this is the first step on the spiritual path. As soon as a person has taken this first step his outlook is changed, his sense of values becomes different, and things to which he had attached great importance become of less importance; things which occupied him a great deal, he no longer concerns himself with. A kind of indifference comes over him. Nevertheless, a thoughtful person keeps to his duty just the same; in fact he is more conscientious. There is greater harmony because he also begins to pity others.

And when he goes another step forward there comes bewilderment. He begins to wonder, 'What is it all for? Much ado about nothing!' I once saw in India a sage whom I knew to be very deep, a man of high attainment, and he was laughing at nothing. I wondered what he was laughing at. Then I stood there and looked around, thinking I must see from his point of view what was making him laugh so much. And I saw people hustling and bustling. For what? Was it not laughable? Every person thinking his particular point of view to be the most important! He pushes others away because he finds his action the most important. Is this not the picture of life? It is the way of the evolved and the unevolved. And what do they reach? Nothing. Empty-handed they leave this world; they have come without anything and they leave without anything.

It is this outlook which bewilders the soul. The sage does not feel proud when he laughs at others, but at the same time he finds it highly amusing. But he is just as amused at himself as at others.

And again another step forward brings a person to an understanding which changes his outlook and manner. Generally what happens is this: from morning till evening man reacts against everything, both good and bad. But good he sees very rarely; he always sees bad things. Or he meets someone who is nervous or excited or domineering or selfish, and so he experiences a jarring effect from everyone he meets. Then, without knowing it, his constant reaction will be one of despising, of hating, or of wishing to get away. This will be his continual feeling; and if he gets into the habit of saying, 'I don't like', 'I dislike', he will soon be saying it from morning till evening with everyone he meets. This reaction he then expresses in word, thought, feeling, or action.

When one reaches this third stage of understanding one begins to understand instead of reacting. Then there is no reaction, for understanding comes and suppresses it. It is just like the anchoring of a boat; it produces tranquillity, stillness, weight in the personality. One no longer sways with every wind that blows; but one stays on the water like a heavy ship, not like a small boat that moves with every wave that passes. This is the stability one reaches in the third stage of unfoldment; and then one is ready to tolerate and to understand both the wise and the foolish.

It is a fact that the foolish person disagrees more with others than does the wise. One would think that he knew more than the wise! But the wise man agrees with both the foolish and the wise; the wise man is ready to understand everybody's point of view. He has his own ideas, his way of looking at things, but he is capable of looking at things from the point of view of others too. One eye alone does not see fully; to make the vision complete two eyes are needed. So the wise can see from two points of view, and if we do not keep our own thoughts and preconceived ideas in check, if we cannot be passive, and if we do not wish to see from the point of view of other people we make a great mistake. This third stage produces a tendency to understand every person one meets.

Then again there is a fourth stage of the unfoldment. In that fourth stage one not only understands, but one sympathizes; one cannot but sympathize, for then one realizes that life in the world is nothing but limitation. Whether a person is rich, in a high position or in wretched circumstances, whatever condition he is in or whatever he is, he has to experience this limitation. This in itself is a great misery, and therefore every person has his problems. And when one begins to see that every person on this earth has a certain problem or burden he has to carry through life, one cannot but sympathize. The one who is awake to the pain of mankind, whether it is of his friend or his foe, cannot help but sympathize with him. Then he develops a tendency of reaching out; he will always wish to reach out to every person he meets. And naturally by his sympathy he looks for good points, for if one looks at a person without sympathy one will always touch his worst points.

And when one goes a step further still, then the way is open to communicate. Just as there is a communication between two people who love each other, so the sympathy of a person who has achieved his soul's unfoldment is so awakened that not only every person but even every object begins to reveal its nature, its character, and secret. To him every man is an open book. We hear stories of saints and sages who talked with rocks and plants and trees. They are not just stories; this is a reality.

All the teachings given by the great prophets and teachers are only interpretations of what they have seen, and they have interpreted in their own language what they have read from this manuscript of nature, what trees, plants, and rocks said to them. Did they only speak with these in the past? No, the soul of man is always capable of that bliss if he only realized it. Once the eyes of the heart are open man begins to read every leaf of the tree as a page of the sacred Book,

THE UNFOLDMENT OF THE SOUL

IT IS IN the unfoldment of the soul that the purpose of life is fulfilled. And it is not only with human beings, but also with the lower creation, even with objects of every kind, that the fulfilment of their existence lies in their unfoldment. The clouds gather, and the purpose of this is shown when it starts raining. It is the unfoldment of that gathering of clouds which shows itself in rain; that purpose was not accomplished in the gathering of the clouds, which was only a preparation. One sees the same thing in nature, which works the whole year round, and in the appropriate season it brings forth its fruits. Not only human beings but even the birds and animals watch and delight in seeing the purpose of nature's continual activity being fulfilled in the spring.

We learn from this that every being and every object is working towards that unfoldment which is the fulfilment of its purpose. As Sa'di has said, 'Every being is intended to be on earth for a certain purpose, and the light of that purpose has been kindled in his heart.'

But behind all the different purposes which we see working through each individual, there seems to be one purpose, and that is the unfoldment of the soul. Knowing this, the ancient Hindus held this ideal before them in all walks of life. Not only those who sought after truth were seeking the soul's unfoldment, but an artist, a scientist, a learned man, a man of industry, of commerce, each one believed that through his particular occupation he would be able to reach that goal. The great misfortune today is that men are so segregated in their different occupations that they have lost the thread which binds humanity into one, and gives that impetus from which all derive benefit. When the scientist stands on his ground strongly and firmly and the artist is absorbed in his sphere, the industrial man in his world, and a man of commerce in the world of commerce, it is natural that their souls do not come in contact with one another, giving them a combined force for the betterment of the whole.

Although a degeneration caused by extreme materialism prevails throughout the whole world, it is not yet too late to find examples of personalities in all walks of life who still wish to arrive at the proper goal. Rabindranath Tagore translated into English a book of verse by Kabir, an uneducated man, a weaver from childhood whose livelihood depended upon his weaving; but through his continual seeking after unfoldment he arrived at the goal. He told his experience in everyday language, but his book is looked upon today by the people as holy scripture.

This makes us wonder whether it is possible for a scientist to arrive through his scientific studies, or an artist through his art and a man of commerce through his trade, at that central truth which concerns every soul. When we look at humanity we find that we can not only divide it into different races and different nations; we can also divide it into people of different occupations. In this age of materialism, the only thing that unites us is our material interest; but how long can we be united by a material interest? A friendship formed in materialism is not a friendship which will endure, nor can such friends depend upon each other. It is sacrifice which enables us to be friends and to co-operate with one another, and in sacrifice the sign of spirituality is seen; but we do not unite together in sacrifice today; our unity is in what we can gain in one way or the other. It is a matter for distress that in order to unite we are holding fast to a lower ideal which will never prove a centre of unity. It is only the high ideal which can unite and in which we can hope to be united.

How can one define the unfoldment of the soul? The soul can be likened to the rose; as a rosebud blooms, so the soul unfolds itself. For the rosebud to bloom five conditions are required: fertile soil, bright sun, water, air, and space; and the same five things are required for the unfoldment of the soul. As a fertile soil is required by the rose-bush in order to grow, so education in the spiritual ideal should be given to the child from the moment it is born. When a child is deprived of that most important education in its childhood, then the soil is taken away from the roots of the rose. I can recall having met so many people who had every possibility and tendency to become interested in all that is spiritual and lofty, but who at the same time were afraid of the

terminology in which it is expressed. What does this show? It
shows that in childhood something was denied them, and now
that they have grown up, although they feel a desire for it, although
they want it, when they look at it in a form they are not accustomed to they are afraid of it.

Is there even one soul, however materialistic, which does not
wish to unfold? There cannot be. Every soul has been born to
unfold itself; it is its innate tendency, it cannot help it. Only, if
the soul is deprived of the right conditions then it ceases to develop.
Very often I have met people who did not believe in any particular religion, did not profess any particular faith, nor adhere to
any outward form, but at the same time I have seen great spiritual
qualities in them.

The water that nourishes the rose is the love element. If
that element is absent from anyone's life, however great his
intellectual knowledge and his desire to seek after truth, he will
still remain backward. Unfortunately this element often seems
to be missing in cultural life. A learned man will say that it has
no place in the world of reason, and thus he separates the outer
learning from the religious ideal which is called the love of God.

What is it that takes the part of the sun in the life of man, as
the sun takes part in the growing of the rose? It is intelligence.
Everyone may not seem to be intelligent, but the soul itself is
intelligence. When the intelligence is covered by the mist of
impressions, of ideas of this earth, that intelligence becomes
drowned in something, buried under something. When it is discovered, then it is as bright as the sun. The mission of Buddha
was mainly intended for this purpose. All that Buddha wished to
teach his disciples was to discover that pure intelligence which is
above all reasoning and which is the essence of all reason.

The place that air occupies in the growth of the soul is this:
air is symbolical of the inspiration which comes to the heart that
is prepared for it. And it is not by outward learning but by what
one learns through inspiration that the soul is raised towards its
unfoldment.

The space which is needed around the rose-bush in order
to let it grow, means symbolically a wide outlook on life. A person
may live a hundred years, but with a narrow outlook he will

never see the light. In order to see life clearly the outlook should be wide. There is much to fight with in life in order to keep our outlook wide, for the nature of our life in the world is such that it drags us down and places us in conditions where we cannot but be narrow. A great person is not great because of his merits, his qualities or reputation; the surest proof that a person can give of his greatness is his vast outlook. And it is wonderful to notice how, even unconsciously, people who have arrived at that stage, in whatever walk of life, automatically begin to show a vast outlook on life. What manures this plant and makes roses bloom is, symbolically, the teaching given by the great masters of humanity.

How can one recognize this development of the soul in which the purpose of life is fulfilled? What are its indications, its signs? The soul becomes like a rose, and begins to show the rose quality. Just as the rose consists of many petals held together, so the person who attains to the unfoldment of the soul begins to show many different qualities. These qualities emit fragrance in the form of a spiritual personality. The rose has a beautiful structure, and the personality which proves the unfoldment of the soul has also a fine structure: in manner, in dealing with others, in speech, in action. The atmosphere of the spiritual being pervades the air like the perfume of the rose.

The rose has seeds in its heart, and so the developed souls have in their heart that seed of development which produces many roses. The rose blooms and fades away, but the essence that is taken from the rose lives and keeps the fragrance that the rose had in its full bloom. Personalities who touch that plane of consciousness may live for a limited time on the earth, but the essence which is left by them will live for thousands and thousands of years, always keeping the same fragrance and giving the same pleasure that the rose once gave.

THE SOUL'S DESIRE

THE DESIRE of the soul is always for the right way, not for the way of darkness. One does not like to be without a candle, a light in one's house. One likes a good light; and this shows that the desire of the soul is for light.

What is lacking with man is that he knows only the passing, the momentary joys, and does not know the greater joys. And for experiencing a passing joy, a joy that lasts only for a few minutes or for a few days, there will be a bill to pay; and the paying of that bill may take ten years. Then man discovers that this passing joy is not what he really wants, that he wants something better, something more lasting. He seeks something else and turns to mysticism. But mysticism may not be for him. He may not be ready or prepared for it. Then he turns to religion, but its dogma and ceremonial do not necessarily satisfy his mind. If he is a devout person he may be satisfied, otherwise he will not.

The work of the Sufi is to help those who are seeking for something else. First there is the improvement of bodily health. Very often weakness or ill-health of the body is the cause of the poor condition of the mind and soul. A very weak man, however intelligent he may be, will give way whenever a strong man addresses him in a commanding tone.

In our fondness for animal food we have gone so far that we do not enquire whether the animal whose flesh we eat was in good condition, nor what were its qualities; yet these act upon us. We see that plants which are supplied with certain substances acquire certain qualities. So it is with animals and fish; and so it is with us. One has only to look at the condition of the Brahmin, who eats nothing but vegetables, and only certain vegetables at that, and who fasts a great deal. His intelligence is very clear.

We see that the effect of opium and of alcohol is so strong that the most intelligent person becomes weak when he takes these; even tea and coffee have an effect. There are many Sufis who while doing certain spiritual practices do not eat at all, not in obedience to any principle but in order to make the body a fitting instrument.

The founders of the different religions have always prescribed what should be eaten and what avoided, as they knew the effect of different foods. As to the question of vegetarianism and the killing of animals, there are two things to be considered in this connection. One is harmlessness. It is a human tendency to hurt and harm, and man has inherited it from the lower creation. That tendency prompts him to kill defenceless creatures and use them as food, in spite of all the vegetables, cereals, fruits, and nuts which nature has provided for him.

The other point is that for the purification of the blood, for the health of the muscles, and for the purity of the body in general, a vegetable diet is far preferable to flesh food. At the same time, the training of the Sufi is a spiritual one, and as a physician sees in every case what is best for that particular person, so the murshid prescribes for his mureeds what is best for them. There are perhaps people for whom a vegetable diet is not sufficient and not suitable; for them meat may be a medicine. So the Sufis do not have such restrictions, and no dogma is made of vegetarianism, for the need of every individual is according to his health.

In ancient times shepherds used to wrap some of their flock in tiger skins in order to protect them from wild animals when moving about in the open. When a kind and good person lives in this world where there are so many different natures, it is more difficult for him to live among the gross vibrations than for others who are perhaps more or less of the same kind. When someone has died young, one often hears it said that he was a good person; and there is generally some truth in this. Many souls coming to the earth from where it is good and beautiful, cannot bear the coarseness of ordinary human nature.

In point of fact what is diet? Diet is not for the soul; it is only for the body. And what is the body? The body is a cover, a blanket. If the body is covered with armour then it can stand the struggle of life; and it was for this reason that the great ones also allowed themselves to partake of flesh food, which in reality was meant for the average person.

Then there is the improvement of the mind. At the present time great attention is paid to physical health, not indeed in an ideal way, since it is only considered from a physical point of view. Much could be done by considering it from a mystical point of view. Doctors tell us about different diseases of the body and how to guard against them, but they tell us little of the diseases of the mind, of the faults that we see so easily in others and not in ourselves.

While we are very young our parents tell us our faults, although there are few parents to be found in the world who are perfect themselves. But later no one tells us our faults. People only think, 'This person is unpleasant, we do not wish to associate with him.' And we do not see our faults ourselves; we are all the time pointing out the faults of others. Our faults may grow so much that when we are old our own children do not wish to be with us any more and that our friends desert us. While youth lasts there is a certain magnetism, a certain amount of charm which covers the faults, but when we are old nothing covers them. Riches or power can cover the faults, but a man's servants will always be watching for a chance to uncover them.

Let us not look at the fault of another; let us not think that a person is stupid or disagreeable; let us look at ourselves. If each person is occupied with his own black record, he will have enough to do, and it is after this that comes the improvement of the soul for everybody. The soul is the faculty of knowing. In its collective aspect it may be called the consciousness, while in its limited aspect it is the intelligence of each individual being. And it is the desire of the soul to know. The soul is very inquisitive. When it sees the sea, it desires to know what the sea is, from whence it comes. It sees a tree, and it wishes to know what the tree is, what are its fruits, how they taste. We are all the same. We want to know about every new flower we chance to find. When the soul is active, a person wants to see what science he can learn, what language, what music. He wants to know about history and geography. He wants to read the newspapers, to know what is happening in other parts of the world. And then his body becomes dim before his consciousness.

The soul may possess knowledge of everything else, but it can never be satisfied without the knowledge of itself: what it is, whence it is. This is the secret of knowledge. The world is always running after the knowledge of outside things, but what the soul needs is the knowledge of itself. When a man has gained this, God Himself is proud of him, the one who, being man, yet has realized God.

THE AWAKENING OF THE SOUL (1)

THERE IS a process of awakening from childhood to youth, and from youth to maturity; and during this development one's point of view, one's outlook on life, is changing. One finds, too, that sometimes one goes through an illness or great suffering, and at the end of it one's whole outlook on life has changed. It also sometimes happens that someone who has travelled far returns apparently quite altered. Again, there often comes a sudden change of outlook after a person has formed a friendship, or has been somebody's pupil, or has married. There are even some cases where the change is so marked that one can say he has become an entirely new person.

We can divide such changes or developments into three classes, of which the first is connected with the physical development, the next with the development of the mind, and the third with the development of the soul. Though few will admit it, many people can recollect experiences in their childhood when in one moment their whole outlook on life changed. Ripening is a desirable result, and it is the aim of every object in life to ripen and to develop; therefore in the awakening of the soul one may recognize the fulfilment of life's purpose.

The first sign of the soul's awakening is just like the birth of an infant. From the time of its birth the infant is interested in hearing things, whatever sound may come, and in seeing things, a colour or light or whatever it may be; and thus a person whose soul has awakened becomes awake to everything he sees and hears. Compared with that person, everyone else seems to have open eyes and yet not to see, to have open ears and yet not to hear. Though there are many with open ears yet there is rarely one who hears, and though there are many with open eyes yet there is hardly one who sees. That is why the natural seeing of the awakened soul is called clairvoyance and its natural hearing clairaudience. The simple English word 'seer' conveys that such a man has eyes, but as well as eyes he has sight.

The moment the soul has awakened music makes an appeal to it, poetry touches it, words move it, art has an influence upon it. It no longer is a sleeping soul, it is awake and it begins to enjoy life to a fuller extent. It is this awakening of the soul which is mentioned in the Bible: unless the soul is born again it will not enter the kingdom of heaven. For the soul to be born again means that it is awakened after having come on earth; and entering the kingdom of heaven means entering this world in which we are now standing, the same kingdom which turns into heaven as soon as the point of view has changed. Is it not interesting and most wonderful to think that the same earth that we walk on is earth to one person and heaven to another? And it is still more interesting to notice that it is we who change it from earth to heaven. This change comes not by study, nor by anything else but by the changing of our point of view. I have known people seek after truth, study books about it, even write many books on philosophy and theology themselves, and in the end they were standing in the same place as before. That shows that all outer efforts are excuses; there is only one thing that brings one face to face with reality, and that is the awakening of the soul.

All the tragedy of life, all the misery and disharmony, are caused by lack of understanding; and lack of understanding comes from lack of penetration. When one does not look at life from the point of view that one should, then one is disappointed because one cannot understand. It is not for the outer world to help us to understand it better, it is we ourselves who should help ourselves.

Then there is a further awakening, a continuation of what I have called the awakening of the soul. And the sign of this awakening is that the awakened person throws a light, the light of his soul, upon every creature and every object, and sees that object, person, or condition in this light. It is his own soul which becomes a torch in his hand; it is his own light that illuminates his path. It is just like directing a searchlight into dark corners which one could not see before, and the corners become clear and illuminated; it is like throwing light upon problems that one did not understand before, like seeing through people with x-rays when they were a riddle before.

As soon as life becomes clear to the awakened soul, it shows another phase of manifestation, and this is that every aspect of life communicates with this person. Life is communicative, the soul is communicative, but they do not communicate until the soul is awakened. Once a soul is awakened it begins to communicate with life. As a young man I had a great desire to visit the shrines of saints and of great teachers, but although I wanted very much to hear something from them and to ask them something, I always held back my questions and sat quietly in their presence. I had a greater satisfaction in that way, and I felt a greater blessing by sitting quietly there, than if I had discussed and argued and talked with them, for in the end I felt that there was a communication which was far more satisfactory than these outer discussions and arguments of people who do not know what they discuss. It was enlightening and refreshing, and it gave the power and inspiration with which one can see life in a better light.

Those who are awakened become guiding lights not only for themselves but also for others. And by their light, often unknowingly, their presence itself helps to make the most difficult problems easy. This makes us realize the fact that man is light, as the scriptures have said, a light whose origin, whose source, is divine. And when this light is kindled, then life becomes quite different. Furthermore, when the soul is awakened, it is as if that person were to wake up in the middle of the night among hundreds and thousands of people who are fast asleep. He is sitting or standing among them, he is looking at them, hearing about their sorrows and miseries and their conditions, hundreds of them moving about in their sleep, in their own dream, not awakened to his condition although he is near them. They may be friends or relations, acquaintances or enemies, whatever be their relationship, but they know little about him as each one is absorbed in his own trouble. This awakened soul, standing among them all, will listen to everyone, will see everyone, will recognize all that they think and feel; but his language no one understands, his thoughts he cannot explain to anyone, his feelings he cannot expect anyone to feel. He feels lonely; but no doubt in this loneliness there is also the sense of perfection, for perfection is always lonely.

When it was said that upon the descent of the Holy Ghost the apostles knew all languages, it did not mean knowing the languages of all countries. I knew a man in Russia who spoke thirty-six languages, but that did not make him spiritual. The apostles, however, knew the language of the soul; for there are many languages which are spoken in different lands, but there are also numberless languages which are spoken by each individual as his own particular language. And that helps us to realize another idea of very great importance: that the outer language can only convey outward things and feelings, but that there is an inner language, a language which can be understood by souls which are awakened. It is a universal language, a language of vibrations, a language of feeling, a language which touches the innermost sense. Heat and cold are different sensations which are called by different names in different countries, and yet they are always essentially the same sensations. Also love and hate, kindness and unkindness, harmony and disharmony, all these ideas are called by different names in different countries, but the feeling is the same with all men.

When in order to know the thought of another person we depend upon his outer word, we probably fail to understand it, for perhaps we do not know that person's language; but if we can communicate with another person soul to soul, we can certainly understand what he means, for before he says one word he has said it within himself; and that inner word reaches us before it is expressed outwardly.

Before the word is spoken the expression says it; before the thought has formed, the feeling speaks of it. And this shows that a feeling forms a thought, a thought that manifests as speech; and even before a feeling manifests it can be caught when one is able to communicate with the soul. This is what may be called communication: to communicate with the innermost being of a person. But who can communicate thus? The one who knows how to communicate with himself, the one who, in other words, is awakened. The personality of an awakened soul becomes different from every other personality. It becomes more magnetic, for it is the living person who has magnetism; a corpse has no magnetism. It is the living who bring joy, and therefore it is the awakened soul who is joyous.

And never for one moment think, as many do, that a spiritual person means a sorrowful, dried up, long-faced person. Spirit is joy, spirit is life; and when that spirit has awakened, all the joy and pleasure that exists are there. As the sun takes away all darkness, so spiritual light removes all worries, anxieties, and doubts. If a spiritual awakening were not so precious, then what would be the use of seeking it in life? A treasure that nobody can take away from us, a light that will always shine and will never be extinguished, that is spiritual awakening, and it is the fulfilment of life's purpose. Certainly, the things a person once valued and considered important become less important; they lose their value, and those which are beautiful lose their colour. It is just like seeing the stage in daylight: all the palaces and other scenery on the stage suddenly mean nothing. But it puts an end to the slavery to which everyone is subjected, for the awakened man becomes master of the things of this world; he need not give them up. Optimism develops naturally, but an optimism with open eyes; power increases naturally, the power of accomplishing things, and he will go on with something until it is accomplished, however small it is.

It is very difficult to judge an awakened soul, as they say in the East, for there is nothing outwardly to prove its condition. The best way of seeing an awakened soul is to wake up oneself, but no one in the world can pretend to be awake when he is still asleep, just as a little child by putting moustaches on its face cannot prove itself to be grown-up. All other pretences one can make, but not the one of being an awakened soul, for it is a living light. Truth is born in the awakening of the soul; and truth is not taught, truth is discovered. The knowledge of truth cannot be compared with the knowledge of forms or ideas; truth is beyond forms and ideas. What is it? It is itself and it is our self.

Very often people make an effort, though in vain, to awaken a friend or a near relation whom they love. But in the first place we do not know if that person is more awakened than we ourselves; we may be trying for nothing. And the other point is, it is possible that a person who is asleep needs that sleep. Waking him in that case would be a sin instead of a virtue. We are only allowed to give our hand to the one who is turning over in his sleep, who desires to wake up; only then a hand is given. It is this giving of the hand which is called initiation. No doubt a teacher who is acquainted with this path may give a hand outwardly to the one who wishes to journey, but inwardly there is the Teacher who has always given and always gives a hand to awakening souls, the same hand which has received the sages and masters of all time in a higher initiation. Verily, the seeker will find sooner or later, if only he keeps steadily on the path until he arrives at his destination.

THE AWAKENING OF THE SOUL (2)

THE WORDS 'awake' and 'asleep' are very familiar to us, as we use them in expressing different states in life. But in reality, when we look at it from the point of view of the soul, we are asleep and awake at the same time. For instance, when we are looking at a certain thing, when our mind is fully absorbed in it, we do not hear anything at that time. And when we are listening to something and are absorbed in what we are hearing, when our sense of hearing is thus focused, though our eyes may be open yet we are not seeing. This shows that when one sense is fully awakened the other senses are asleep. In the same way the mind is absent while we are experiencing a sensation through the body; and when we have a sensation we are experiencing something through the mind, while the body takes no part in it. The more we look at sleeping and waking from the psychological point of view, the more we will find that they are not what we commonly understand by these words, but that every moment of the day and night we are both awake and asleep at the same time. Also, when a person is asleep and experiencing a dream he is awake to something and yet asleep to the outer things. To one world he is asleep; to the other awake.

According to the mystics there are five stages of consciousness. One stage is our experience through the senses. In this condition our eyes are ready to see, our ears to hear; and we are awake to the outer world. This is the only aspect of wakefulness which we recognize as such, but there are four other aspects besides this one. The second aspect is when a person is asleep and yet is experiencing life exactly as he does on this plane of the physical world. This is the dream state; we call it a dream when we have woken up and have passed that stage. At the time of dreaming that state is as real as this state in the physical world, and nothing is lacking in the dream that we find here. While dreaming we never think that it is a dream, but many things which we cannot find here on the physical plane we can find in the dream state. All the limitations and all that we lack in this life are provided for in the dream state. All that we are fond of, all that we would like to be, and all that we need in our life, are easier to find in a dream than in the wakeful state. When we wake up and return to this life, we call it real and the other a dream, and we say that it was imagination, without any reality; we think that only on this physical plane are we awake, that only this is real. But is yesterday as real as today? Everything that has happened from the moment we came to earth, all that is past, is all yesterday; only just now is today. If it is not a dream, then what is it? We only recognize that which we saw in the dream as being just a dream; but all that is past is in reality nothing but a dream. It is 'just now' which gives us the feeling of reality, and it is that which we are experiencing which becomes real to us, whereas that which we are not experiencing, of which we are not conscious, does not exist for us at this moment.

Thus everyone has his own life and his own world. His world is that of which he is conscious; and in this way everyone has his heaven and his hell made by himself. We live in the world to which we are awakened, and to the world to which we are not awakened we are asleep. We are asleep to that part of life which we do not know.

Another experience is that of the man who lives in the world of music, whose thoughts and imaginings are about the composition of music, who enjoys it, to whom music is a language. He lives under the same sun as everybody else, and yet his world is different. Beethoven, who could no longer hear music with his ears, enjoyed the music he read and played, while perhaps another man with excellent hearing did not hear it. Beethoven's soul was in it, and the music was in himself.

Thus there is the kind of experience we have through our senses, our five senses; but this is one world, one plane of existence, and there is the other existence which we experience in the dream, and that is a world too, a different world, with different laws. Those who consider the dream only as a dream do not know the importance, the greatness, the wonder of it. The dream plane is more wonderful than the physical plane, because the physical plane is crude, limited, and poor, and is subject to death and disease; the other plane which one experiences in the dream is better, purer, and one has a greater freedom there.

The third stage of consciousness is situated between spirit and matter. It is this which we experience as sleep, that condition which one calls deep sleep, when one does not even dream. There is so little said about it, and very few think about it. Once a person studies this question of sleep he will find that it is the greatest marvel in the world. It is a living phenomenon. The rest and peace, vitality and vigour, intelligence and life that come to man during the time of sleep are beyond explanation. And yet man is so ungrateful, he is never thankful for this experience which is given to him every day; he is only unhappy when he has lost it. Then nothing in the world can satisfy him, no wealth, no comfort, no home, no position, nothing in the world can replace that experience which is as simple as sleeping, which means nothing and yet is everything.

The further we study the phenomenon of deep sleep the more we will come to understand the mystery of life. It gives a key to the mystery of life, for it is an experience which divides our spiritual consciousness between the physical and spiritual worlds. It stands as a barrier between two experiences, one in this world, and one which is reached by spiritual attainment. The great Persian poet Rumi has written about sleep; he says, 'O sleep! It is thou who makest the king unaware of his kingdom and the suffering patient forget his illness, and prisoners are free when they are asleep.' All pains and sorrows and limitations of life, all the tragedy of life, all sufferings and agitations are washed away when one experiences that deep sleep.

It is a great pity that the mechanical and artificial life that we live in this world today is depriving us of that natural experience of deep sleep. Our first fault is that we congregate and live in one city all crowded together. Besides there are motor-cars, trains, and tramways, and houses of twenty stories shaking every moment of the day and night. Every vehicle is shaking; and we are a race at the present time which is unaware of the comfort, the bliss, and the peace known to the ancient ones who lived simply with nature, far from our mechanical and artificial life. We are so far removed from the old ways that it has become our habit. We do not know any other comfort except the comfort we can experience in the kind of life we live; but at the same time this shows that the soul is capable of attaining to greater comfort, pleasure, and joy, to greater peace, rest, and bliss only by living naturally.

These three stages of consciousness—physical, dream, and deep sleep—are each nothing but an experience of the soul in an awakened state; but when a person is awake outwardly he is asleep to the inner world, and when he is fast asleep he is awakened to that particular plane and asleep both to dreamland and to the physical state.

When we have been looking at a bright light, and then that bright light is shut off, we see darkness. In reality there is no darkness, it only seems so; if there had not been a bright light before there would not be darkness but some light, for it is the contrast that makes it seem dark. Thus the experience which we have in our deep sleep is an experience of a higher and greater kind, and yet it is so fine, so subtle and unusual, because our consciousness is so accustomed to the rigid experiences of the physical world, and when we are in that other state the experience is too fine to perceive and to bring back to the physical world.

Every experience can be made intelligible by contrast. If there were no straight line we could not say high and low, or right and left. It is the straight line which makes us recognize them as such. If there were no sun we could not say south, north, east, or west. Therefore with every conception there must be some object to focus upon and with which to check our conception. With regard to deep sleep we have nothing in physical existence to compare it with, and therefore the experience of deep sleep remains only as a great satisfaction, joy, and upliftment, and as something that has vitalized us and created energy and enthusiasm. This shows that there is something we have received from it. We do not come back empty-handed from there; we have gained something we cannot obtain from the physical plane. We get something we cannot interpret in everyday language, more precious, more valuable and vital than anything from the physical and mental planes.

There is a still higher plane or experience of consciousness, different from these three experiences which everybody knows. more or less; and this fourth experience is that of the mystic. It is an experience of seeing without the help of the eyes, hearing without the help of the ears, and experiencing a plane without the help of the physical body, in a way similar to that of the physical body but at the same time independent of it. And as soon as one arrives at this experience one begins to believe in the hereafter, for it gives one the conviction that when the physical body is discarded the soul still remains; that it is independent of the physical body and is capable of seeing, living, and experiencing, and of doing so more freely and fully. Therefore this stage of experience is called the consciousness of the mystic.

People become frightened when they hear about Nirvana or Mukti. Nirvana means to become nothing, and everyone wants to become something; no one wants to be nothing. There are hundreds and thousands interested in Eastern philosophy, but when it comes to being nothing they find it a difficult thing to grasp, and they consider it most frightening to think that one day they will be nothing. But they do not know that it is the solving of this question that makes a person into a being, because what he believes himself to be is a mortal thing that will one day expire, and he will no more find himself to be what he thought himself to be.

Nirvana, therefore, is the fifth consciousness. It is a consciousness of a similar kind to that of a person in deep sleep. But in deep sleep one is asleep outwardly, that is to say in the physical body, while the mental body is also asleep. In this condition of Nirvana or highest consciousness, however, one is conscious all through of the body as much as of the soul. During this experience a person lives fully, as the consciousness is evenly divided and yet he remains conscious of the highest stage.

To conclude, what does the soul's awakening mean? The body's awakening means to feel sensation; the mind's awakening means to think and to feel; the soul's awakening means that the soul becomes conscious of itself. Normally man is conscious of his affairs, of the conditions of life, of his body and mind, but not of his soul. In order to become conscious of the soul one has to work in a certain way, because the soul has become unconscious of itself. By working through its vehicles, body and mind, it has become unaware of its own freedom, of its own beauty.

The first stage in the awakening of the soul is a feeling of dissatisfaction with all that one knows, with all the knowledge one may have, whether of science, art, philosophy, or literature. A person comes to a stage where he feels there is something else he must know that books, dogmas, and beliefs cannot teach, something higher and greater that words cannot explain. That is what he wants to know. It does not depend on age. It may be a child who has that inclination or a man who may have already reached a considerable age. It depends upon the soul; therefore in the East they call a child an old soul when it begins to show that inclination, when it is not satisfied with the knowledge of names and forms.

Then there comes a second stage, and that stage is bewilderment. Imagine an evolved person being more bewildered than an unevolved one! And yet it is so, for at this stage a man begins to see that things are not as they seem to be but as they are. This causes a kind of conflict; he does not know whether to call a thing good or bad, love or hate. There comes a time when all that he had accepted in his mind, all that he believed in, now appears to be quite the contrary to what it seemed before: his friend, his relations, those whom he loved, everything; wealth, position, all the things he has pursued, all change their appearance and sometimes seem to become quite the opposite of what they were.

Once in Chicago a lady came to see me, trembling, in a very sorrowful state of mind. I asked her what was the matter. She said she had had an accident. The house in which she lived had been burnt down and she had had to break a window in order to get out. She had hurt her hand, and it had all upset her very much. But then she said, 'It is not the fire that has upset me so.' I asked, 'What, then?' She said, 'The way that all my friends and neighbours, whom I loved and liked, acted when the fire started has impressed me so that the whole world is quite different now.' What does this mean? That friendship, relationship, love, or devotion may not be the same as they appeared when it comes to the time of test. There comes a time when our consciousness changes our outlook on life; and it changes as soon as our soul has opened its eyes. Then our whole life changes; we live in the same world and yet do not live in it; it becomes quite a different world.

And the next stage after this bewilderment is the stage of sympathy. We begin to appreciate things more and sympathize more, for up to now when we walked on thorns we did not feel them. But at this stage we begin to feel them, and seeing that others are walking on the same thorns we forget our pain and begin to sympathize with them. The evolved ones become sympathetic; they develop a natural tendency of outpouring. Troubles, sufferings, and limitations—everyone has to go through them, everyone has to face the same difficulties. And not only the good; the wicked have still greater difficulties. They live in the same world with their wickedness, they have a great load to carry. If one can see this one naturally becomes forgiving and sympathetic.

And as one goes further in the soul's unfoldment one finally arrives at the stage of revelation. Life begins to reveal itself, and the whole of life becomes communicative. The evolved soul will feel the vibrations of every other soul; and every condition, every soul, every object in the world will reveal its nature and character to him.

THE AWAKENING OF THE SOUL (3)

DAY and night are not conditions of the sun; they are conditions in themselves. The sun neither rises nor sets; it is our conception; it is more convenient to speak of the rising of the sun and the setting of the sun. If anything rises and sets, it is the world, and not the sun. When the world turns its back to the sun, it is night; when the world turns its face to the sun, it is day.

It is the same with the soul's awakening. The soul is always awake. But what is it awake to? Someone may be looking with open eyes; but what is he looking at? Is he looking upward or downward or sideways? A person is only conscious of the direction in which he is looking.

To speak of the soul's awakening, therefore, is for the sake of convenience. What part of us is it which may be called 'soul'? As it is not our body, then what is it? It is something which is beyond the body and beyond the mind. It is conscious, and at the same time its consciousness is not as we understand it, for the word 'consciousness' conveys that one is conscious of something. Though not everyone knows what consciousness means, everyone knows what he is conscious of. For instance a mirror in which something is reflected is not only a mirror, but it is a mirror with a reflection, which means it is occupied, it is not empty. When a person speaks of consciousness he cannot think of the original condition; he can think only of the consciousness which is conscious of something. As soon as we distinguish between the consciousness and what it is conscious of, we separate them, as we separate the mirror from what is reflected in it.

When one has realized this, one will come to the conclusion that the soul of the wise and of the foolish, of the sinner and the virtuous is one and the same. The wickedness of the wicked and the goodness of the good, the ignorance of the foolish and the wisdom of the wise, are apart from the soul: the soul is conscious of it. When another person is conscious of it, he may say that here is a wise or an ignorant soul. But the soul is the same; it is not the soul which is ignorant or wise, wicked, or virtuous, but what is reflected in it. At the same time one should know that if an elephant is looking into a mirror, the mirror is not the elephant, but one can see an elephant in the mirror. But if a man does not know what a mirror is, he will say that here is an elephant, although it is only its reflection; it is nothing but a mirror when it is free from this reflection. The moment the reflection is removed, the mirror will again be just a mirror.

And so it is with the soul. Man makes it miserable, wicked, ignorant, wise, or illuminated by being conscious of these things. The soul is neither the one nor the other. The soul is only soul. This misconception creates great difficulties.

If the soul is conscious, what is it then? The best explanation one can give is that it is the essence of all things; it is life. But not life in the sense we understand it; that is only a suggestion of life. The soul is the real life. We say of one who moves and sees and hears and acts that he is a living being, but what is living in him is the soul. The soul is not seen, and therefore life is not seen. Life has touched a person, and therefore on seeing the effect of that touch one says, 'He is living, it is life'. But what we see is only a suggestion of life which appears and disappears. Life is living and never dies.

We have the same problem with intelligence as with consciousness. One knows intelligence as something which is intelligent; there is a difference between intelligence and something which is intelligent. Intelligence in which a certain consciousness is reflected becomes intelligent, but intelligence need not know, in the same way that consciousness need not be conscious of anything; it is the knowing faculty. If one keeps a person in a dark room with striking colours and beautiful pictures, he cannot see them. His eyes are open, his sight is all right, but what is before him is not reflected in his sight. What is there is sight, but nothing is reflected in it. So it is with consciousness and so it is with intelligence; intelligence which is consciousness and consciousness which is the soul.

Science today says that there is a gradual awakening of matter towards consciousness and that matter becomes fully intelligent in man. The mystic does not deny this; but where does matter come from? What is it? Matter is intelligence just the same. It is only a process, so if intelligence manifests in man it is the development of matter. But intelligence which is intelligent, begins with intelligence and culminates in intelligence. Spirit is the source and soul of all things. If matter did not have spirit in it, it would not awaken, it would not develop. In matter life unfolds, discovers, realizes the consciousness which has been so to speak buried in it for thousands of years. By a gradual process it is realized through the vegetable and animal kingdoms and unfolds itself in man, and then resumes its original condition. The only difference is that in this completion, this fulfilment of the spirit which manifests in man, there is variety. There is such a large number of beings, millions and billions, but their origin is only one Being; therefore spirit is one when unmanifested, and many in the realm of manifestation; the appearance of this world is variety. The first impression man gets is that of many lives, and this produces what we call illusion, which keeps man ignorant of the human being. The root from whence he comes, the original state of his being, man does not know. He is all the time under the illusion of the world of variety, which keeps him absorbed and interested and busy, and at the same time ignorant of his real condition, for as long as he is asleep to one side of life and awakened to the other, asleep to the inner and awakened to the outer.

One may ask how one awakens to this inner life, what makes one awaken, and whether it is necessary for one to be awakened. The answer is that the whole of creation was made in order to awaken. But this awakening is chiefly of two kinds: one kind is called birth, the birth of the body when the soul awakens in a condition where it is limited, in the physical sphere, in the physical body, and by this man becomes captive; and there is another awakening, which is to awaken to reality, and that is called the birth of the soul. The one awakening is to the world of illusion, the other to the world of reality.

But one must know that there is a time for everything, and when one does not pay heed to this one makes a mistake. When one wakes a person at two o'clock in the morning his sleep is broken; he ought to sleep all night, he needs this. Very often people, not knowing this, try to wake someone up, it may be their wife, their husband, their friend, their relation, or their child. Someone may feel very anxious to awaken another. Often he feels lonely and thinks, 'He is close to me; he should be awake too.' It is the same with the one who smokes or drinks: he likes someone else to do it with him, just as it is dull for a person in a cheerful mood if another person cannot see the joke. Naturally, therefore, the desire and tendency of the one who awakens to the higher life, to reality, is to awaken others. He cannot help it; it is natural. If it were not, he would say, 'Well, I experience it, I enjoy it; is not that enough? Why must I trouble about others who stand in front of me like stone walls?' Such people have toiled their whole life and they have been exiled and flayed and martyred and crucified, and when they have awakened to a certain sphere where they enjoy harmony and peace they wish that others too may experience it and enjoy it in the same way. But very often we are too impatient and unreasonable, and want to awaken people before it is time.

The other day I was touched to see a play in which a student of the light, of the higher ideals, pronounces the Word, the sacred Word, and dies. And the remarkable thing was that there was a sage in the play who saw it and said, 'He saw beyond and died.'*

What does death mean? Turning. The soul is always awake and therefore it is always living, but it may turn from one side to the other side. If there is some beautiful voice coming from behind to which it wishes to listen, then it turns towards it and in the same way when it is attracted to a certain sphere to which it had been asleep before, that is called awakening.

We see that the time for nature to awaken is the spring. It is asleep all winter and it awakens in the spring. And there is a time for the sea to awaken; when the wind blows and brings good tidings as if to awaken it from sleep, then the waves rise. All this shows struggle, shows that something has touched the soul which makes it uneasy, restless, that makes it want liberation, release. Every atom, every object, every condition, and every living being has a time of awakening. Sometimes this is a gradual awakening and sometimes it is sudden. To some people it comes in a moment's time by some blow or disappointment, or because their heart

* Hazrat Inayat Khan refers to Ansky's play, *The Dybbuk*.

has broken through something that happened suddenly. It may have appeared cruel, but at the same time the result was a sudden awakening, and this awakening brought a blessing beyond words. The outlook changed, the insight deepened; joy, quiet, indifference, and freedom were felt and compassion showed in the attitude. A person who would never forgive, who liked to take revenge, who was easily displeased, who would measure and weigh everything, when his soul is awakened, becomes in one moment a different person. As Mahmud Ghasnavi the emperor poet of India has said in most beautiful words, 'I, the emperor, have thousands of slaves awaiting my command, but the moment love had sprung in my heart I considered myself the slave of my servants.'

The whole attitude changes. Only, the question is what one awakens to, in which sphere, in what plane, to which reality. Sometimes, after one has made a mistake, by the loss that mistake has caused the outlook becomes different. In business, in one's profession, in wordly life, a certain experience, just like a blow, has broken something in someone; and with that breaking a light has come, a new life. But it is not right to awaken someone by mistake. No doubt very often awakening comes by a blow, by great pain; but at the same time it is not necessary to look for a blow. Life has enough blows in store for us, we need not look for them.

In order to get a clear idea of awakening one should consider the condition which we call dreaming. Many attach little importance to it. If somebody says, 'That person is dreamy', he means to say that he is not conscious of anything. But is there in reality anything which we can call a dream? The real meaning of dream is that which is past. Yesterday is as much a dream as the experience of the night: it is past. When a person is dreaming, does he think that he is in a dream, does he think that it is unimportant, does he give it any less importance than his everyday life at that moment? He looks at it as a dream when he has awakened to this other sphere, although in that sphere he will not call it a dream. If a person were asked when he is dreaming, 'What about the experience of yesterday?' He would say, 'It was a dream'—'And what about everyday life?' 'It was all a dream.'

The more one thinks of it, the more one happens to glance into the hereafter, the more one will realize that what the hereafter is, what is behind the veil of death, is the awakening to another sphere, a sphere as real as this one or even more real. For what is real? It is the soul, the consciousness itself, which is real. What is past is a dream, what will come is hope. What one experiences seems real, but it is only a suggestion. The soul is real, and its aim is to realize itself; its liberation, its freedom, its harmony, its peace all depend upon its own unfoldment. No outer experience can make the soul realize the real.

Why cannot we see the soul as we can see the body? From our thought we can understand that we have a mind, because thought manifests to us in the form of a mental picture, but why do we not see the soul? The answer is that as the eyes cannot see themselves, so it is with the soul: it is sight itself, and therefore it sees all. The moment it closes its eyes to all it sees, its own light makes it manifest to its own view. It is for this reason that people take the path of meditation, the path by which they get in touch with themselves; they realize the independence and the continuity of life, which is immortal life, by getting in touch with their soul.

As to those who come into this world in a miserable condition, while others come in good conditions, this is not something in the soul. It is something the soul has carried along with it like the camel's load which is on its back and not in the camel itself.

In spiritual awakening the first thing that comes to man is a lifting of the veil, and that means the lifting of an apparent condition. Then a person no longer sees every condition as it appears to be, but behind every condition he sees its deeper meaning. Generally man has an opinion about everything that appears before him. He does not wait one moment to look patiently, he immediately forms an opinion about every person, every action he sees; whether it is wrong or right, he immediately forms an opinion without knowing what is beyond. It takes a long time for God to weigh and measure; but for man it takes no time to judge! When, however, the veil of immediate reason is lifted, then one reaches the cause, then one is not awakened to the surface but to what is behind the surface.

Then there comes another step in awakening. In this man does not even see the cause, but he comes to the realization of the adjustment of things; how every activity of life, whether it appears to be wrong or right, adjusts itself. By the time a person arrives at this condition he has lost much of his false self. That is what brings him there, for the more one is conscious of the false self, the further one is removed from reality; these two things cannot go together. It is dark or it is light; if it is light there is no darkness. The more the false conception of self is destroyed, the more light there is. It is for this reason that a person who is on the path sees life more clearly.

Another form of awakening is the awakening of the real self. Then one begins to see what one's thoughts and one's feelings mean, what right and wrong mean. Then man begins to weigh and measure all that springs up within himself. The further one goes, the more one sees behind things, the more one becomes attached to all planes of existence, not only living on the surface of life. This is a new kind of awakening; then a person has only to be awakened to the other world; he need not go there. He need not experience what death is, for he can bring about a condition where he rises above life. Then he comes to the conclusion that there are many worlds in one world; he closes his eyes to the dimensions of the outer world and finds within his own self, in his own heart, the centre of all worlds. And the only thing that is necessary is turning; not awakening, but turning.

Man has become motionless, stagnant, by attaching himself to this world into which he is born and in which he has become interested. If he can make his soul more supple and thus be able to turn away from all this, he can experience all that has been said of the various planes of different worlds, which are in reality different planes of consciousness. Only by being able to make his soul supple, by making his soul able to turn, will he find the whole mystery within himself.

The Sufis distinguish fourteen planes of existence, which they call *Choudatabaq*. It is a mystical conception: these planes are the expression of the fourteen different states of consciousness experienced by the help of meditation; the lowest of them is called *Pataloka*. In the experience of these fourteen planes the jinn plane and the angelic plane are also touched.

We need not awaken ourselves to every particular plane; we should awaken to every plane as we go on in life's journey. What is necessary is to be wide awake in life and to see what is asked of us by our friend, by our neighbour, or by the stranger who is travelling with us; becoming more and more considerate and observing what is expected of us; asking ourselves: do we harm him or do we serve him; are we kind to that person or do we hurt him? For we try to get what we do not have in life, and in doing so we are often inclined to forget whom we push away and to whom we are unkind. The one who observes this rule reduces his mistakes from a thousand to a hundred; it does not mean that he will become faultless, but if he can avoid nine hundred mistakes out of a thousand it is already something.

But no deed, however good it may appear, is a virtue unless it is willingly done, because in the willingness of doing, even in a sacrifice, one expresses the breath of freedom. A virtue forced upon ourselves or upon another is no virtue. It loses its beauty. We must do what we think is good.

A Sufi poet showed wherein lies the solution of this problem when he said, 'You yourself it is who have made yourself a captive and it is you yourself who will try to make yourself free.'

THE MATURITY OF THE SOUL

THE MATURITY of the soul may be pictured as when a little girl, beginning to grow up, no longer gives the same importance and attention to her dolls: her sentiments and her desires have changed. It does not mean that she did not have love or sentiment before; she had those; but with maturity her consciousness developed, and the result of that development was that all the toys and dolls and the various things that she used to pay so much attention to, did not matter any more.

This maturity does not depend upon a certain age, but it does depend upon certain surroundings; it is just like a fruit which ripens when put in a warm place. Environment helps the maturing of the soul; nevertheless the ideal is that the fruit should ripen on the tree, for that is the place for fruit to ripen. All the different attempts to make the soul ripen may help, though it is like fruit no longer on the tree but put in some warm place.

There are people who think that by renouncing the world one will arrive at the maturity of the soul. There are others who think it can be achieved by inflicting all kinds of torments and suffering upon oneself. Often people have asked me if some kind of suffering, some kind of torture, would help to mature their soul. I told them that if they wanted to torture themselves I could tell them a thousand ways, or they might themselves think of a thousand things, but that as far as I knew there was no necessity. If one wants to torture oneself for the sake of torture one may do so, but not for spiritual perfection.

As fruit ripens in the course of nature, so it is in the course of nature that the soul should mature; and it is no use being disappointed or disheartened about ourselves and about those near and dear to us, worrying because our husband, wife, father, or mother does not look at spiritual matters in the same way as we do. In the first place no man, however wise or pious, has the right to judge another soul. Who knows what is hidden behind every action, appearance, speech, and manner? No one. And when a

person begins to know what is hidden in the human soul, in spite
of all deluding appearances he will have respect, a respect for
mankind, as he realizes that in the depth of every soul is He whom
one worships.

No one knows what is a person's inner religion, his inner conception. And one will find many true souls whose heart is enclosed
in a kind of hard shell, and no one knows that the very essence of
God is in their heart, as the outer shell is so hard that no one can
understand it. That is why a Sufi from Persia said, 'I went among
the pious and the godly and was so often deceived; and I went
among those who were looked down upon by others and among
them I found real souls.' It is easy to blame, it is easy to look down
upon someone, but it is difficult really to know how deep someone's soul is.

No doubt there are signs of maturity, but who knows them, and
how does one recognize them? The signs of maturity are like the
subtlety one sees between youthful lovers. For the soul to mature
a passion must have awakened it, a passion for the incomprehensible, for that which is the longing of every soul.

Life on earth is just like Gulliver's travels, where all the people
seem to belong to a different world, to be of a different size.
Before the traveller there are numberless little children, and before
him there appear many drunken people, drunken souls. There is
a saying of the Prophet Mohammad that there will appear in the
hereafter, on the Day of Judgment, a being in the form of a
witch, and man will be frightened at the sight of this witch and
will cry out, 'O Lord, what a horrible sight is this! Who is this?'
And he will receive the answer from the angels, 'This is the same
world, the world which attracted you throughout your life,
which you have worshipped, adored, and esteemed as most
valuable, and which was all you desired. This is the same world
that is before you.' All people's desires, whether they concern
wealth, rank, possession, position, honour, or pleasure, all these
fade away with the maturity of the soul. All claims to love such
as 'I am your brother, or your sister, or your son, or your daughter',
mean very little to the mature soul. A mature soul does not need
to wait for the day in the hereafter when he sees the world in the
form of a witch; he sees it now. No sooner has the soul matured

than he sees the unreality of the world which man has always considered real, and all such words that one uses in everyday language become meaningless.

All distinctions and differences, such as sect and creed and community, mean little to the soul who has awakened. The experience of the mature soul is like the experience of the man who watched a play performed on the stage at night, and in the morning he saw the same stage in the sun and saw that all the palaces and gardens and the actors' costumes were unreal.

When a soul has arrived at this stage, at this maturity, what happens? It is the same as when a person grows up: he takes either the right way or the wrong way. His reaction to this realization of life has three aspects. One reaction is that in answer to every claim of love and attention and respect, he says, 'O, no! I don't believe you, I have had enough. I understand what your claims are. I don't belong to you. I won't listen!' About that which attracts him he thinks, 'You are a temptation. Go away, leave me. I want to be alone. I know what you are.' And by this he becomes more and more indifferent to the world, and isolated in the crowd. He feels solitary; he goes to the cave in the mountain or into the forest; he retires from the world and lives the life of an ascetic, at war with the world although at peace with God.

There is another aspect of this reaction, and it is that a man who understands the reality of all things becomes more sympathetic to his fellow-men. It is this man who out of sympathy sacrifices his love for solitude, his love for being exclusive, and goes into the crowd among those who do not understand him, continually trying to understand them from morning till evening. And the more he advances on this path the more he develops love. He mourns over the unreality, over the falsehood of life, but at the same time he is there, he is in the midst of it. His work is to help those who may be disappointed at the results of all the little expectations they had of their love and devotion. For such people every disappointment, every heartbreak is a surprise, a shock, something that suddenly comes upon them, while for him it is normal, it is the nature of life. He stands beside the disappointed ones, he comforts them, he strengthens them. In the realm of religion for instance, if he happens to be among those who have a certain belief or dogma, he may be above it, but he will stand beside them in that particular belief or dogma; he does not consider that he is different or above them. If he happens to be in business, in some industry, in worldly affairs, although he does not aim at any profit he stands with the others in order to keep harmony. He will even sacrifice his life in this way, and he enjoys doing all things while caring nothing for them.

This is the manner of an actor on the stage. If he is made a king he is not very proud of his kingship; if he is made a servant he is not impressed by that, for he knows and understands in his king's robe or servant's livery, that he is neither a king nor a servant; he is himself. In reality it is such souls who come to save the world. They are like the elder brothers of humanity who help the younger. To them there is no feeling of position, title, or spiritual grade. They are one with all and they take part in the pain and joy of all.

But then there is a third reaction upon a soul, and that is the thought, 'If all that I touch, all that I see, and all that I perceive are unreal, I must find out as best I can what is the real.' Such a person is a warrior, for he has a battle before him to fight. And what is this battle? It is seeking after the truth. It is just like a person swimming, making his way: at every stroke he advances, at every effort he makes in going forward, the waves come to push him back; and in the same way life is a continual struggle for the seeker for truth.

Even in things that might seem to be covering the truth the seeker may be deluded. For there is a very important thing that he has to consider. Christ has said, 'I am the way and the truth . . .' This shows that there are two things: there is the way and there is the truth. The way may lead a person to the goal, but the way may also become like a maze to him. It shows how careful one has to be, that even through the way that seems to lead to the truth one may become puzzled. For in reality life is a maze, a continual puzzle, and it is for love of the puzzle that man goes into it; even a seeker after truth does so, as it is his nature to go into the maze first. If a knower of truth were to call a seeker and tell him, 'Here is the truth', he would say, 'This is something unheard of! Truth at the first step! How is it possible? It should be many years before I can arrive at it. One life is not sufficient, I must live a thousand lives in order to realize the truth!' But verily, for the lover of the puzzle, even a thousand lives are not enough. Besides every man is not ready to accept the bare truth; he is not accustomed to it. On hearing the truth he says, 'It is too simple. I want something which I cannot understand.'

In point of fact truth is simple; it is man who makes it difficult for himself. For all other aspects of knowledge he has to get from outside, but truth is something which is within man himself. It is something which is nearest to us though we imagine it to be farthest; it is something which is within though we imagine it to be outside; it is knowledge itself we want to acquire. Thus the seeker is engaged in a continual struggle: struggle with himself, struggle with others, and struggle with life. And at the end of the journey he always finds that he has travelled because it was his destiny to travel, and he discovers that his starting-point is the same as his final goal.

THE DANCE OF THE SOUL

WE SEE in the life of an infant that there comes a moment when it smiles to itself and moves its little feet and legs as if dancing, bringing delight to the one who looks on and creating life in the atmosphere. What is it that suddenly springs into being in the heart of the infant, ignorant of the pains and pleasures of life, that gives expression to its eyes, that inspires its movements and voice? In ancient times people said, 'This is the spirit coming'; they thought it was an angel or fairy speaking to the child. But in reality it is the soul which at that moment rises in ecstasy, making all things dance. There are many delightful experiences in life, but joy is something greater and deeper than delight; it springs from the innermost being, and there can be no better description of the spring of joy than the dance of the soul.

One finds in the life of every person, sorrowful or happy, wise or foolish, moments when he begins to sing or move. Joy may be expressed by a smile, it may even be expressed in tears, but in all it is the dance of the soul. This heavenly bliss is not only for mankind; it comes to all beings. Man lives his life in an artificial world and seldom has a chance to see the beauty of nature; this ecstasy is to be found in the forests, in the wilderness where the great yogis, sages, saints, seers, and prophets received their inspiration. One can see it in what is called in the East the dance of the peacocks, the peacocks expressing the impulse of joy, inspired and blessed by the sublime beauty around them. Birds and animals all have their moment of joy, and one can hear this in their voices, in their song, but its greatest expression is in their dance. To nearly all animals there come moments when the blessing of heaven descends upon them, and they respond by dancing.

This blessing is revealed in every aspect of life, even in inanimate objects such as trees and plants; even there we see in the spring the rising of life. Flowers and plants are but different expressions of the one life, the source of all harmony, beauty, and joy. Someone asked the Prophet for a definition of the soul, and he answered in one sentence, 'The soul is an action of God.' Nothing could be more expressive. Thus joy is the action of the inner or divine life, and when it shows itself in any form it is the reaction to the action of God. It is this which may be called the dance of the soul, and it has inspired all the great musicians and poets. Why do the music of Wagner or Beethoven and the words of Shakespeare live so long, and continually give new joy and inspiration? Why has not all music and poetry the same effect? Because poetry is one thing, and the dance of the soul another. The dance of the soul is beyond mere poetry, and when music expresses itself as the dance of the soul it becomes something higher than music. Man is accustomed to external knowledge, wanting to learn and understand this thing and that, but beauty does not come so naturally, because beauty is beyond all knowledge; it is intended to prepare man to express his soul.

How often do we confuse these two things: inspiration and education. Education is the preparation for inspiration. Education prepares the mind to be a better means of expression for the natural spring which is to be found in the heart. When education becomes a hobby and inspiration is forgotten, then the soul becomes choked, and where there is no life man is mechanical, unreal; he may write poetry, compose music, and paint pictures, but they will all be lifeless, for he himself is a machine. It is the soul itself which is life, knowledge, and beauty.

Kalidasa was the most learned poet of the Sanskrit age; he had never been educated. The language of Kabir, another poet of India, was most ordinary, and yet when those who attached importance to the delicacy and conventions of Hindi heard his words they forgot all conventions; for his poetry brought life, it sprang from the soul, it was spirit. His grammar was faulty, but nevertheless his verses made that impression because the words were living, the soul was dancing. The purpose of life is to become more living, to allow the soul to live more; and that is the lesson given by Christ when he tells us to raise our light on high. It means allowing the soul to express itself. It does not matter what our life is, what our pursuit is; in order to fulfil the purpose of life we need not be in a temple or a church. Whatever our life's pursuit, we can be as spiritual as a priest or a clergymen living a life of

continual praise. Our work should be our religion, whatever our
occupation may be. The soul should express itself in every aspect
of life, and then it will surely fulfil its purpose. Life comes naturally to the soul, if only we open ourselves for the spirit to rise.

There is an old story from India that expresses this philosophy.
The Hindu heaven or paradise is called Indraloka, where the God
Indra is king, and where there are Peris, the angels or fairies whose
task is to dance before Indra. There was one fairy from Indraloka
who descended to earth, and loved an earthly being. By the power
of her magic she brought this earthly being to paradise; but when
this became known to Indra she was cast out from paradise and the
lovers were separated.

This legend is symbolic of the human soul. Originally the Peri,
who represents the soul, belonged to Indraloka, the kingdom of
God, the sphere full of peace, joy, and happiness. Life there is
nothing but joy; it is a dance. Life and love come from God, and
raise every soul till it dances. In its pure condition the soul is
joy, and when it is without joy its natural condition is changed;
then it depends upon the names and forms of the earth and is
deprived of the dance of the soul, and therein lies the whole
tragedy of life. The wrath of Indra symbolizes the breach of the
law that the highest love must be for God alone. It is natural that
the soul is attracted to the spirit and that the true joy of every soul
lies in the realization of the divine spirit.

The absence of this realization keeps the soul in despair. In the
life of every poet, thinker, artist, or scientist there come moments
when ideas or words are given to him; they are given at that
time and at no other. This is the moment when unconsciously
the soul has an opportunity to breathe. Man does not usually
allow his soul to breathe; the portal is closed up in the life of the
earth. Man closes it by ignorance; he is absorbed in things of
much less importance, so when the door opens and the soul is
able to breathe even one breath, it becomes alive in that one
single moment, and what emerges is beauty and joy, making man
express himself in song or dance. In that way heavenly beauty
comes on earth.

The things that catch man's mind are always living things. The
poems of Rumi have lived for eight hundred years and they are

still living; they bring joy and ecstasy whenever they are sung or recited. They are ever-living life, expressing an everlasting beauty. It is the power of God, and it is a mistake for man ever to presume it to be possible to produce that by study. It is impossible; it is the power of God above which brings out the perfection of beauty. Man can never make the soul dance, but he can make himself a fit instrument for the expression of his soul. The question is, in what way can he do so?

The soul is the spirit of God, and the spirit of God lives within the shrine of the heart; this shrine can be closed or it can be open. There are some things in life that open it, and some that close it. The things which close the heart are those which are contrary to love, tolerance, and forgiveness; such as coldness, bitterness, ill-will, and a strong sense of duality. The world is more disturbed today than ever before; in many ways man seems to be going from bad to worse, and yet he thinks that he is progressing. It is not lack of organization or of civilization; he has both these things; but what he lacks is the expression of the soul. He closes his door to his fellow-man, he closes the shrine of the heart, and by doing so keeps God away from himself and others. Nation is set against nation, race against race, religion against religion. Therefore more than ever before there is a need for the realization of this philosophy. It is not that all religions should become one nor all races; that can never be; but what is needed is undivided progress, and the making of ourselves into examples of love and tolerance.

It will not come by talking about it, by discussing and arguing, but by self-realization, by making ourselves examples of what we should be, by giving love, accepting love, and showing in our action gentleness, consideration, and the desire for service, for the sake of the God in whom we can all unite beyond the narrow barriers of race and creed.

'I passed into nothingness, I vanished; and lo! I was all living.' All who have realized this secret of life understand that life is one, but that it exists in two aspects: first as immortal, all-pervading, and silent life; and secondly as mortal, active, and manifested in variety. The soul, being of the first aspect, becomes deluded, helpless, and captive by experiencing life in contact with the mind and body, which are of the next aspect. The gratification of the desires of the body and the fancies of the mind does not suffice the purpose of the soul, which is the experience of its own phenomena in the seen and the unseen, but whose inclination is to be itself and nothing else. When delusion makes it feel that it is helpless, mortal, and captive, it finds itself out of place. This is the tragedy of life which keeps all the strong and the weak, the rich and the poor, dissatisfied, constantly looking for something, they do not know what. The Sufi, realizing this, takes the path of annihilation, and by the guidance of a teacher on the path he finds at the end of his journey that the destination was himself.

'I wandered in the pursuit of my own self. I was the traveller, and I am the destination', says Iqbal.

THE AIMS OF THE SUFI MOVEMENT

The Movement is based upon the Sufi Message brought to the Western world by Hazrat Inayat Khan in 1910.

In his studies as an initiate in one of the ancient Sufi orders, Inayat Khan recognised the basic love and wisdom through which humanity may realize the purpose of life. He saw these two principles as enshrined in the ideals of all religions. He held that by honouring all, and respecting their differences, a basis for mutual understanding could be reached which would not be possible by seeking to convert one to the views of another.

In pursuance of his vision he came to the West, and taught in Europe and America until 1926 when, shortly before his passing, he returned to India. He called his teaching the Sufi Message and to propagate it he founded a body called the International Sufi Movement. In the constitution are enshrined the following Sufi Thoughts:

1. There is one God, the Eternal, the Only Being; none else exists save He.
2. There is one Master, the Guiding Spirit of all souls, who constantly leads his followers towards the light.
3. There is one Holy Book, the sacred manuscript of nature, the only scripture which can enlighten the reader.
4. There is one Religion, the unswerving progress in the right direction towards the ideal, which fulfils the life's purpose of every soul.
5. There is one Law, the Law of Reciprocity, which can be observed by a selfless conscience together with a sense of awakened justice.
6. There is one Brotherhood, the human brotherhood, which unites the children of earth indiscriminately in the fatherhood of God.
7. There is one Moral Principle, the love which springs forth from self-denial, and blooms in deeds of beneficence.
8. There is one Object of Praise, the beauty which uplifts the heart of its worshipper through all aspects from the seen to the unseen.
9. There is one Truth, the true knowledge of our being within and without which is the essence of all wisdom.

10. There is one Path, the annihilation of the false ego in the real, which raises the mortal to immortality and in which resides all perfection.

The Movement has the following Objects:

1. To realize and spread the knowledge of unity, the religion of love and wisdom, so that the bias of faiths and beliefs may of itself fall away, the human heart may overflow with love, and all hatred caused by distinctions and differences may be rooted out.
2. To discover the light and power latent in man, the secret of all religion, the power of mysticism, and the essence of philosophy, without interfering with customs or belief.
3. To help to bring the world's two opposite poles, East and West, closer together by the interchange of thought and ideals, that the Universal Brotherhood may form of itself, and man may meet with man beyond the narrow national and racial boundaries.

Regarding the aims of the Movement, we quote as follows from the words of Inayat Khan:

"The purpose of the Sufi Movement is to work towards unity. Its main object is to bring humanity, divided as it is into so many different sections, closer together in the deeper understanding of life. It is a preparation for a world service, chiefly in three ways. One way is the philosophical understanding of life; another is bringing about brotherhood among races, nations, and creeds; and the third way is the meeting of the world's greatest need, which is the religion of the day. Its work is to bring to the world that natural religion which has always been the religion of humanity: to respect one another's belief, scripture, and teacher. The Sufi message is the echo of the same divine message which has always come and will always come to enlighten humanity. It is not a new religion; it is the same message which is being given to humanity. It is the continuation of the same ancient religion which has always existed and will always exist, a religion which belongs to all teachers and all the scriptures.

Sufism in itself is not a religion nor even a cult with a distinct or definite doctrine. No better explanation of Sufism can be given than by saying that any person who has a knowledge of both outer and inner life is a Sufi. Thus there has never at any period of the world's history been a founder of Sufism, yet Sufism has existed at all times.

The present-day Sufi Movement is a movement of members of different nations and races united together in the ideal of wisdom; they believe that wisdom does not belong to any particular religion or race, but to the human race as a whole. It is a divine property which mankind has inherited; and it is in this realization that the Sufis, in spite of belonging to different nationalities, races, beliefs, and faiths, still unite and work for humanity in the ideal of wisdom.

The Sufi message warns humanity to get to know life better and to achieve freedom in life; it warns man to accomplish what he considers good, just, and desirable; it warns him before every action to note its consequences by studying the situation, his own attitude, and the method he should adopt.

Sufism not only guides those who are religious, mystical, or visionary, but the Sufi message gives to the world the religion of the day: and that is to make one's life a religion, to turn one's occupation or profession into a religion, to make one's ideal a religious ideal. The object of Sufism is the uniting of life and religion, which so far seem to have been kept apart. When a man goes to church once a week, and devotes all the other days of the week to his business, how can he benefit by religion? Therefore, the teaching of Sufism is to transform everyday life into a religion, so that every action may bear some spiritual fruit.

The method of world reform which various institutions have adopted today is not the method of the Sufi Movement. Sufis believe that if evil is contagious, goodness must be even more so. The depth of every soul is good; every soul is searching for good, and by the effort of individuals who wish to do good in the world much can be done, even more than a materialistic institution can achieve. No doubt for the general good there are political and commercial problems to be solved; but that must not debar individuals from progress, for it is the individual progress through the spiritual path which alone can bring about the desired condition in the world.

The Sufi message is not for a particular race, nation, or church. It is a call to unite in wisdom. The Sufi Movement is a group of people belonging to different religions, who have not left their religions but who have learned to understand them better, and their love is the love for God and humanity instead of for a particular section of it. The principal work that the Sufi Movement has to accomplish is to bring about a better understanding between East and West, and between the nations and races of his world. And the note that the sufi message is striking at the present time is the note which sounds the divinity of the human soul. If there is any moral principle that the Sufi Movement brings, it is this; that the whole of humanity is like one body, and any organ of that body which is hurt or troubled can indirectly cause damage to the whole body. And as the health of the whole body depends upon the health of each part, so the health of the whole of humanity depends upon the health of every nation. Besides, to those who are awakening and feel that now is the moment to learn more of the deeper side of life, of truth, the Sufi Movement extends a helping hand without asking to what religion, sect, or dogma they belong. The knowledge of the Sufi is helpful to every person, not only in living his life rightly but in regard to his own religion. The Sufi Movement does not call a man away from his belief or chruch: it calls him to live it. In short, it is a movement intended by God to unite humanity in brotherhood and in wisdom."

From *The Sufi Message of Hazrat Inayat Khan,* Volume IX

HAZRAT INAYAT KHAN MEMORIAL TRUST

The Hazrat Inayat Khan Memorial Trust, located in New Delhi, has been created for religious and charitable purposes. It is founded on the Sufi Message of love, harmony and beauty, as brought by Hazrat Inayat Khan (1882—1927).

Its goal is twofold: It wants to unite all people longing for love, harmony and beauty; and it wants to create not only a physical opportunity for this to happen, but also to create the appropriate atmosphere.

Its original and first activity was—and remains to be—to take care of the Dargah (memorial tomb) of this Sufi saint and master, who has been working for human brotherhood, religious tolerance, mysticism in daily life, the unity of religious ideals and a practical life philosophy. Apart from his being an active and famous musician in the first decade of this century in India, he has been working mainly in the West, bringing about a greater understanding for the values, the philosophy and the music of India, thus preparing ground for later positive developments.

The Trust further undertakes, within the limits set by the donations by Sufis and others, to render financial, material and spiritual help to the needy and destitute, particularly around the Dargah. This help is given to improve the physical health, to leniate immediate suffering, to provide for better living conditions through education, and by providing food to children and other needy persons. The Trust also looks after housing problems in some cases.

During the last fifteen years the Trust has succeeded to make the Dargah into a dignified place and to start making it suitable for the Sufi work. It is becoming a place of peace and happiness, for silence and meditation, a home for everybody looking for these experiences within or without, its atmosphere charging every open-hearted visitor with upliftment and new energy. It is intended to become an ecumenical meeting ground in the real sense of the word for Hindus, Buddhists, Parsis, Sikhs, Jains, Jews, Christians, Muslims, and all others with sympathy in their hearts. At the same time it must be a place for help to our fellow-men. Here everyone can feel at home and free, and can meet people from other circles on 'neutral' yet warm and inspired ground. It is a centre for the spreading of the ecumenical Sufi Message of love, harmony and beauty: a Message of universal brotherhood and tolerance, a basis for inter-religious brotherhood, a platform for inter-communal understanding, a spiritual centre, and a 'akasha' for love, harmony and beauty.

Gradually, the land around the Dargah had become completely occupied by temporary dwellings, refugees and others. To enlarge the area for our direct use was a very difficult and expensive task, because the Trust wanted to help the tenants living on the spot in acquiring better accommodation, even with financial assistance to these tenants living in the very poor huts in this area. In other cases, the Trust has given some help to a tenant in starting a business.

In this way it became also possible to make some space available for the social, medical and educative programmes of the Hope Project Charitable Trust, another Sufi organisation working in the name of Hazrat Inayat Khan. The work of this Trust is to provide free social services to those living in the community around the Dargah. It includes the Hazrat Inayat Khan Health Centre, where medical treatment and referral services are provided; two dispensaries are being run, one homeopathic, the other allopathic, which help about 250 patients a day. In the Milk programme milk is distributed everyday to infants, pregnant mothers and the infirm. The Hazrat Inayat Khan Education Centre offers educational and vocational training for children and adults from the Basti; there is a school for women, girls and little boys for educational and vocational training, free of charge. The social work programme offers help to those who are in crisis situations, financial troubles, the disabled and anyone who is in need.

This is quite in the tradition of Sufi Dargahs in India: besides spiritual activities also the material requirements of those in need are provided for.

In 1988 the new Dargah building was inaugurated. It is constructed around the original mazaar (tomb) by ASEMA architects in close contact with the Trust. Its simple design in beautiful material and harmonious proportions may be a symbol for the scope each individual has for the design of his life and the development of his heart. With this new building new opportunities are opening up.

Even before that time the activities of the Trust have grown steadily, and have become more intense. During a greater part of the year there are daily prayers and meditations, weekly qawalli concerts, weekly classes of the Inner School; each month Universal Worship is held, where texts from the sacred scriptures of the major world religions are read; occasionally there are concerts of spiritual classical Indian music, music playing such an important role in Inayat Khan's Message; regularly lectures and courses on modern Sufism are being given. On special occasions there is langar, the free distribution of food to the local population. There is a small library in a preliminary form, on the fields of Sufism, philosophy, psychology, mysticism and (comparative) religion.

Further new activities are being envisaged. The first of these is realised by the publication of this series of volumes on the Sufi Message by Hazrat Inayat Khan. Brotherhood meetings will be organised amongst followers of different religions in order to increase mutual tolerance through understanding and realisation of the essentials we have in common. Courses will be developed on the Sufi Message on subjects such as: the unity of religious ideals, moral culture as the way to God, the development of personality; the tuning of mind, heart and spirit, etc. Further opportunities will be created to participate in meditation, silence, prayer, and spiritual music in order to develop the feeling of sympathy within so that it may radiate. Staging concerts of spiritual classical Indian music will be continued, following the tradition of the great musician, Hazrat Inayat Khan has been. The library may develop into a scholarly one. In close contact with the Hope Charitable Trust further facilities will be offered in the field of social and welfare programmes.

In 1987 the Circle of Friends of Hazrat Sufi Inayat Khan was inaugurated. It is open to all those sympathising with the Sufi Message of today, who feel stirred by the ideas and ideals of love, harmony and beauty, balance and tolerance, understanding and moral culture; those who look for spiritual development yet standing in the world; who want to strengthen the unity of religious ideals; to all those, therefore, who want to unite with other friends in order to share and to contribute to the development of these ideals within oneself, amongst one another, and around, on a foundation of ever growing sympathy. In the meantime meetings of the Circle of Friends are taking place regularly.

For further information on the work of the Trust or on its Circle of Friends apply to:

Hazrat Inayat Khan Memorial Trust
129, Basti Hazrat Nizamuddin Aulia
(opposite Lodhi Hotel)
New Delhi 110 013
Tel. 4625883

ABOUT THE SERIES

Volume I. *The Way of Illumination*
The traditional Sufic outlook on life's values and purpose is re-expressed by Hazrat Inayat Khan in universal and contemporary concepts.
Included are: *The Way of Illumination; The Inner Life; The Soul; Whence and Whither;* and *The Purpose of Life.*

Volume II. *The Mysticism of Music, Sound and Word*
Sufism traditionally used music as a means of transmitting the essence of mystical insight. Hazrat Inayat Khan integrates this concept of music with elements like sound and silence, vibration and the word, thoughts and inspiration, creating new dimensions for our lives, and thereby recomposing a musical concept extending beyond the tradition of time and culture.

Volume III. *The Art of Personality*
This volume contains the substances of Hazrat Inayat Khan's teaching on our Divine heritage and human relationships, including the science of life's forces. He suggests that the art of personality is the completion of nature and the culmination of heredity. Development of the personality is taken from before birth to the deepest aspects of consciousness.
Included are: *Education; Rasa Shastra; Character-Building and the Art of Personality; Moral Culture.*

Volume IV. *Mental Purification and Healing*
In this volume the Sufi principles are explained concerning the influence the mind may exert on the body, in relation to the spiritual power within us, and concerning the possibilities of spiritual healing in conjunction with modern science.
Included are: *Health; Mental Purification; The Mind World.*

Volume V. *Spiritual Liberty*
This volume contains a wealth of information about different aspects of Sufi mysticism.
Included are: *A Sufi Message of Spiritual Liberty: Aqibat: Life after Death; The Phenomenon of the Soul; Love, Human and Divine; Pearls from the Ocean Unseen.*

Volume VI. *The Alchemy of Happiness*
Hazrat Inayat Khan always insisted that spiritual or mystical aspirations
are of no avail if one's life is not lived as it should be. Under this title, forty
lectures are collected that deal with life in all its aspects.

Volume VII. *In an Eastern Rose Garden*
Talks given by Hazrat Inayat Khan on a variety of subjects. His ability to
communicate the unity and relativity of his viewpoint on diverse subjects
illustrates the essence of his mystical perception of life.

Volume VIII. *Sufi Teachings*
A collection of talks on various practical and esoteric aspects of traditional Sufi teachings developed by Hazrat Inayat Khan in a modern and
universal context.

Volume IX. *The Unity of Religious Ideals*
A systematically arranged collection of Hazrat Inayat Khan's addresses
on what is perhaps the most important part of his teaching: the underlying
unity of all religious thought and experience.

Volume X. *Sufi Mysticism*
Hazrat Inayat Khan situates the traditional concepts of initiation, dis-
cipleship, spiritual teaching and other esoteric aspects of Sufism in
today's world. Besides the main part consisting of: *Sufi Mysticism* and
The Path of Initiation and Discipleship, these subjects are included: *Sufi
Poetry, Art: Yesterday, Today and Tomorrow; The Problem of the Day.*

Volume XI. *Philosophy, Psychology, Mysticism*
These later talks by Hazrat Inayat Khan, given during the last two years
before his death, contain a clear overview of these topics in terms of his
Sufic vision. This series of lectures may be considered his *magnum opus.*
The Aphorisms at the end are sayings noted down by his pupils which
Hazrat Inayat Khan expressed at different times and places to soothe or
clarify the seeker.

Volume XII. *The Divinity of the Human Soul*
The first part of this volume deals with the relationship of man and God.
The second part is autobiographical. The third part contains four short
plays written by Hazrat Inayat Khan for his pupils.
Included are: *The Vision of God and Man; Confessions; Four Plays.*

Volume XIII. *Sacred Readings: The Gatha's*
This volume contains the teachings derived from classes given by Hazrat Inayat Khan to his pupils at the earlier stages of their training.

Volume XIV. *Index to Volumes I-XIII*
The volume is published for the first time. It will be of great interest for the student of Sufism.

The Dance of the Soul
This collection of aphorisms is just a gem of wisdom and mysticism with a touch of humour. It helps you to discover your very being at the same time as hinting practical solutions for your daily life: feeling, thinking, speaking, acting.

Bowl of Saki (1994)
Wisdom for everyday. The book contains one saying for each day of the year. Space is left open to accommodate the signatures of your friends.

Those desiring particulars regarding the activities in all countries of the Sufi Movement founded by Hazrat Inayat Khan should apply to the International Headquarters of the Movement as follows:

(for activities in India)	(for activities outside India)
Sufi Movement India,	General Secretariat,
Dargah Hzt. Inayat Khan	Sufi Movement,
129, Basti Hzt. Nizamuddin	Anna Paulownastraat 78
New Delhi 110 013	2518 BJ The Hague
	Holland